Essential Readings ON Early Literacy

Compiled and introduced by Dorothy S. Strickland

INTERNATIONAL
Reading Association
800 BARKSDALE ROAD, PO BOX 8139
NEWARK, DE 19714-8139, USA
www.reading.org

The International Reading Association attempts, through its publications, to provide a forum for a wide spectrum of opinions on reading. This policy permits divergent viewpoints without implying the endorsement of the Association.

Executive Editor, Books   Corinne M. Mooney
Developmental Editor   Charlene M. Nichols
Developmental Editor   Tori Mello Bachman
Developmental Editor   Stacey L. Reid
Editorial Production Manager   Shannon T. Fortner
Design and Composition Manager   Anette Schuetz

Project Editors   Wesley Ford

Cover   Linda Steere

Library of Congress Cataloging-in-Publication Data
Essential readings on early literacy / compiled and introduced by
Dorothy S. Strickland.
   p. cm.
 ISBN 978-0-87207-809-3
 1. Reading (Early childhood) I. Strickland, Dorothy S.
 LB1139.5.R43E78 2010
 372.4'049--dc22

2009050066

Contents

Assessment

Making Home-School Connections

About the Editor

Dorothy S. Strickland is the Samuel DeWitt Proctor Professor of Education Emerita and Distinguished Research Fellow of the National Institute for Early Education Research at Rutgers, The State University of New Jersey, New Brunswick, USA. A former classroom teacher and learning disabilities specialist, she has authored and edited numerous publications concerning language development and reading. Recent publications include *Literacy Leadership in Early Childhood: The Essential Guide*; *Learning About Print in Preschool: Working With Letters, Words, and Beginning Links With Phonemic Awareness*; *Improving Reading Achievement Through Professional Development*; and *The Administration and Supervision of Reading Programs* (3rd edition).

A past president of both the International Reading Association (IRA) and the Reading Hall of Fame, Dorothy is the recipient of IRA's Outstanding Teacher Educator in Reading Award, the National Council of Teachers of English Award for Outstanding Educator in the English Language Arts, the Rewey Belle Inglis Award as Outstanding Woman in English Education, and the National-Louis University Ferguson Award for Outstanding Contributions to Early Childhood Education.

In 2008, she presented the annual Jeanne Chall Distinguished Address at Harvard University, and she is a frequent visiting professor and lecturer at other institutions. She has served on numerous boards and committees, including the National Early Literacy Panel and the panels that produced *Becoming a Nation of Readers: The Report of the Commission on Reading*, *Preventing Reading Difficulties in Young Children*, and *Reading for Understanding: Toward an R&D Program in Reading Comprehension*. She currently serves on a National Academy of Science panel on teacher preparation and the Validation Committee for the Common Core Standards. She was appointed by the governor to the New Jersey State Board of Education in 2008.

Introduction

Dorothy S. Strickland

There is substantial agreement among educators, policymakers, and the general public that a strong foundation in early literacy is critical for success in school. Indeed, literacy education is the most prominent aspect of the curriculum for which the public demands high achievement and high accountability. Today's early literacy educators—that is, educators working in preschool through the primary grades—face numerous challenges and require knowledgeable and thoughtful leadership to initiate wise policy decisions and support effective classroom instruction (Strickland & Riley-Ayers, 2007). The following are some of these challenges:

- The very notion of what it means to be literate in our society has changed. While it is still true that becoming literate involves the development of some very basic skills and strategies, such things as surface-level decoding and the recall of information are hardly enough. Even very young children are presented with texts of endless variety—books, magazines, and pamphlets of every conceivable design. They are exposed to e-mail and surface mail, to images and text on television screens, computer screens, and numerous other electronic displays in their kitchens, living rooms, and other rooms at home. Today's young learners need to acquire literacy skills to read and write texts of all kinds and that help them adapt to constant change.

- Expectations have increased for what young readers and writers should know and be able to do. Public awareness of the critical need for literacy proficiency has never been greater. The concerns extend well beyond the educational community to include parents and policymakers. That interest has stimulated an unprecedented amount of attention and discussion about the content of the early literacy curriculum and the need to ensure that young children get off to a good start.

- Expectations for teacher performance have also increased. Content standards and performance expectations for students are often accompanied by corresponding standards for teacher preparation, professional development, and overall teacher performance. Efforts to improve teacher quality in the areas of language arts and literacy often receive special attention.

- Accountability for student achievement is at the center of school reform. Reform efforts at the local, state, and national levels generally include requirements for some type of formalized method of accountability so that trends in achievement can be tracked and the progress of various groups can be compared. Effective classroom instruction is expected to include some form of systematic monitoring and documentation of student progress.

- The demographics of the student population have changed. Today's challenges are compounded by a growing diversity among the student body. This diversity reflects a changing population that is increasingly rich in its multicultural and multilingual nature. Today's educators are expected to know and implement successful strategies for working with students from diverse cultural and linguistic backgrounds.

Essential Readings on Early Literacy, introduced and complied by Dorothy S. Strickland. © 2010 by the International Reading Association

• Coordination across prekindergarten and primary-grade programs has increased. As initiatives to make preschool more widely available become increasingly prevalent, more and more public schools are involved with staffing, monitoring, and supervising prekindergarten programs. The need to provide a coherent curriculum and smooth transition from one level to another has caused many states to expand their core curriculum standards to cover prekindergarten through grade 12. It has also inspired professional development efforts that encourage prekindergarten, kindergarten, and primary-grade teachers to work together on common issues.

With all of the attention given to early literacy, perhaps the greatest challenge for classroom teachers is the need to provide students with the core content associated with beginning reading and writing instruction in ways that are age and developmentally appropriate. With that in mind, a brief discussion of changing perspectives on the development of early literacy follows, along with an overview of key reports on relevant research in the areas of early literacy and developmentally appropriate practice.

From "Readiness" to "Emergent Literacy"

Until the late 1980s, reading readiness was the approach embraced by most early literacy teachers to provide a foundation for formal reading instruction, which generally began in first grade. In traditional readiness programs, prescribed skills such as knowledge of the alphabet, word recognition, vocabulary knowledge, and visual discrimination were directly taught to get children "ready" to read. Teale and Yokota (2000) suggest that, even then, reading readiness was pursued by educators along two different paths. Down one path went those who were convinced that readiness was essentially a result of maturation or "neural ripeness." Down the other path

were educators who believed that appropriate experiences created readiness or accelerated it.

By the late 1980s, the view that reading readiness was a prerequisite for beginning literacy instruction was seriously challenged, and the notion of emergent literacy took hold. Emergent literacy looks at both reading and writing as emerging processes in the everyday lives of children beginning from their earliest years (Teale & Sulzby, 1986). Thus, children begin to acquire knowledge about oral and written language long before formal instruction begins. Children who have had many meaningful experiences with print, such as being read to often and experimenting with writing, are more "ready" for school literacy programs than those who have not had such exposures.

Overview of Influential Research Reports on Early Literacy: A Historical Frame

There is a strong empirically based consensus about what beginning readers are expected to know and be able to do to be successful learners and about the instructional opportunities required to support their development. Virtually all of the readings included or suggested in this book are connected in some way to this rich body of work. Very brief descriptions are provided here in the hope that some readers will dig further to investigate those research reports that interest them. At the very least, they provide the evidence base that informs our knowledge of early literacy learning and teaching. (For more complete descriptions and discussions of most of these studies, see Cowen, 2003.)

"Success in First Grade Reading" (Durrell, Nicholson, Olson, Gavel, & Linehan, 1958) was one of the earliest major studies focused on beginning reading. To the credit of Durrell and his colleagues, much of the succeeding work in this area has confirmed their findings. This research had multiple purposes: to assure reading success among the first-grade students involved in the study, to evaluate reading readiness practices and concepts, and to study the relationships among various aspects of reading growth. The following are the four key findings of this study:

1. Most reading difficulties can be prevented by an instructional program that provides early instruction in letter names and sounds, followed by applied phonics and accompanied by suitable practice in meaningful sight vocabulary and aids to attentive silent reading.

2. Testing of letter names at school entrance is the best predictor of achievement at the middle and end of the year (February and June).

3. There is a great variability among children in key elements of readiness for reading instruction. Children who enter first grade "ready" for instruction make greater progress when conventional reading readiness materials are omitted from their reading programs.

4. There appears to be no basis for the assumption that a prescribed number of sight vocabulary words must be taught before the beginning of instruction in word analysis skills.

The findings of Durrell and his associates (1958) are still among the recurring themes that dominate research on early literacy today. Issues related to the prevention of reading difficulties, the key components of early literacy instruction, the predictors of literacy success, and the need to address learner variability with differentiated instruction are among the research topics addressed by the reports briefly described in what follows.

In "The Cooperative Research Program in First-Grade Reading Instruction" Bond and Dykstra (1967) seek to compare the effectiveness of existing alternative reading programs and to investigate how students, teachers, schools, and communities might also contribute to the reading achievement of first-grade students. The ability to recognize letters at the beginning of first grade was related to reading success in all of the methods and programs examined. These researchers also point out the importance of the

ability to discriminate between word sounds (phonemic awareness) and that an integrated approach, which combined systematic phonics with reading for meaning and writing, far surpassed lock-step approaches that may not be satisfactory for all children.

Chall's (1967) *Learning to Read: The Great Debate* confirms the importance of systematic phonics as a superior approach to what was termed the *whole-word* approach. However, it is important to note that while Chall supports an early code emphasis, she also emphasizes reading for meaning. Once again, the importance of specific foundational skills was confirmed. Chall was also struck by the great variability in the backgrounds of beginning readers. She makes specific suggestions related to children from lower socioeconomic status (SES) homes and to children with lower level abilities.

Becoming a Nation of Readers: The Report of the Commission on Reading (Anderson, Hiebert, Scott, & Wilkinson, 1985) stresses the importance of a balanced approach to reading instruction with an early emphasis on phonics and phonemic awareness. However, these researchers also emphasize the need to teach students the alphabetic principle to enable them to see the relationship between the letters and sounds and apply that knowledge to sound out and blend letters to read words. The need to help students identify words in meaningful sentences and stories was stressed. This report helped to frame the discussion beyond the content of instruction to include the way in which instruction is delivered.

In *Beginning to Read: Thinking and Learning About Print*, Adams (1990) also confirms the finding that the ability to identify sounds in words is a key predictor of success in reading. She also stresses the need to teach both phonemic awareness and the alphabetic principle. This work had a profound effect on the inclusion of phonemic awareness as a key component of the beginning reading program. Adams pays direct attention to the importance of home and community in supporting children's literacy development.

Preventing Reading Difficulties in Young Children (Snow, Burns, & Griffin, 1998), an exhaustive review of the literature, is concerned with the best ways to prevent reading difficulties at the inception of instruction. Knowledge of how sounds are represented alphabetically, the structure of spoken words, and the nature of the alphabetic writing system are found to be required for success in reading. In addition, opportunities to obtain meaning from print and sufficient background knowledge and vocabulary to render written texts meaningful are considered essential. This study focuses heavily on the needs of children at risk for failure. As such, it provides considerable information on the individual and group risk factors related to children from low SES levels, English-language learners, and other causal problems that may predict reading difficulties.

The report of the National Reading Panel (National Institute of Child Health and Human Development, 2000), arguably one of the most influential studies on reading, also confirms many of the studies that preceded it. Alphabetics (phonemic awareness instruction and phonics) is once again mentioned as a key foundational aspect of learning to read. Attention to fluency, comprehension, and vocabulary instruction is also stressed. This report confirms the need for meaningful practice. Comprehension is described as the construction of meaning through the application of intentional, problem-solving processes while interacting with written text. Comprehension involves all the elements of the reading process acting together: phonemic awareness, phonics, fluency, vocabulary, and text comprehension.

Developing Early Literacy: Report of the National Early Literacy Panel (National Institute for Literacy, 2008) provides a synthesis of research on the development of early literacy in young children, prior to first grade. The researchers sought to determine the skills and abilities young children require to help them grow into successful readers and writers. Once again, this study has the prevention of reading difficulties as a primary focus. Key predictive skills and abilities found to be related to success in reading are alphabet knowledge, phonological/phonemic awareness, knowledge about print, and oral language development. Effective instructional strategies include shared reading that encouraged reader–child interaction and one-on-one and small-group instructional interventions. Successful parent and home programs were found to foster children's oral language and cognitive development. Also see Strickland and Shanahan (2004) for a discussion of the preliminary findings of this work and its implications for instruction.

Perspectives on Developmentally Appropriate Practice

It is important to place this reading research within the field of early childhood education and the long-held views about what is developmentally appropriate practice. The report *Developmentally Appropriate Practice in Early Childhood Programs Serving Children from Birth Through Age 8* (National Association for the Education of Young Children, 2009) offers principles and guidelines for educators in the field of early childhood education. Grounded in research on child development and educational effectiveness, this report offers an important perspective on how educators might bring research and practice together. The report addresses several strands of development—physical, social and emotional, cognitive, and language and literacy—with separate sections on the preschool years, the kindergarten year, and the primary grades. Key messages include the following:

- *The importance of the principles of best practice*—best practice is based on knowledge, not on assumptions, of how children learn and develop. Basic principles of child development apply regardless of the content of instruction.

- *The need to reduce the achievement gap*—young children who have not had the learning opportunities they require to succeed in school need more extended, enriched, and intensive learning experiences.

- *The need for a comprehensive, effective curriculum*—all the domains of a child's development are interrelated. Teachers must maintain high expectations while setting challenging, achievable goals with learning experiences integrated across the curriculum.
- *The need to improve teaching and learning*—effective teachers are intentional in their use of a variety of approaches and strategies to support children's interests and abilities in all learning domains. "To ensure that teachers are able to provide care and education of high quality, they must be well prepared, participate in ongoing professional development, and receive sufficient support and compensation" (National Association for the Education of Young Children, 2009, p. xiii).

In This Book

The challenges faced by today's early literacy educators and the research reports described in the preceding section of this Introduction have helped to inform the content and structural frame for this book. The readings fall under three major headings: Instructional Strategies, Assessment, and Making Home–School Connections. In each main section, additional recommended readings are listed along with brief descriptions of the articles selected for inclusion in the book. I selected the readings based on two criteria: they must be relevant to the topic of early literacy (prekindergarten through early primary grades), both in terms of learning and teaching; and they must be written in a straightforward style accessible for any educator, whether experienced or new to the field. Some ideas for the use of this book as a tool for professional development have been included in the final section.

Instructional Strategies

The suggested readings on instructional strategies organized around five general categories: using children's literature to foster early literacy development, comprehension and fluency, vocabulary development and word study, writing development, and addressing linguistic and cultural diversity. However, it is apparent that the categories overlap considerably. Children's literature, for example, is treated as a separate category although it is a central ingredient throughout early literacy instruction. The articles included in this category focus on reading literature aloud to children, a staple of the literacy curriculum. Throughout all categories, the strategies very appropriately address more than one aspect of the curriculum—for example, the recommended article on word study by Yopp and Stapleton (2008) with its emphasis on English-language learners.

Using Children's Literature to Foster Early Literacy Development. Exposure to an abundance of children's literature is a staple of the early literacy curriculum. Literature helps broaden children's background knowledge, vocabulary, and sense of how texts are constructed. Listening to teachers model fluent reading and responding to material read aloud is at the heart of building comprehension abilities and a love of reading. Both narrative and informational texts have been used in a variety of ways to build early literacy strategies. Read-aloud strategies are among the most important instructional tools used to promote early literacy. The readings included here, McGee and Schickedanz's "Repeated Interactive Read-Alouds in Preschool and Kindergarten" and Lane and Wright's "Maximizing the Effectiveness of Reading Aloud," offer specific suggestions for conducting effective read-aloud activities to foster a range of literacy skills and learner strategies.

The following are additional recommended resources:

- Welsch, J.G. (2008). Playing Within and Beyond the Story: Encouraging Book-Related Pretend Play. *The Reading Teacher*, *62*(2), 138–148.
- Stephens, K.E. (2008). A Quick Guide to Selecting Great Informational Books for Young Children. *The Reading Teacher*, *61*(6), 488–490.

Comprehension and Fluency. Comprehension is the ultimate goal of reading. Research shows that comprehension can improve when children are taught to use specific cognitive strategies and reason strategically when they encounter difficulties in understanding what they are reading. Skilled readers are fluent readers. They recognize words with automaticity, which frees resources to group words into meaningful units (phrases), attend to punctuation, and, ultimately, gain meaning from what they are reading. There is a close relationship between fluency and reading comprehension. That relationship is effectively applied, along with a variety of other early literacy strategies, in the instructional activities described in Fingeret's "*March of the Penguins*: Building Knowledge in a Kindergarden Classroom," Kuhn's "Helping Students Become Accurate, Expressive Readers: Fluency Instruction for Small Groups," and Santoro and colleagues' "Making the *Very* Most of Classroom Read-Alouds to Promote Comprehension and Vocabulary."

These recommended readings expand upon this topic:

- McIntyre, E. (2007). Story Discussion in the Primary Grades: Balancing Authenticity and Explicit Teaching. *The Reading Teacher. 60*(7), 610–620.
- Myers, P.A. (2005). The Princess Storyteller, Clara Clarifier, Quincy Questioner, and the Wizard: Reciprocal Teaching Adapted for Kindergarten Students. *The Reading Teacher*, *59*(4), 314–324.
- Richards, M. (2000). Be a Good Detective: Solve the Case of Oral Reading Fluency. *The Reading Teacher, 53*(7), 534–539.
- Williams, T.L. (2007). "Reading" the Painting: Exploring Visual Literacy in the Primary Grades. *The Reading Teacher, 60*(7), 636–642.

Vocabulary Development and Word Study: Alphabet Knowledge, Phonemic Awareness, and Phonics. *Phonemic awareness* is the ability to distinguish and manipulate the individual sounds—phonemes—in spoken language. *Phonics* refers to the relationship between the letters of written language and the sounds (phonemes) of spoken language. It is different from phonemic awareness because it involves the letters themselves and how these relate to the sounds of the language. Phonemic awareness should be taught because it supports new readers in developing and using their knowledge of phonics, which directly aids word-reading and builds a base for fluency and the comprehension of text. Blachowicz and Obrochta's "Vocabulary Visits: Virtual Field Trips for Content Vocabulary Development" is included in this section, and suggestions for using alphabet books for a variety of purposes that go well beyond letter naming is the focus of the Bradley and Jones article, "Sharing Alphabet Books in Early Childhood Classrooms." Other recommended readings describe a wide range of creative activities that extend vocabulary development into the content areas for building background knowledge. Many specific suggestions for phonemic awareness and phonics are included as well:

- Labbo, L.D., Love, M.S., and Ryan, T. (2007). A Vocabulary Flood: Making Words "Sticky" With Computer-Response Activities. *The Reading Teacher, 60*(6), 582–588.
- Manyak, P.C. (2008). Phonemes in Use: Multiple Activities for a Critical Process. *The Reading Teacher, 61*(8), 659–662.
- McCarthy, P. (2008). Using Sound Boxes Systematically to Develop Phonemic Awareness. *The Reading Teacher, 62*(4), 346–349.
- Rasinski, T., Rupley, W.H., and Nichols, W.D. (2008). Two Essential Ingredients: Phonics and Fluency Getting to Know Each Other. *The Reading Teacher, 62*(3), 257–260.

Writing Development. Most young children begin to write by drawing and scribbling. They write messages, grocery lists, stories, and notes, and they "pretend read" what they have written to anyone who will listen. As soon as they can write a few letters, they begin to add these and other letter-like marks to their drawings and scribbles, showing that they know writing is not completely arbitrary but that it involves certain kinds of special marks. When their informal exposure to written language through environmental print is supported by experiences with print such as interactive reading and writing, children begin to internalize the alphabetic principle.

As active learners, children invent spellings according to their own phonemic rules, for example, *chran* for *train*, and *swm* for *swim*. Standard spellings are soon mixed with invented spellings. Personal content tends to dominate the writing of very young children. However, given the opportunity, young children can write informational texts and stories and are aware of how they are different. The development of reading and writing is highly interrelated. Gibson's "An Effective Framework for Primary-Grade Guided Writing Instruction" and Williams and Lundstrom's "Strategy Instruction During Word Study and Interactive Writing Activities," along with the following additional recommended reading, offer advice for encouraging children's early emergent writing and strategies for moving them toward successful independent writing:

- Patterson, E., Schaller, M., and Clemens, J. (2008). A Closer Look at Interactive Writing. *The Reading Teacher*, *61*(6), 496–497.

Addressing Linguistic and Cultural Diversity. Effective early literacy programs foster an atmosphere that is culturally and linguistically responsive. Both the leadership and the day-by-day classroom instruction should demonstrate a welcoming attitude to parents and children of all backgrounds. All teachers should be urged to learn as much as they can about the home language and culture of the students they teach, as described in Manyak's "What's Your News? Portraits of a Rich Language and Literacy Activity for English-Language Learners" and Teale and colleagues' "Beginning Reading Instruction in Urban Schools: The Curriculum

Gap Ensures a Continuing Achievement Gap." Professional development activities should include special attention to the needs of English learners.

Here are some addition resources:

- Al-Hazza, T.C., and Bucher, K.T. (2008). Building Arab Americans' Cultural Identity and Acceptance With Children's Literature. *The Reading Teacher*, *62*(3), 210–219.
- Mohr, K.A.J., and Mohr, E.S. (2007). Extending English-Language Learners' Classroom Interactions Using the Response Protocol. *The Reading Teacher*, *60*(5), 440–450.
- Yopp, H.K. and Stapleton, L. (2008). Conciencia Fonemica en Español (Phonemic Awareness in Spanish). *The Reading Teacher*, *61*(5), 374–382.

Assessment

Monitoring and assessing student development is an important part of a comprehensive early literacy program. Assessment has a number of purposes. It is used to monitor students' learning, to guide teacher planning and decision making, to identify students who might benefit from special services, and to report to and communicate with others responsible for each child's development, such as parents and administrators. Helpful assessments reveal what children *can* do as well as what they cannot do. Many of today's early literacy programs make use of multiple methods of assessment. Reilly's "Choice of Action: Using Data to Make Instructional Decisions in Kindergarten" focuses on linking instruction and assessment in the classroom, as do these additional recommended readings:

- Boyd-Batstone, P. (2004). Focused Anecdotal Records Assessment: A Tool for Standards-Based, Authentic Assessment. *The Reading Teacher, 58*(3), 230–239.
- Nilsson, N.L. (2008). A Critical Analysis of Eight Informal Reading Inventories. *The Reading Teacher*, *61*(7), 526–536.

- Teale, W.H. (2008). What Counts? Literacy Assessment in Urban Schools. *The Reading Teacher, 62*(4), 358–361.

Making Home-School Connections

The link between supportive parental involvement and children's early literacy development is well established. Children from homes where parents model the uses of literacy and encourage activities that promote basic understandings about literacy are better prepared for school. Educators are sometimes challenged to get the message across to all parents that everyday activities of all sorts, accompanied by interesting talk with lots of new vocabulary words, can play an important part in their children's language and literacy development. Successful parent involvement programs help parents understand the importance of their role as "first teachers" and equip them with the skills and strategies to foster their children's language and literacy development. Key understandings include the knowledge that a child's capacity for learning is not determined at birth and that there is a great deal parents can do to enhance it. Parents should also be aware that there are many informal and enjoyable ways that language and literacy skills can be developed in the home.

Ortiz and Ordoñez-Jasis's "*Leyendo Juntos* (Reading Together): New Directions for Latino Parents' Early Literacy Involvement" and Padak and Rasinski's "Is Being Wild About Harry Enough? Encouraging Independent Reading at Home" offer practical suggestions for linking home and school. Also worth reading is the following:

- McTavish, M. (2007). Constructing the Big Picture: A Working Class Family Supports Their Daughter's Pathways to Literacy. *The Reading Teacher, 60*(5), 476–485.

Using This Book for Professional Development

The books in the Essential Readings series are meant to be used as tools for professional development. The articles included here can be used with long-term, teacher study groups or by individual teachers as a catalyst for improving instruction.

A review of recent literature addressing professional development for teachers of reading reveals considerable agreement about the features of effective professional development programs (c.f., Duffy, 2004; Strickland & Kamil, 2004; Strickland & Riley-Ayers, 2007). Suggestions for implementing an effective study group model include the following:

- Designate someone as the "official" leader of the group. Though the leadership may be shared, it is important to designate someone to keep the effort on track.

- Hold regularly scheduled meetings to reflect on and discuss ongoing efforts with others.

- Focus on a well-articulated purpose that is clear to all participants. Participants need to understand how they are expected to apply the knowledge shared.

- Follow a cycle of Read → Discuss → Apply → Share → Reapply → Share Again.

- Meet in the schools or classrooms where teachers work and where demonstrations of techniques and approaches will be applied.

- Involve everyone in a school, group of schools, or school district whose responsibilities relate to the topic. This includes administrators and supervisors, teachers across age/grade levels and years of experience, special service providers, English-language specialists, and educational support personnel.

- Plan for implementation that is long-term and sustained.

- Provide participants with a variety of experiences, including small-group and individualized support, and with opportunities for discussion, analysis, reflection, and evaluation.

You may wish to begin by reading, responding to, and discussing the sections in this introduction on literacy development and the overview of key research reports. Then, prioritize and select from topics as desired by the group. "Questions for Reflection" at the end of each article suggest themes to think about or discuss, but in each case, your study should be guided by the particular needs of the children you teach.

References

Adams, M.J. (1990). *Beginning to read: Thinking and learning about print.* Cambridge, MA: MIT Press.

Anderson, R.C., Hiebert, E.H., Scott, J.A., & Wilkinson, I.A.G. (1985). *Becoming a nation of readers: The report of the Commission on Reading.* Washington, DC: National Institute of Education.

Bond, G.L., & Dykstra, R. (1967). The cooperative research program in first-grade reading instruction. *Reading Research Quarterly, 2*(4), 5–142. doi:10.2307/746948

Chall, J.S. (1967). *Learning to read: The great debate.* New York: McGraw-Hill.

Cowen, J.E. (2003). *A balanced approach to beginning reading instruction: A synthesis of six major U.S. research studies.* Newark, DE: International Reading Association.

Duffy, G.G. (2004). Teachers who improve reading achievement: What research says about what they do and how to develop them. In D.S. Strickland & M. Kamil (Eds.), *Improving reading achievement through professional development* (p. 3–22). Norwood, NJ: Christopher-Gordon.

Durrell, D.D., Nicholson, A., Olson, A.V., Gavel, S.R., & Linehan, E.B. (1958). Success in first grade reading. *Journal of Education, 140*(3), 1–48.

National Association for the Education of Young Children. (2009). *Developmentally appropriate practice in early childhood programs serving children from birth through grade 8* (3rd ed.). Washington, DC: Author.

National Institute for Literacy. (2008). *Developing early literacy: Report of the National Early Literacy Panel.* Washington, DC: Author.

National Institute of Child Health and Human Development. (2000). *Report of the National Reading Panel: Teaching children to read: An evidence-based assessment of the scientific research literature on reading and its implications for reading instruction* (NIH Publication No. 00–4769). Washington, DC: U.S. Government Printing Office.

Snow, C.E., Burns, M.S., & Griffin, P. (Eds.). (1998). *Preventing reading difficulties in young children.* Washington, DC: National Academy Press.

Strickland, D.S. & Kamil, M. (Eds.). (2004). *Improving reading achievement through professional development.* Norwood, NJ: Christopher-Gordon.

Strickland, D.S., & Riley-Ayers, S. (2007). *Literacy leadership in early childhood: The essential guide.* New York: Teachers College Press; Washington, DC: The National Association for the Education of Young Children.

Strickland, D.S., & Shanahan, T. (2004). Laying the groundwork for literacy. *Educational Leadership, 61*(6), 74–77.

Teale, W.H., & Sulzby, E. (Eds.). (1986). *Emergent literacy: Writing and reading.* Norwood, NJ: Ablex.

Teale, W.H., & Yokota, J. (2000). Beginning reading and writing: Perspectives on instruction. In D.S. Strickland & L.M. Morrow (Eds.), *Beginning reading and writing* (pp. 1–15). Newark, DE: International Reading Association.

Additional Recommended Resources

Enz, B.J., & Morrow, L.M. (2009). *Assessing preschool literacy development: Informal and formal measures to guide instruction.* (2nd ed.). Newark, DE: International Reading Association.

Morrow, L.M., Freitag, E., & Gambrell, L.B. (2009). *Using children's literature in preschool to develop comprehension: Understanding and enjoying books* (2nd ed.). Newark, DE: International Reading Association.

Roskos, K.A., Tabors, P.O., & Lenhart, L.A. (2009). *Oral language and early literacy in preschool: Talking, reading, and writing* (2nd ed.). Newark, DE: International Reading Association.

Schickedanz, J.A., & Casbergue, R.M. (2009). *Writing in preschool: Learning to orchestrate meaning and marks* (2nd ed.). Newark, DE: International Reading Association.

Strickland, D.S. (1998). *Teaching phonics today: A primer for educators.* Newark, DE: International Reading Association.

Strickland, D.S., & Schickedanz, J.A. (2009). *Learning about print in preschool: Working with letters, words, and beginning links with phonemic awareness* (2nd ed.). Newark, DE: International Reading Association.

Vukelich, C., & Christie, J. (2009). *Building a foundation for preschool literacy: Effective instruction for children's reading and writing development* (2nd ed.). Newark, DE: International Reading Association.

Repeated Interactive Read-Alouds in Preschool and Kindergarten

Lea M. McGee and Judith A. Schickedanz

Research is mixed on the value of reading aloud to children aged 3 to 6. On one hand, researchers have validated that reading aloud affects vocabulary development (Robbins & Ehri, 1994; Whitehurst et al., 1999), acquisition of literary syntax and vocabulary (Purcell-Gates, McIntyre, & Freppon, 1995), story recall (Morrow & Smith, 1990), and sensitivity to the linguistic and organizational structures of narrative and informational text (Duke & Kays, 1998). Studies have shown that preschoolers make gains in expressive language even when the duration of story reading interventions is short (e.g., Hargrave & Sénéchal, 2000). In contrast, researchers have found only a modest relationship between the frequency and quality of parent–child read-alouds during preschool and later first-grade reading achievement (Scarborough & Dobrich, 1994). Researchers have also found a negative relationship between the amount of time teachers spend reading aloud in kindergarten and children's decoding skills (Meyer, Wardrop, Stahl, & Linn, 1994). These studies suggest that merely reading books aloud is not sufficient for accelerating children's oral vocabulary development and listening comprehension. Instead, the way books are shared with children matters.

Effective Read-Aloud Techniques

Research has demonstrated that the most effective read-alouds are those in which children are actively involved asking and answering questions and making predictions rather than passively listening (Dickinson, 2001). These read-alouds are called interactive or dialogic and result in gains in vocabulary (Hargrave & Sénéchal, 2000), comprehension strategies and story schema (Van den Broek, 2001), and concept development (Wasik & Bond, 2001). Merely inviting children to talk during interactive read-alouds, however, is not sufficient to accelerate their literacy development. Instead, growth is related to how frequently they engage in analytic talk (Dickinson & Smith, 1994). Analytic talk involves making predictions or inferences that explain a character's motivation or connect events from different parts of the story. Teachers prompt children to engage in analytical thinking by making comments that model such thinking and then asking thoughtful questions.

Other activities boost the value of reading aloud to young children. For example, research has demonstrated that the following activities increase comprehension and language development: inviting preschoolers and kindergartners to retell or dramatize stories (Cornell, Sénéchal, & Brodo, 1988; Pellegrini & Galda, 1982); reading several books on a similar topic and inviting children to play with objects related to the concepts or characters introduced in these books (Rowe, 1998; Wasik & Bond, 2001); reading a book repeatedly (Crago & Crago, 1976); inserting short definitions for some words while reading aloud (Collins, 2004; Elley, 1989); and encouraging children to use these same words when they answer questions, discuss book events

Reprinted from McGee, L.M., & Schickedanz, J.A. (2007). Repeated interactive read-alouds in preschool and kindergarten. *The Reading Teacher, 60*(8), 742-751.

(Hargrave & Sénéchal, 2000; Robbins & Ehri, 1994), or describe illustrations (Reese & Cox, 1999). Thus, effective interactive read-alouds include a systematic approach that incorporates teachers' modeling of higher-level thinking, asking thoughtful questions calling for analytic talk, prompting children to recall a story in some way within a reasonable time frame, reading a single book repeatedly, and reading books related by topic. It also involves a systematic approach to developing children's understanding of vocabulary, such as inserting short definitions of words and phrases during reading.

Two recent methods for reading aloud to children aged 3 to 6 include many of these research-based techniques. Klesius and Griffith (1996) described a technique for reading aloud to small groups of at-risk kindergartners that they claimed extended children's talk about books. Using interactive read-alouds, teachers point to details in illustrations and ask questions about vocabulary words as they read. They extend children's responses by asking them to clarify and explain. After reading, children recall a portion of, or the entire, story. Beck and McKeown (2001) developed a similar technique, called Text Talk, to help kindergarten and primary-grade children expand vocabulary. As teachers read, they draw attention to a few vocabulary words by inserting short definitions. They also ask open-ended questions in which children must provide explanations rather than one- or two-word responses. After reading, teachers discuss vocabulary words in the context of the story and in other contexts.

Our Experiences With Effective Read-Aloud Practices

As researchers and practitioners of early literacy development, we have demonstrated and observed teachers reading aloud in hundreds of preschool and kindergarten classrooms over the last three decades. Despite the wealth of research on effective read-alouds and practical models for such approaches, we have noticed that fewer teachers seem to be attempting to read what we consider sophisticated stories and nonfiction books in pre-school and kindergarten in favor of reading easier, predictable, and concept books (often in Big Book format), especially in classrooms with high percentages of at-risk children. Sophisticated picture books include, for example, stories in which readers must infer characters' motivations and thoughts and connect them to actions (i.e., causes and effects). These books have a rich repertoire of vocabulary. Examples include *Henny Penny* (Galdone, 1968), *Oonga Boonga* (Wishinsky, 2001), and *Owl Moon* (Yolen, 1987). These books can be contrasted with predictable books in which readers do not need to infer character motivation, feelings, or thoughts in order to enjoy the repeated words and actions. Examples include *Brown Bear, Brown Bear, What Do You See?* (Martin, 1967) or *Over in the Meadow* (Wadsworth, 1992). While predictable books have a role in preschool and kindergarten literacy programs, sophisticated picture books play an additional role of expanding vocabulary and enhancing oral comprehension.

Because we were aware that fewer teachers seemed to be reading sophisticated picture books as a daily part of their early literacy programs, we worried that many children were not engaging in analytic talk. As we wondered how we could help teachers systematically promote this kind of talk, we considered Cochran-Smith's (1984) argument that effective teachers model the role of ideal reader as they read aloud. An ideal reader is one who intuitively and unconsciously makes appropriate inferences and predictions and constantly rethinks current events in a story in relation to past events. Thus, effective teachers model what ideal readers do by explicitly talking aloud as they read, making children aware that they are predicting, making an inference, or changing their ideas about what is happening in a story. While thinking aloud is a frequently used technique to help children interpret literature in the elementary grades (e.g., Keene & Zimmerman, 1997; Miller, 2002), we wanted to adapt this technique for much younger children. We wanted teachers to model making comments that would reveal implicit information that preschool and kindergarten children would not likely be able to produce on their own. Therefore, we crafted an approach to reading aloud to reflect insights drawn from current research and theories of an ideal reader as well as our own experiences. The purpose of this article is to describe what we call repeated interactive read-alouds using sophisticated storybooks.

Repeated Interactive Read-Alouds: First Reading of a Picture Storybook

The first read-aloud includes four components: book introduction, vocabulary support techniques, analytical comments and questions, and an after-reading "why" question. These techniques have been carefully selected to help children build a stronger first understanding of the story, including some of its vocabulary.

Book Introductions

Research has shown that effective readers quickly begin to infer story problems and use their tentative ideas about problems to process story information (Van den Broek, 2001). However, problems present challenges for young children: They are often not directly stated in the text (Paris & Paris, 2003; Stein & Glenn, 1979), and young children are relatively insensitive to problems and goals compared to characters and actions (Benson, 1997; Stein & Glenn). Because young children are not likely to focus on the story problem, we craft book introductions to make the problem explicit.

For example, *Henny Penny* (Galdone, 1968) is about a hen who mistakenly believes that a piece of sky has fallen on her head. She is so upset by this event that she acts foolishly and rushes to tell the king about this occurrence. She does not recognize the danger posed by the fox when he invites her and her friends to take a short cut right into his cave (the actual problem of the story, which only readers and not the characters realize). In order to construct a three- or four-sentence introduction we either explicitly state or strongly imply the main problem of the story. For example, to introduce Henny Penny we might say,

> In this story you are going to meet a silly, foolish hen who makes a big mistake. She thinks a catastrophe, a really bad disaster, is about to happen and runs to tell the king about it. A lot of her friends believe her mistake, and they all get in trouble because they are so silly.

As we give the book introduction, we show the front cover and sometimes the back cover or end papers and the title page (rather than all the illustrations as is done in a picture walk). For example, the front cover of *Henny Penny* illustrates the main character and the end papers depict Henny Penny running up a hill toward a castle. As we show these pages we complete the book introduction:

> Here is Henny Penny running to tell the king about the catastrophe. But I have to warn you, she never makes it to the castle. Let's find out what happens to her on the way to tell the king about the catastrophe.

We do not recommend that, during a first read, teachers have children identify book parts such as the front and back cover or top and bottom of the page, tell what the author or illustrator does, or discuss the dedication page. We have found that these activities divert children's attention away from the main goal of a first read-aloud—to enjoy a good story by focusing on its meaning. As we read a book during a first read, we use expression, gestures and dramatic pauses, variations in the pace of reading, and plenty of eye contact. We have found these techniques highly effective at capturing and maintaining children's interest and enjoyment, even when reading longer and more sophisticated books.

Inserting Vocabulary Support

Before reading the book aloud, we select 5 to 10 vocabulary words or phrases from the book that we will highlight or define during reading. These words are critical to understanding the story and are likely to be encountered in other books or useful in nonbook contexts (Beck, McKeown, & Kucan, 2002). Sometimes the book does not include specific vocabulary that ideal readers would use in their analytical thinking about this particular book, so we insert these additional vocabulary words into the book introduction and our comments as we read aloud. For example, we would insert the words *mistake*, *catastrophe*, *disaster*, and *foolish* while reading *Henny Penny* because these words are critical for analyzing the problem in relationship to the main character's motivations and traits. Once we select vocabulary words and phrases, we highlight the words or enhance word and phrase meanings in one or more of five ways:

1. We insert a short phrase or sentence that defines or explains a word, such as saying "*Feast*, that's a really big dinner."

2. We point to salient parts of the illustration that help clarify a word or phrase meaning, such as pointing to the illustration of an acorn as we read the word in the text.

3. We use dramatic gestures, such as demonstrating the meaning of *shrugged* by shrugging our shoulders as we read.

4. We use voice, such as making clear the fox's sly intentions by reading the text with a droll voice.

5. We vary the pacing with which we read words or phrases, such as reading more quickly what Henny Penny says to demonstrate her foolish rush.

It only takes a few moments to plan how to support children's understanding of each word, but the most effective read-alouds are ones in which we actually decide which of the vocabulary enhancers we will use for each vocabulary word. For words that are to be clarified verbally, we plan short explanations that are "slipped" into the story reading so the definitions are part of the actual story without interrupting the flow of reading.

Comments and Questions to Support and Extend Comprehension

During reading we make comments that demonstrate analytic thinking at three or four junctures

in which ideal readers would make inferences about a character's thoughts, feelings, or motivations, or we predict upcoming events. When we comment about the story, we often use language to signal our mental activity by using the phrase "I'm thinking." For example, in the scene where Henny Penny exclaims, "The sky is falling. I must go and tell the king" (unpaged), we may comment, "I'm thinking this is where the hen is doing something really foolish. She isn't even looking down to try and find out what really hit her. I think she is looking up instead of down." Then we would go on to ask, "Why does the hen think a piece of the sky has fallen on her head?" We have found that children's answers to questions following our analytical comments are more likely to be related to the story. This teaching sequence provides a deliberate and systematic approach toward expanding children's comprehension. We have noticed that most young children are not yet capable of engaging in analytic thinking and talking without teacher modeling or questioning.

After-Reading Questions

After reading the entire book, we ask a "why" question requiring children to make inferences about and explain several story events. Then we use follow-up probing questions to support children's ability to answer broader explanation questions. For example, after a first reading of *Henny Penny*, we might ask the explanation question "Why didn't Foxy Loxy just jump up and eat those silly birds? Why did he lead them into his cave?" In order to help children answer this question we might comment, "I'm thinking that even though the fox is strong and has big teeth, there are a lot of birds. How many friends were with Henny Penny?" Recalling the number of birds will help children infer that the fox may have only been able to catch and eat one of the birds and the others might have escaped. We also help children consider this question by using illustrations to support their thinking. In this version of the story, the last illustration shows Foxy Loxy and Mrs. Loxy and their seven children peering out from the cave. We turn to this illustration and say, "You know I'm remembering this illustration right here. This might give me a hint about why the fox led the birds into the cave. What is the hint?" This comment might help children infer that Foxy led the birds into the cave so that his children would also have a dinner, and his wife could help catch the birds.

Second Interactive Read-Aloud

Second read-alouds occur a day or two after first reads. The purpose is to enrich children's comprehension of the story and provide further opportunities for children to engage in analytic talk. During second book introductions, we remind children that they have read this book before and that they will remember some things from the book; for example, we might say,

> We read this book yesterday, and you probably remember that it is about a hen who misinterprets something that happened to her. Who can remember what she thought happened to her? What was the catastrophe, and what did she decide to do about it?

We continue to highlight the same vocabulary; however, in a second read we verbally define more words. For example, during a first read of *Owl Moon*, in which a father and a child go owling in the woods late one night, we might simply dramatize how the owl pumped his wings. During the second read, we would dramatize *pumped* and insert a verbal explanation (e.g., "That means he flapped his wings up and down very hard").

During the second read, we continue modeling analytic comments, but we ask more frequent questions that help children make additional inferences. In the first read, our comments focus on getting children to infer what the main character is thinking and feeling or to connect main events with their causes. Thus, our comments and questions during the second read might focus on the other characters' motivations or thoughts. Just as in a first read, we prepare children to answer analytical questions by first modeling analytic comments that make explicit some, but not all, of the information needed to

adequately answer the question. For example, in *Henny Penny*, after Cocky Locky asks to join Henny Penny on her way to tell the king that the sky is falling, we might comment, "I'm thinking that Cocky Locky believes that a piece of the sky really did fall on Henny Penny's head." Later, when Ducky Lucky joins Henny Penny and Cocky Locky, we comment, "Henny Penny has now convinced two other birds that the sky is falling." Then we could ask, "If they had been with Henny Penny when the acorn fell on her head, what do you think they would have said when she shouted, 'Oh, my, the sky is falling, we must go and tell the king'?"

Like first reads, we end second reads by asking another explanation question. Sometimes we ask children about something that might happen beyond the story. For example, we might ask, "What do you think the king would have done if Henny Penny had managed to get to the castle and told him the sky was falling?"

Third Interactive Read-Aloud

Third reads occur a few days after the second read when the story is still fresh in children's minds but when they must remember information across some time. This close repetition is also important for reinforcing vocabulary carefully developed during the first and second read. Third interactive read-alouds differ from first and second read-alouds because they integrate a guided reconstruction of the story with the teacher's reading of some of the story text. Reconstructions are retellings of story events along with explanations about what caused those events and what characters are thinking during the events. Therefore, guided reconstructions are more effective than mere retellings because children use analytical talk to explain why events occurred.

In third read-aloud book introductions, we again acknowledge that children are familiar with the book and its content and ask questions about the title or characters, such as "We've read this book two times before, so I know you know its title. What is it?" We usually allow children to respond together to this easily answered question. We might continue to prompt children to reconstruct information by asking, "What other details do we see on the cover that we know are important for the story?" (e.g., prompting children to notice the acorn on the front cover of *Henny Penny*). We continue to focus on the story problem by asking, "We all remember Henny Penny's problem, don't we? Who would like to share that with us?" We are very careful with the number of questions we ask both during book introductions and during guided reconstruction. We have found that third read-alouds can become deadly when teachers overwhelm students with a barrage of questions.

We use two general prompts in guiding reconstruction of texts. Before reading some pages of the story, we point to the illustration and ask, "What's happening here?" We use this prompt as we show a double-spread illustration. Sometimes we use the second question "Do you remember what will happen next?" before turning to the next illustration. We only use this question when the next event is causally related to the event the children have just recalled. For example, in *Owl Moon* after reconstructing the event in which the characters hear the owl hoot in response to the dad's call, we might ask, "Do you remember what happens next?" because this scene provides a connection to the next event: seeing the owl.

After children reconstruct the events on one double spread, we might read the text. On longer books, we reread many pages of the text and have children reconstruct only a few pages; on shorter books, we allow children to reconstruct more of the story and read only a few pages of the text. The length of the book and children's responses guide our decisions of whether to read more or engage children in more reconstruction.

In third reads, teachers continue to insert verbal explanations of words, point to illustrations, and make dramatic motions. To further emphasize vocabulary in a third read, teachers extend some word meanings to a familiar context but not one included in the story. For example, to extend children's understanding of the word *pumped* in *Owl Moon*, we might say,

Sometimes, when you are on the swings outside and want help, we tell you to "pump your legs," and you move them back and forth to make yourself go up and back on the swing. The owl was moving his wings—pumping them up and down to fly through the sky.

Thus, each day of the repeated interactive read-aloud systematically builds and extends children's awareness and understanding of vocabulary. Table 1 presents an overview of the components for the three days of repeated interactive read-alouds.

Repeated Interactive Read-Alouds in Action

Across three days of reading the same book, the strategies used in repeated interactive read-alouds provide children with an opportunity to engage more actively in the reading experience. During a first read, teachers take a more active role by reading the text and making comments; children are actively listening and sometimes comment or answer questions. During a second read, children participate more verbally by answering questions and commenting more frequently. In the third read-aloud, children take a highly active role as they reconstruct the story with teacher guidance. The following excerpts are taken from book introductions in a first, second, and third read of a story. They demonstrate how children's participation changes across time.

First Read-Aloud: Book Introduction

In the story *Oonga Boonga*, no one can quiet Baby Louise who is crying so loudly that pictures fall off walls, neighborhood animals flee, and neighbors come calling to help. Despite attempts by every family member, only Louise's brother Daniel can soothe her. We read this book three times to a group of 4-year-olds in a Head Start center.

Teacher: Today I'm going to read you a book called *Oonga Boonga*, and this story is about Baby Louise (points to front cover with illustration of Baby Louise

Table 1
Components of Repeated Interactive Read-Aloud

	First read-aloud	Second read-aloud	Third read-aloud: Guided reconstruction
Book introduction	Give a few sentences introducing the main character and central problem. Use illustrations on the book cover, back, and title page as needed.	Remind children that they know the characters and some things the character does. Ask questions about the characters and problem.	Invite children to identify the problem and describe the solution. Have children recall the title of the book.
Book reading	Insert vocabulary enhancements for 5-10 vocabulary words by pointing to illustrations, gesturing dramatically, or inserting a few definitions. Make comments that reveal what the main character is thinking or feeling. Ask a few follow-up analytical questions based on your comments.	Insert vocabulary enhancements for the same vocabulary, including more verbal definitions. Make comments that reveal what other characters are thinking or feeling. Ask more analytical follow-up questions.	Before reading a double page, show the illustration and ask, "What is happening here?" Follow up children's comments by extending comments or asking for clarification. Read some of the pages of text. When appropriate, before turning to the next page, ask, "Who remembers what will happen next?" Call attention to some vocabulary in different contexts.
After-reading discussion	Ask a "why" question that calls for explanation. Use follow-up questions to prompt answers. Demonstrate how to answer the question by saying, "I'm thinking...."	Ask another "why" question or ask, "What would have happened if...?" Use follow-up questions to prompt children's thinking.	Ask another "why" question or ask, "What would have happened if...?"

and Daniel smiling at one another, then turns to the back cover and points to illustration of Baby Louise crying). Baby Louise is unhappy. She's crying and crying, and no one can stop her. I know one reason why babies cry; they cry because they're hungry. They cry when they're bored and want to see something funny. We're going to find out why Baby Louise is crying and what will help her stop crying. (Turns back to front cover) Here is Baby Louise and she's not crying is she? This might give us a hint about what stops her from crying.

In this book introduction, Lea (first author) provided reasons why babies might cry and hinted strongly at what would make Baby Louise stop crying by showing the front illustration of Daniel and Louise. She did all the talking while the children were actively listening.

Second Read-Aloud: Book Introduction

The following day Lea read the book a second time to the children. She prompted the children to take a more active role in constructing the book introduction.

Teacher:	(Holds book up)
Children:	(Overlapping responses) Oonga boonga, oonga boonga, that baby was crying, her brother came back, he say oonga boonga.
Teacher:	That's right, yes (making eye contact with many different children to affirm their comments about the story). Now, in this story Baby Louise has a big problem.
Child:	She crying.
Teacher:	She *is* crying. She is very upset. Now the front of this book (pointing) shows us the solution to the problem.
Child:	She happy.
Teacher:	She *is* happy. What is the solution to the problem of Baby Louise *crying*? (Flips to back cover)
Several children:	Oonga boonga.
Teacher:	(Flips to front cover) Yes, Daniel (points to him on the cover) says, "oonga boonga" and makes her feel good. We're going to read the story again today and watch and see what all the other people do to try and soothe Baby Louise. Baby Louise is very upset. She's wailing and crying. Nobody could make her stop.
Several children:	Oonga boonga.

The second book introduction was jointly constructed by Lea and the children. Lea allowed and encouraged spontaneous comments and prompted the children to recall what they knew about the story.

Third Read-Aloud: Guided Reconstruction Book Introduction

In the book introduction for the third read, Lea again prompted children's active engagement by asking them to reconstruct more of the story. The children remembered much of the discussion they had during the second read-aloud and included speculations of what might have happened if Daniel had tried alternative ways to quiet Baby Louise.

Teacher:	I know you remember the title of this book.
Several children:	*Oonga Boonga*.
Teacher:	Yes, *Oonga Boonga*. And who can remember the problem in the story?
Children:	(Overlapping responses) Crying, brother Daniel stopped the crying, oonga boonga.
Teacher:	Yes the baby is crying and crying. Can mother stop the baby crying?
Many children:	No, no.
Teacher:	Can father stop her?
Many children:	No, no, her brother.
Teacher:	Yes, Daniel stopped the baby from crying, and he stops her crying in two ways. The first way....
Several children:	Oonga boonga.
Teacher:	Yes, he says, "Oonga boonga." The second way he stops her crying? Do you remember?
Child:	Tickles her tummy.
Teacher:	Yes, we did talk that he *might* have tickled her tummy when we read this two days ago.
Child:	Sings a song.
Teacher:	Yes, we did talk about that he *might* have sung a lullaby. But he *actually* whispered something else.
Many children:	Bonka wonka.
Teacher:	Yes, he said another silly thing: Bonka wonka.

Thus, across these three introductions, it is clear that the children are building a richer, more detailed understanding of the story. By the third read, the children are clearly using analytic talk to move beyond what actually happened in the story to what might have happened.

Analytic Talk in First and Third Read "Why" Questions

In the next section, we show how children's ability to use analytic talk increases from a first to a third interactive read-aloud. Here is their response to a "why" question during the first read:

Teacher: Why was Louise crying all the time?

Child: 'Cause her brother was, her brother was gone.

Teacher: Her brother wasn't there, and why was Louise crying?

Child: 'Cause she was crying.

Teacher: But *why* was she crying?

Child: She wanted her brother to say, "oonga boonga."

Teacher: She did want her brother. Did she want the words "oonga boonga" or did she want her brother?

Child: Her brother.

Teacher: Yes, she just wanted her brother.

The children were able to make explicit that Baby Louise was crying because she wanted her brother. They were beginning to grasp that the silly words her brother said had nothing to do with Louise stopping crying; it was her brother she wanted. Lea continued to explore this inference in both the second and third read with different "why" questions. By the third read, most children engaged in a more extended analytic discussion.

Teacher: Now, let's think about this. Remember I said yesterday, "What if Daniel had tickled her belly instead of saying 'Bonka wonka.'" Would Louise have stopped crying?

Children: (Overlapping responses) No, no. He whispered in her ear. Yes.

Teacher: I think she would have stopped crying.

Child: He whistled in her ear.

Teacher: You know, maybe if he would've whistled in her ear and tickled the baby, I think she would have stopped crying. Because he was her brother, and he, well, let me ask you this: What if her brother took her in his arms like this (turns to picture of the mother rocking baby) and rocked her and sang her a lullaby. Do you think she would've stopped crying?

Children: (Overlapping responses) Yes, yes, no.

Teacher: (Looks at one child) I do, too. I think she would have stopped crying. What if Daniel had taken her in his arms like this (shows illustration of grandfather) and made a funny face at her. Do you think she would have stopped crying?

Children: (Overlapping responses) Yes, yes, no.

Teacher: I think so. If Daniel played the harmonica, would it work for him?

Child: It did.

Teacher: I think it would work. What if Daniel gave the baby a bottle? Do you think it would've stopped her crying?

Child: Yes.

Teacher: She really liked it when Daniel said silly words, but I think she just likes her brother.

Child: She don't care about oonga boona. She care about her brother.

While Lea's original "why" question seemed beyond the children's understanding, turning to specific illustrations and posing alternative questions allowed children to be more successful in both understanding the questions and making the inferences needed to answer them. Most children realized that Daniel, not the silly words, was the key to getting Baby Louise to stop crying.

As shown in the excerpts from the three repeated readings of *Oonga Boonga*, our experiences suggest it is a powerful technique for extending children's vocabulary, their use of comprehension strategies, and their engagement with literature. We are consultants and directors of several Early Reading First grants currently using a repeated interactive read-aloud approach. While repeated interactive story reading is certainly not the only strategy used to enhance vocabulary and comprehension in these programs, it is the most systematic approach.

The repeated interactive read-aloud approach requires that teachers study closely each book they read. They must craft effective comments and questions and be able to respond on the spot to children's answers, which often indicate misinterpretations and misunderstandings. However, it is critical that teachers use these strategies so that children engage in analytical thinking. We recommend that teachers read aloud a sophisticated picture book daily, along with many other kinds of books, including predictable books. Teachers with whom we have worked include repeated interactive read-alouds of a sophisticated storybook or nonfiction as a part of their daily whole-group literacy instruction.

Final Thoughts

We have shown that the repeated interactive read-aloud technique is a research-based approach to comprehension and vocabulary development in preschool and kindergarten. We developed this approach to help teachers share picture books with young children, especially children with few home literary experiences, in ways that will allow them to enjoy our most sophisticated literature. It challenges both teachers and children to extend their thinking and their literary understanding in analytic discussions.

References

Beck, I.L., & McKeown, M.G. (2001). Text talk: Capturing the benefits of read-aloud experiences for young children. *The Reading Teacher, 55*, 10–20.

Beck, I.L., McKeown, M.G., & Kucan, L. (2002). *Bringing words to life: Robust vocabulary instruction. Solving problems in the teaching of literacy.* New York: Guilford.

Benson, M.S. (1997). Psychological causation and goal-based episodes: Low-income children's emerging narrative skills. *Early Childhood Research Quarterly, 12*, 439–457.

Cochran-Smith, M. (1984). *The making of a reader.* Norwood, NJ: Ablex.

Collins, M. (2004). *ESL preschoolers' English vocabulary acquisition and story comprehension from storybook reading.* Unpublished doctoral dissertation, Boston University.

Cornell, E.H., Sénéchal, M., & Brodo, L.S. (1988). Recall of picture books by 3-year-old children: Testing and repetition effects in joint reading activities. *Journal of Educational Psychology, 80*, 537–542.

Crago, H., & Crago, M. (1976). The untrained eye? A preschool child explores Felix Hoffman's "Rapunzel." *Children's Literature in Education, 22*, 135–151.

Dickinson, D. (2001). Book reading in preschool classrooms: Is recommended practice common? In D.K Dickinson & P.O. Tabors (Eds.), *Building literacy with language: Young children learning at home and school* (pp. 175–203). Baltimore: Brookes.

Dickinson, D.K., & Smith, M.W. (1994). Long-term effects of preschool teachers' book readings on low-income children's vocabulary and story comprehension. *Reading Research Quarterly, 29*, 104–122.

Duke, N.K., & Kays, J. (1998). "Can I say 'once upon a time'?": Kindergarten children developing knowledge of information book language. *Early Childhood Research Quarterly, 13*, 295–318.

Elley, W. (1989). Vocabulary acquisition from listening to stories. *Reading Research Quarterly, 24*, 174–187.

Hargrave, A.C., & Sénéchal, M. (2000). A book reading intervention with preschool children who have limited vocabularies: The benefits of regular reading and dialogic reading. *Early Childhood Research Quarterly, 15*, 75–90.

Keene, E.O., & Zimmermann, S. (1997). *Mosaic of thought: Teaching comprehension in a reader's workshop.* Portsmouth, NH: Heinemann.

Klesius, J.P., & Griffith, P.L. (1996). Interactive storybook reading for at-risk learners. *The Reading Teacher, 49*, 552–560.

Meyer, L.A., Wardrop, J.S., Stahl, S.A., & Linn, R.L. (1994). Effects of reading storybooks aloud to children. *Journal of Educational Research, 88*, 69–85.

Miller, D. (2002). *Reading with meaning: Teaching comprehension in the primary grades.* Portland, ME: Stenhouse.

Morrow, L.M., & Smith, J.K. (1990). The effects of group size on interactive storybook reading. *Reading Research Quarterly, 25*, 213–231.

Paris, A.H., & Paris, S.G. (2003). Assessing narrative comprehension in young children. *Reading Research Quarterly, 38*, 36–76.

Pellegrini, A.D., & Galda, L. (1982). The effects of thematic-fantasy play training on the development of children's story comprehension. *American Educational Research Journal, 19*, 443–452.

Purcell-Gates, V., McIntyre, E., & Freppon, P.A. (1995). Learning written storybook language in school: A comparison of low–SES children in skills-based and whole language classrooms. *American Educational Research Journal, 32,* 659–685.

Reese, E., & Cox, A. (1999). Quality of adult book reading affects children's emergent literacy. *Developmental Psychology, 35,* 20–28.

Robbins, C., & Ehri, L.C. (1994). Reading storybooks to kindergartners helps them learn new vocabulary words. *Journal of Educational Psychology, 86,* 54–64.

Rowe, D. (1998). The literate potentials of book-related dramatic play. *Reading Research Quarterly, 33,* 10–35.

Scarborough, H.S., & Dobrich, W., (1994). On the efficacy of reading to preschoolers. *Developmental Review, 14,* 245–302.

Stein, N.L., & Glenn, C.G. (1979). An analysis of story comprehension in elementary school children. In R.O. Freedle (Ed.), *New directions in discourse processing* (Vol. 2, pp. 53–120). Norwood, NJ: Ablex.

Van den Broek, P. (2001). *The role of television viewing in the development of reading comprehension.* Washington, DC: U.S. Department of Education.

Wasik, B.A., & Bond, M.A. (2001). Beyond the pages of a book: Interactive book reading and language development in preschool classrooms. *Journal of Educational Psychology, 93,* 243–250.

Whitehurst, G.J., Crone, D.A., Zevnbergen, A.A., Schultz, M.D., Velting, O.N., & Fischel, J.E. (1999). Outcomes of an emergent literacy intervention from Head Start through second grade. *Journal of Educational Psychology, 91,* 261–272.

Literature Cited

Galdone, P. (1968). *Henny Penny.* New York: Seabury Press.

Martin, Jr, B. (1967). *Brown bear, brown bear, what do you see?* New York: Holt, Rinehart and Winston.

Wadsworth, O. (1992). *Over in the meadow: An old counting rhyme.* New York: Scholastic.

Wishinsky, F. (2001). *Oonga boonga.* New York: Puffin.

Yolen, J. (1987). *Owl moon.* New York: Philomel Books.

Questions for Reflection

• The authors highlight the importance of using sophisticated picture books and guiding children to active participation and high levels of thinking. Interactive read-alouds are intended to move from teacher-dominated talk to shared talk to child-dominated talk. Think about how you read aloud to young children, or ask a colleague to watch as you read aloud and then discuss your technique with him or her. Are the books you select engaging for your learners? What are you doing—or not doing—to ensure children's active participation in high levels of thinking?

• Are there ways in which you could engage parents in this technique? What might you develop to send home to parents that would help them improve their at-home reading to their children?

Maximizing the Effectiveness of Reading Aloud

Holly B. Lane and Tyran L. Wright

Two decades ago, in *Becoming a Nation of Readers* (Anderson, Hiebert, Scott, & Wilkinson, 1985), reading aloud gained a new level of emphasis. It was called "the single most important activity for building the knowledge required for eventual success in reading" (p. 23). Since that time, parents and teachers have heard much more about the importance of reading aloud. Trelease's *Read-Aloud Handbook* (1982) became quite popular. Programs such as Reading is Fundamental produced public service announcements touting the benefits of reading aloud to children. The National Parent Teacher Association and the National Education Association promoted reading aloud through their parent guide (2004). The Reach Out and Read program began using pediatricians as an avenue to provide parents books and tips for reading aloud to their children (www.reachoutandread.org).

With such widespread promotion, most parents and teachers have come to believe that reading aloud to children is an important part of early literacy development (Roberts & Burchinal, 2002), and many parents and teachers spend a good deal of time engaged in read-aloud activities (Teale, 2003). Despite this common acceptance of the importance of reading aloud, many children continue to start school with extremely limited experience with books (Anderson-Yockel & Haynes, 1994). The most frequently cited barriers to reading aloud are lack of time (Smith, 1989) and limited access to children's books (Dickinson, McCabe, & Anastasopoulos, 2003; Strickland, 2002). Adams (1990) explained that children may begin school with as little as 25 hours or as much as 1,500 hours of read-aloud experiences.

Effects of Reading Aloud to Children

The public interest in reading aloud to children sparked a new wave of research. Some of the findings were surprising. For example, despite being labeled the "single most important activity" (Anderson et al., 1985, p. 23), Scarborough and Dobrich (1994) found that reading aloud accounts for only 8% of the variance in reading ability in the primary grades. The researchers suggested that more studies should be conducted to determine what specific behaviors during read-aloud sessions contribute to later literacy development. Meyer, Wardrop, Linn, and Hastings (1993) found that there are low to moderate negative correlations between time teachers spend reading aloud and their students' reading achievement. That is, in classrooms where teachers spend more time reading aloud to children, students' reading achievement tends to be worse than in classrooms where less time is devoted to read-aloud activities. In classrooms where reading aloud was taking place, there were fewer interactions with students, and students spent less time reading on their own. On the surface, these studies seem to indicate that reading aloud may not be particularly beneficial to children.

On the other hand, there is ample evidence of the benefits of reading aloud to children. For example, several researchers have demonstrated that reading aloud to children can increase their

Reprinted from Lane, H.B., & Wright, T.L. (2007). Maximizing the effectiveness of reading aloud. *The Reading Teacher, 60*(7), 668–675.

vocabulary (Beck, McKeown, & Kucan, 2002; Brabham & Lynch-Brown, 2002; De Temple & Snow, 2003; Sénéchal, 1997; Sharif, Ozuah, Dinkevich, & Mulvihill, 2003). We also have evidence that reading aloud to children can increase their listening comprehension skills (Morrow & Gambrell, 2002; Stanovich, Cunningham, & West, 1998; Teale, 1986). We know that reading aloud to children can promote their syntactic development (Chomsky, 1972). It is also clear that reading aloud to children can increase their ability to recognize words (Stahl, 2003). Reading aloud promotes a variety of skills and abilities related to emergent literacy, and, in fact, children's own emergent readings demonstrate evidence of having had books read to them (Elster, 1994).

So, how can we make sense of these apparently contradictory findings? We can start by examining the conditions under which reading aloud to children has been effective. The most positive results of reading aloud have typically been found with researcher-designed methods, as opposed to naturally occurring methods. This suggests that teachers and parents could be more productive in their read-aloud activities if they employed some of the more systematic methods that researchers use.

Maximizing the Effectiveness of Read-Alouds

Given the pressures of accountability in today's school climate, it is essential that instructional time be spent wisely. To ensure that reading aloud does not get lost in the press for higher student achievement, teachers must maximize the effectiveness of their read-aloud activities. To make read-alouds as effective as possible, Teale (2003) suggested that teachers consider (a) the amount of read-aloud time, (b) the choice of text for read-aloud activities, (c) the method of reading aloud, and (d) the fit of the read-aloud in the curriculum.

Time for Reading Aloud

To determine how much reading aloud is appropriate, teachers should consider what reading aloud adds and what, if anything, is given up.

Often, multiple instructional goals can be accomplished with one read-aloud, which can actually save instructional time. Different children have different needs based on their prior experiences, so the amount of read-aloud time appropriate in a high-poverty school may be different than what would be appropriate in a school with a more affluent population. Teale (2003) recommended that teachers reflect on the amount of time spent to ensure that it is time spent wisely.

Choosing Text for Reading Aloud

It is important to consider the quality of books selected for read-aloud activities. Books that are well written, books with engaging characters and plots, and books that offer the teacher many opportunities to model fluent and expressive reading are the best choices. Including an assortment of text genres exposes children to more literary variety. Teachers should consider the instructional goals of the read-aloud when selecting books. For example, alphabet books are excellent for teaching about letters, and storybooks are useful for developing vocabulary. Informational books can help children develop content knowledge and enhance their motivation for reading. Word play books are useful for developing metalinguistic abilities such as phonological awareness.

Methods for Reading Aloud

There are several general methods that should be used to make read-alouds effective (Teale, 2003). For example, teachers should encourage children to use their background knowledge to develop understanding of the text and ask questions that keep children engaged. Reading in a lively, engaging way, using voices, gestures, and expressions can enhance understanding. It is helpful to encourage children to predict what will happen in a story, but teachers should be careful to help children confirm or refute their predictions using the text. Especially for younger children, it is important to focus on important ideas from the text and avoid discussions that are too tangential.

Dickinson and Tabors (2001) suggested that teachers and parents should engage children in both immediate and nonimmediate talk. Immediate talk focuses on answering literal questions and labeling pictures. Nonimmediate talk extends beyond the text. It includes discussions of word meanings, making predictions and inferences, and relating the text to personal experiences. It is important that individual children have multiple opportunities to engage in nonimmediate talk during read-alouds.

Examining Book Reading in the Classroom

Dickinson et al. (2003) suggested that it is important for teachers to examine their own book reading in the classroom. For example, it is helpful to have a designated read-aloud area in the classroom, and that area should be inviting and comfortable. There should also be plentiful time for adult–child book reading, and there should be strong connections between home and classroom read-aloud activities.

Read-aloud activities should be integrated throughout the curriculum. Teachers should match read-aloud texts to curriculum goals and consider how the book fits into the unit being studied. Developing connections across books makes learning more connected and meaningful. Teachers can extend the read-aloud experience beyond the book itself through activities, discussions, and projects. Finally, using research-based methods of reading aloud should increase the likelihood that read-aloud activities will achieve the desired results.

Research-Based Read-Aloud Methods

Although substantial research efforts have been devoted to examining the effects of reading aloud, only a few researchers have developed and tested specific techniques for reading aloud to children. Three methods that have emerged as particularly compelling approaches to reading aloud are dialogic reading (Whitehurst, Arnold, Epstein, & Angell, 1994), text talk (Beck & McKeown, 2001), and print referencing (Ezell &

Justice, 2000). These methods incorporate critical elements of language development, vocabulary growth, and knowledge about books in ways that promote learning without detracting from children's enjoyment.

Dialogic Reading

Dialogic reading, developed and refined by Whitehurst and his colleagues (Arnold, Lonigan, Whitehurst, & Epstein, 1994; Lonigan & Whitehurst, 1998; Valdez-Menchaca & Whitehurst, 1992; Whitehurst et al., 1988; Whitehurst et al., 1999), provides a simple structure for making parent–child or teacher–child read-alouds more effective and productive. This method is most commonly used with preschool children, but it is appropriate for older children as well. Dialogic reading is based on three principles: (a) encouraging the child to become an active learner during book reading, (b) providing feedback that models more sophisticated language, and (c) challenging the child's knowledge and skills by raising the complexity of the conversation to a level just above his current ability (De Temple & Snow, 2003).

According to Whitehurst et al. (1988), as parents or teachers begin using dialogic reading, the emphasis should be on asking "what" questions, following answers with questions, repeating what the child says, and providing help and praise. As the read-aloud interactions become more sophisticated, specific types of prompts are implemented. Completion prompts are fill-in-the-blank prompts (e.g., "When Lucy reached the shed she...."). Recall prompts require the child to remember specific details from the story (e.g., "Can you remember what they saw at the zoo?"). Open-ended prompts are statements or questions that encourage responses in the child's own words (e.g., "What do you think she should do next?"). *Wh-* prompts are *what*, *where*, and *why* questions. Distancing prompts are statements or questions that require the child to relate the content of the book to life outside the book (e.g., "Have you ever lost something special like

Table 1
Examples of Prompts to Use During a Read-Aloud

Prompt type	Example
Completion	When the little pig wouldn't open the door, the wolf said.... The last little pig's house wouldn't blow down because....
Recall	What did the wolf say? What was the first little pig's house made of?
Open ended	Why wouldn't the little pig open the door for the wolf? What was the real reason the wolf wanted the pig to open the door?
Distancing	Has a stranger ever come knocking on your door? What kind of house would you like to build when you grow up?

Adam did?"). Table 1 provides more examples of prompts. As children become accustomed to this type of dialogue, eventually open-ended questions become enough to sustain meaningful storybook interactions.

Text Talk

Text talk, developed by Beck and McKeown and their colleagues (Beck & McKeown, 2001; Beck et al., 2002), is a read-aloud strategy that focuses on vocabulary development. (See Table 2 for an explanation of the text talk strategy.) This strategy is most typically used in the primary grades. By engaging children in meaningful discussions about books, teachers can use text talk read-alouds to provide a context for teaching new words. A teacher begins a text talk lesson by reading a story aloud and engaging in rich discussion with children. The teacher then targets several words from the story to discuss in more depth. Deep learning of these words becomes the focus of the lesson.

Selecting Words to Teach. The selection of appropriate words is one of the most important aspects of a good text talk lesson. The teacher should choose words that can be connected to what students know, can be explained with words they know, and will be useful and interesting to students. Beck (2004) explained that there are three "tiers" of word utility. Tier 1 words are common, everyday words that the children prob-

ably already know (e.g., *baby*, *school*, *hungry*, *ceiling*, *quickly*). Tier 2 words are less common words but ones that mature speakers of the language use and understand readily (e.g., *solemn*, *coincidence*, *trivial*, *devour*, *avoid*). Tier 3 words are relatively infrequent words that are most typically associated with a specific content area (e.g., *isotope*, *peninsula*, *filibuster*, *fricative*, *photosynthesis*). Because they are both useful and probably not already known, Beck suggested targeting Tier 2 words for instruction.

Creating Child-Friendly Definitions. To communicate the meanings of the target words, dictionary definitions are usually not very helpful for children. Beck et al. (2002) suggested teachers create their own definitions to make the word meanings more accessible. A child-friendly definition uses everyday language to explain the meaning of the word. To create a child-friendly definition, Beck suggested teachers ask themselves, "When do I use this word?" "Why do we have this word?" Staying focused on the central meaning or concept of the word rather than the multiple meanings of the word promotes understandings. Finally, Beck et al. recommended including *something*, *someone*, or *describes* in a child-friendly definition to clarify how the word is used (see Table 3 for examples). As a resource for generating definitions that children can understand and use, Beck (2004) recommended the *Collins Cobuild Student Dictionary* (Collins Cobuild, 2002).

Table 2
Elements of the Text Talk Strategy

Read and discuss the story with children.	During the book reading, ask children questions that focus on understanding the story. After reading the book, conduct a minilesson about a few key words from the text.
Introduce the target words one at a time.	During each lesson, focus on three to five Tier 2 words. Choose words that will be most likely to be useful to children later. Write the word on the chalkboard or on a pocket-chart card to display.
Ask children to repeat each word.	It is important for children to have a clear phonological representation of the words. For more difficult words, you may want to have children say the word several times.
Introduce a child-friendly definition.	Explain the central meaning of the word using words the children already know. Use complete sentences and, whenever possible, include the words *someone*, *something*, or *describes*.
Share examples of the word in contexts that are *different* from the context in the story.	Expand children's understanding of the word by using it in a variety of contexts. For words with multiple meanings, make sure your examples use the central word meaning.
Engage children in thinking about and using the meaning of the word.	Guide children in activities that require them to use the word. You may ask them, "Have you ever...?" Or, you might ask them to agree or disagree with comments using the word. Or, you might ask children to turn to a partner and tell them something they know about the word. Be sure children use the word in their explanations.
Ask children to repeat the word again to reinforce its phonological representation.	Be sure every child has an opportunity to say the word several times, especially in meaningful contexts.
Repeat these steps for each target word.	

Adapted from Beck, McKeown, & Kucan (2002).

Table 3
Examples of Child-Friendly Definitions

Word	Child-friendly definition
Guardian	A *guardian* is someone who takes care of you.
Nuisance	A *nuisance* is something or someone that bothers you.
Obvious	*Obvious* describes something that is clear and easy to understand.
Expert	An *expert* is someone who knows a lot more than other people about a particular topic.
Avoid	When someone *avoids* something, they try to keep away from it or keep it from happening.
Proposal	A *proposal* is an idea or suggestion that you really want someone to agree to.
Extraordinary	*Extraordinary* describes something that is very special or unusual–something out of the ordinary.
Drowsy	*Drowsy* describes that feeling when you are getting sleepy and you have trouble keeping your eyes open.

Using Target Words in Other Contexts.
According to Beck et al. (2002), after explaining in child-friendly language what a target word means, the teacher should require students to use and interact with the word by thinking about its meaning. These contexts should be sentences or paragraphs designed to make word meaning transparent, and they should be used along with (not instead of) child-friendly explanations. The goal of this portion of the text talk lesson is to make word meaning explicit and clear and to engage students in actively thinking about and using the meanings right away. A teacher might elect to ask children to use the word themselves or to respond to the teacher's use of the word.

Print Referencing

Print referencing refers to the verbal and non-verbal cues, such as tracking print or pointing to print in pictures, adults use to call children's attention to important aspects of the text, including its forms, features, and functions (Justice & Ezell, 2004). The purpose of print referencing is to increase the metalinguistic focus of reading aloud, thereby increasing print interest. With increased print interest, "children come to view written language as an object distinctly worthy of attention" (Justice & Ezell, 2004, p. 186). Cues can be explicit or implicit and are embedded within the storybook reading interaction. They can be verbal cues (e.g., commenting or questioning about print) or nonverbal cues (e.g., pointing to each word in a line of text during reading). Print referencing can promote children's development of print concepts, concept of word, and alphabet knowledge (Justice & Ezell, 2002). Table 4 provides examples of print references that facilitate development in each of these areas.

Justice and Ezell (2004) cautioned that too much print referencing during reading can detract from the child's enjoyment, and they suggested three to five references during a single storybook. They suggested, however, that to promote literacy development, these print references should be used regularly, or at least once during each storybook reading session. These may include nonverbal references that call attention to features of print without requiring a response from the child (e.g., pointing to print in pictures). Finally, they also suggested that the adult should be sure to keep cues within the child's zone of proximal development.

Helping Parents Maximize the Effectiveness of Read-Alouds at Home

Teachers and schools can assist parents in their read-aloud efforts by ensuring plentiful access to appropriate books. This can be accomplished with school or classroom take-home books,

Table 4
Examples of Print-Referencing Cues During Storybook Reading

Type of cue	Example
Verbal cues	
Questions about print	"Can you find the title of this book?"
Request about print	"Show me where I should start reading on this page."
Comments about print	"That word is *stop*."
Nonverbal cues	
Pointing to print	Teacher points to a word on a page or to print within an illustration.
Tracking print	Teacher tracks her finger under the words as she reads the text.

Adapted from Justice & Ezell (2004).

through book fairs and book give-aways, and in connections with public library events and bookmobiles.

In addition to the methods mentioned previously, other useful ways to engage children during read-alouds are recommended by Cole, Maddox, Notari-Syverson, and Ross (1998). In *Talking & Books*, their video for parents, they suggested using the C.A.R. strategy with children: Comment and wait, Ask questions and wait, and Respond by adding a little more. "Comment and wait" involves the adult making comments that reflect a child's focus of interest in the book, then giving the child time to think before responding or asking a question. "Ask questions and wait" includes asking both closed questions (i.e., ones that require a yes or no answer) and open-ended questions (i.e., ones that require the child to construct an answer). Parents must remember to provide a child more time to think when open-ended questions are asked. "Respond by adding a little more" involves a parent repeating a child's response and then adding one or two new words or phrases. This action reinforces a child's talking and provides new information. Waiting com-

municates that the adult is interested in what the child has to say.

Helping parents make the most out of read-aloud activities can be aligned with research-based practices. Researchers have successfully taught parents to implement research-based methods (Jordan, Snow, & Porche, 2000; Lonigan & Whitehurst, 1998; Whitehurst et al., 1998). Schools can do this by providing specific training to assist parents. Parent workshops and meetings are appropriate times to discuss key methods for reading aloud and why they are important (see Table 5 for suggested topics to discuss at parent meetings).

Final Thoughts

Read-alouds provide a wonderful opportunity to promote children's love of literature, and they can be a treasured time together. As demonstrated through the research on dialogic reading, text talk, and print referencing, a systematic approach to reading aloud can yield important academic benefits for children. Educators and parents should ensure, however, that attempts to build literacy through read-alouds do not detract from

Table 5 Suggested Topics for Parent Meetings	
Physical engagement with books	Encourage parents to make read-aloud sessions a positive experience where children are allowed to reference pictures and to point to words as they read.
Elaborating	Parents should help children to make connections between the read-aloud story and their own life. Parents should also encourage the child to expand on ideas as they read.
Questioning	In addition to asking children open-ended questions about read-aloud stories, parents should encourage children to ask questions during storybook reading sessions.
Wait time	Waiting after a question or comment invites the child to respond, using and expanding oral language skills and increasing engagement with text.
Child-friendly explanation of new words	Encourage parents to explain the meaning of new words in ways that are child friendly—use words that children already know to help them understand new words. Discussion of how to select words to teach would also be useful for most parents.
Print referencing	Explain to parents how to call children's attention to important features of the text in ways that keep the child engaged and promote print awareness.

children's enjoyment of good books. Socially and emotionally rewarding literacy interactions can lead to a positive attitude toward reading and can serve to motivate children to engage in other literacy activities on their own. Reading aloud to children can be a very powerful way to increase their vocabulary, listening comprehension, syntactic development, and word-recognition skills. By employing research-based methods, teachers and parents can maximize the effectiveness of reading aloud, thereby enhancing the reading experiences and the achievement of students.

References

Adams, M.J. (1990). *Beginning to read: Thinking and learning about print*. Cambridge, MA: MIT Press.

Anderson, R.C., Hiebert, E.H., Scott, J.A., & Wilkinson, I.A.G. (1985). *Becoming a nation of readers: The report of the Commission on Reading*. Washington, DC: National Institute of Education.

Anderson-Yockel, J., & Haynes, W.O. (1994). Joint book-reading strategies in working-class African American and white mother-toddler dyads. *Journal of Speech and Hearing Research, 37*, 583–593.

Arnold, D.H., Lonigan, C.J., Whitehurst, G.J., & Epstein, J.N. (1994). Accelerating language development through picture book reading: Replication and extension to a videotape training format. *Journal of Educational Psychology, 86*, 235–243.

Beck, I.L. (2004, April). *Igniting students' knowledge of and interest in words*. Presentation at the Florida Middle School Reading Leadership Conference, Orlando, FL.

Beck, I.L., & McKeown, M.G. (2001). Text talk: Capturing the benefits of read-aloud experiences for young children. *The Reading Teacher, 55*, 10–20.

Beck, I.L, McKeown, M.G., & Kucan, L. (2002). *Bringing words to life: Robust vocabulary instruction*. New York: Guilford.

Brabham, E.G., & Lynch-Brown, C. (2002). Effects of teachers' reading-aloud styles on vocabulary acquisition and comprehension of students in early elementary grades. *Journal of Educational Psychology, 94*, 465–473.

Chomsky, C. (1972). Stages in language development and reading exposure. *Harvard Educational Review, 42*, 1–33.

Cole, K.N., Maddox, M.E., Notari-Syverson, A. (Writers/Producers), & Ross, A. (Director). (1998). *Talking and books* [Motion picture]. (Available from Washington Learning Systems, 2212 Queen Anne Ave North, #726, Seattle, WA 98109, USA)

Collins Cobuild. (2002). *Collins Cobuild new student's dictionary* (2nd ed.). Toronto, ON: HarperCollins Canada.

De Temple, J., & Snow, C.E. (2003). Learning words from books. In A. van Kleeck, S.A. Stahl, & E.B. Bauer (Eds.), *On reading books to children: Parents and teachers* (pp. 16–36). Mahwah, NJ: Erlbaum.

Dickinson, D.K., McCabe, A., & Anastasopoulos, L. (2003). A framework for examining book reading in early childhood classrooms. In A. van Kleeck, S.A. Stahl, & E.B. Bauer (Eds.), *On reading books to children: Parents and teachers* (pp. 95–113). Mahwah, NJ: Erlbaum.

Dickinson, D.K., & Tabors, P.O. (2001). *Beginning literacy with language*. Baltimore: Brookes.

Elster, C.A. (1994). "I guess they do listen": Young children's emergent readings after adult read-alouds. *Young Children, 49*(3), 27–31.

Ezell, H.K., & Justice, L.M. (2000). Increasing the print focus of adult–child shared book reading through observational learning. *American Journal of Speech-Language Pathology, 9*, 36–47.

Jordan, G.E., Snow, C.E., & Porche, M.V. (2000). Project EASE: The effect of a family literacy project on kindergarten students' early literacy skills. *Reading Research Quarterly, 35*, 524–546.

Justice, L.M., & Ezell, H.K. (2002). Use of storybook reading to increase print awareness in at-risk children. *American Journal of Speech-Language Pathology, 11*, 17–29.

Justice, L.M., & Ezell, H.K. (2004). Print referencing: An emergent literacy enhancement strategy and its clinical applications. *Language, Speech, and Hearing Services in Schools, 35*, 185–193.

Lonigan, C.J., & Whitehurst, G.J. (1998). Relative efficacy of parent and teacher involvement in a shared-reading intervention for preschool children from low-income backgrounds. *Early Childhood Research Quarterly, 13*, 263–290.

Meyer, L.A., Wardrop, J.L., Linn, R.L., & Hastings, C.N. (1993). Effects of ability and settings on kindergartners' reading performance. *Journal of Educational Research, 86*, 142–160.

Morrow, L.M., & Gambrell, L.B. (2002). Literature-based instruction in the early years. In S.B. Neuman & D.K. Dickinson (Eds.), *Handbook of early literacy research* (pp. 348–360). New York: Guilford.

National Education Association. (2004). *A parent's guide to helping your child learn to read*. Retrieved December 1, 2006, from http://www.okea.org/ESEA/resource/PDF/ParGdeHelpChildRead.pdf

Roberts, J.E., & Burchinal, M.R. (2002). The complex interplay between biology and environment: Otitis media and mediating effects on early literacy development. In S.B. Neuman & D.K. Dickinson (Eds.), *Handbook of early literacy research* (pp. 232–241). New York: Guilford.

Scarborough, H.S., & Dobrich, W. (1994). On the efficacy of reading to preschoolers. *Developmental Review, 14*, 245–302.

Sénéchal, M. (1997). The differential effect of storybook reading on preschoolers' acquisition of expressive and receptive vocabulary. *Journal of Child Language, 24*, 123–138.

Sharif, I., Ozuah, P.O., Dinkevich, E.I., & Mulvihill, M. (2003). Impact of a brief literacy intervention on urban preschoolers. *Early Childhood Education Journal, 30*, 177–180.

Smith, J.P. (1989). Children among the poor. *Demography, 26*, 235–248.

Stahl, S.A. (2003). What do we expect storybook reading to do? How storybook reading impacts word recognition. In A. van Kleeck, S.A. Stahl, & E.B. Bauer (Eds.), *On reading books to children: Parents and teachers* (pp. 363–383). Mahwah, NJ: Erlbaum.

Stanovich, K.E., Cunningham, A.E., & West, R.F. (1998). Literacy experiences and the shaping of cognition. In S.G. Paris & H.M. Wellman (Eds.), *Global prospects for education: Development, culture, and schooling* (pp. 253–288). Washington, DC: American Psychological Association.

Strickland, D.S. (2002). Early intervention for African American children considered to be at risk. In S.B. Neuman & D.K. Dickinson (Eds.), *Handbook of early literacy research* (pp. 322–332). New York: Guilford.

Teale, W.H. (1986). Home background and young children's literacy development. In W.H. Teale & E. Sulzby (Eds.), *Emergent literacy: Writing and reading* (pp. 173–206). Norwood, NJ: Ablex.

Teale, W.H. (2003). Reading aloud to young children as a classroom instructional activity: Insight from research and practice. In A. van Kleeck, S.A. Stahl, & E.B. Bauer (Eds.), *On reading books to children: Parents and teachers* (pp. 114–139). Mahwah, NJ: Erlbaum.

Trelease, J. (1982). *The read-aloud handbook.* Harmondsworth, England: Penguin.

Valdez-Menchaca, M.C., & Whitehurst, G.J. (1992). Accelerating language development through picture book reading: A systematic extension to Mexican day care. *Developmental Psychology, 28*, 1106–1114.

Whitehurst, G.J., Arnold, D.S., Epstein, J.N., & Angell, A.L. (1994). A picture book reading intervention in day care and home for children from low-income families. *Developmental Psychology, 30*, 679–689.

Whitehurst, G.J., Falco, F.I., Lonigan, C.J., Fischel, J.E., DeBaryshe, B.D., Valdez-Menchaca, M.C., et al. (1988). Accelerating language development through picture book reading. *Developmental Psychology, 24*, 552–559.

Whitehurst, G.J., Zevenbergen, A.A., Crone, D.A., Schultz, M.D., Velting, O.N., & Fischel, J.E. (1999). Outcomes of an emergent literacy intervention from Head Start through second grade. *Journal of Educational Psychology, 91*, 261–272.

Questions for Reflection

• In the preceding article, published after this piece by Lane and Wright, McGee and Schickedanz describe another research-based method of reading aloud to young children. How does their repeated interactive read-aloud approach compare to the methods of dialogic reading, text talk, and print referencing described here? What would be the benefits of each for the children you teach? Would any of the methods be more or less challenging to implement in your classroom? Why?

• In describing their method, Justice and Ezell (2004) suggest using only three or four print references in a single read-aloud because more could detract from children's enjoyment of and engagement with the story. With each of the methods described here, how can you ensure that you strike the right balance in your reading aloud, meeting instructional goals without detracting from children's active listening and involvement in text?

March of the Penguins: Building Knowledge in a Kindergarten Classroom

Lauren Fingeret

It is a commonly held belief among literacy researchers and practitioners alike that using content-rich texts for classroom read-alouds is an effective way to enrich students' knowledge. As reading researchers and teachers, we assume that experiencing high-quality literature and films, specifically those containing abundant historical and scientific information, produces substantial increases in students' content knowledge. For example, the research on effective schools demonstrates that successful teachers choose content-rich texts for classroom read-alouds as well as for students' independent reading (Fisher, Flood, Lapp, & Frey, 2004; Pressley et al., 2001; Pressley, Raphael, Gallagher, & DiBella, 2004). However, this research does not enlighten us as to what knowledge students gain from these rich read-aloud experiences. Interestingly, in spite of these encouraging examples that lead us to presume that experiencing content-rich texts and films builds knowledge and improves reading comprehension, there is no empirical evidence to support this assumption.

For multiple reasons, it is important for literacy teachers and researchers to learn more about how to build knowledge in students as well as how to integrate science and social studies content into literacy curricula. There has long been evidence, in reading comprehension research and instruction, that activating students' prior knowledge is a good way to help them comprehend text (Duke, Pressley, & Hilden, 2004; Keene & Zimmermann, 1997; Pressley, 2006). Sometimes called "schema theory," the idea is that, by activating students' schema, or background knowledge, students will be able to more easily make inferences and predictions when reading new texts (Anderson, 1984; Anderson & Pearson, 1984; McKoon & Ratcliff, 1992; van den Broek, 1994). Furthermore, students will be able to assimilate new information into their existing schema to deepen their knowledge on a topic (Kintsch, 1998).

Although the reading research and teaching communities have extensively investigated the ways in which prior knowledge assists with reading comprehension, there has been less of an emphasis on researching how to build and improve students' bodies of prior knowledge. Students certainly accrue knowledge in the subject areas, but the subject areas are merging with literacy instruction more than ever, both at the mutual urging of science education and literacy researchers (e.g., Casteel & Isom, 1994; El-Hindi, 2003; Short & Armstrong, 1993) and because of the pressures of recent state and federal mandates in the United States to have 90-minute reading blocks every day. As a result, we need to know as much as possible about how to effectively build students' knowledge during literacy-based instruction.

In this study, I followed a kindergarten class in which the teacher used a film, rather than a book, for a read-aloud. Although this may initially sound counterintuitive, the teacher chose a high-quality film to introduce a complex unit on penguins to her young class. She was so impressed with *March of the Penguins* that she wondered if she could treat the film like a text in her classroom. The unabridged *March of the Penguins* book was also available to the students and they consulted it frequently, but she did not

Reprinted from Fingeret, L. (2008). *March of the Penguins*: Building knowledge in a kindergarten classroom. *The Reading Teacher, 62*(2), 96-103.

read it to them. This teacher was confident about how to use the film as a text and felt it may be a better medium than a book because her students were so young. The teacher showed *March of the Penguins* in 20-minute increments and used the same techniques for building vocabulary and comprehension that she used during oral read-alouds (which will be discussed in detail). I gave pretests, posttests, and retention tests to the students and also conducted multiple observations in the classroom. I found that the students not only learned a tremendous amount of facts about penguins through watching the film and experiencing the unit, but they also retained a tremendous amount as well.

March of the Penguins

As most readers likely know, *March of the Penguins* is the story of the mating rituals of emperor penguins. It was shot entirely on location in Antarctica by a team of French biologists and documentary filmmakers, and it is narrated in English by Morgan Freeman. Despite its seemingly dry source material—even its narrator wondered, incredulously, "Penguins? Penguins?!" (Jacquet, 2005)—the movie won critical acclaim and enormous commercial success. Some critics have noted that the film anthropomorphizes penguins to an unrealistic degree, particularly in regard to their feelings and motives, but no one suggests that the information is inaccurate.

Setting and Participants

This study took place in a half-day kindergarten classroom with 19 students. The teacher who participated in the study, Mrs. Evans, had been previously identified as a master teacher (Pressley, Mohan, Raphael, & Fingeret, 2007) in a study of an effective suburban school. She had been teaching in the primary grades for 13 years, but this was her first year teaching kindergarten. She described the class as "bright and enthusiastic" and considered it a "joy" to work with them. The students were from a diverse range of socioeconomic and cultural backgrounds as well as from a range of literacy abilities. Nevertheless,

most of the students, about 75%, were at grade level or above in reading and writing. Most of the students were reading short, simple books on their own, following along with their fingers while listening to others read, and writing short, one- or two-sentence journal entries using invented spelling. Two of the students were English-language learners (ELLs). One student left the school between the time of the posttest and the retention test, reducing the total number of students to 18.

Methods: Assessment, Observation, Interviews

There were two primary modes of data collection in this study: the content assessments and classroom observations with informal teacher interviews. By using these forms of collection, I hoped to get information about what the students were learning from the film and how the teacher was supporting the use of the film in her curriculum. These methods were intentionally disparate; by combining an essentially quantitative assessment and analysis of the assessment with a thoroughly qualitative series of observations and field notes, I was seeking to learn about how the students and teacher were handling—teaching, learning, using, adapting—their new knowledge from deliberately different angles. Furthermore, although the assessment data spoke for themselves in terms of what the students learned from the film, I was also able to round out my sense of what they had learned from observing their activities, writing, and even play about penguins. These data are more anecdotal than the evidence from the assessments, but they does help to show how the students were able to use their knowledge about penguins in the authentic setting of the classroom (as opposed to the artifice inherent in answering questions on a test).

The assessment was designed to take about 10–15 minutes. I administered it orally, one to one, with each of the 19 students. This method was more time consuming than it would have been to give the assessment as a group, but I wanted to make sure I was assessing what the students knew about penguins, rather than what the students were able to read or write on a test (Shepard, 1994). I administered the assessment three times: immediately prior to the viewing of the film, within a week after the class finished the film, and again four months later. Only the students who had not seen the film previously were given the pretest ($n = 9$).

Prior to the assessments, the students were told that the assessments were not related to their grades and that they could say as much or as little as they wished for an answer. They were also told that it was OK if they did not know an answer. If a student paused for more than 15 seconds, I would ask if he or she was finished or ready for another question. These sessions were recorded on audiotape and transcribed.

The nine-item assessment began with an intentionally broad question: "Please tell me everything you know about penguins." From there, the questions grew progressively more specific. Some of the questions required only short, literal answers, such as "Do penguins have predators? If so, what are they?" There was an explicit vocabulary item, "Can you tell me what *nesting ground* means?" and other items also implicitly tested vocabulary, such as with the use of the word *predator*. Finally, some items required critical thinking and inferencing, as in "In what season do penguins go swimming for the first time?" and "How do father penguins protect their eggs and babies from the cold?" In the first example, it is mentioned in the film that the penguins first swim in spring, but there is more emphasis on the fact that the ice has melted so much that it is a shorter journey from the nesting ground to the sea than it was in the winter. If the students picked up on this detail about the warmer weather, they may have been able to infer that the penguins left the nesting ground in the spring. In short, the assessment was a fairly complex battery of questions and tested knowledge that reached much deeper than whether, for example, penguins are black and white.

In addition to using the assessments to collect data on the students' knowledge about penguins, I also collected data on how Mrs. Evans showed the film, shared the book, and otherwise used these texts as part of her instruction. To a lesser extent than with the assessments, and as mentioned previously, I also used these observations to learn about how the students were using their new knowledge. To do so, I observed in the classroom on eight separate occasions and collected field notes. During these times, I did not interact with the students or Mrs. Evans; instead, I sat quietly and observed without input. I tried to take notes on everything that Mrs. Evans and the students said, doing my best to record it verbatim, or as close as possible. I did not record or code pauses, repetitions, or "ums" or "uhs," but I tried to write down everything substantive. Before and after these observations, I talked with Mrs. Evans about her plans and her thoughts about how the unit was going. Because I was in the classroom so frequently, I became a regular fixture. The students smiled and greeted me by name (or as "The Penguin Lady") when they saw me but were otherwise undistracted by my presence. Finally, I collected copies of the students' written work about penguins. Although these artifacts do not figure into the assessment results, they do augment the findings on the kind of teaching Mrs. Evans was doing and the kind of thinking the students were doing about penguins.

Scoring the Tests

Because the answers to the open-ended assessment questions could have much longer responses than the short-answer items, I scored them in a way that weighted the answers more equitably. In the initial scoring, for example, each piece of correct information to the item "Please tell me everything you know about penguins" was worth 1 point. On the post- and retention tests, some students gave 15 or more pieces of correct information—one student gave 22! If I had left the scores in that form, the first question could have been worth more than the rest of the test combined, which may have obfuscated the students' performance on the vocabulary and inferential items. Therefore, I scaled the answers to three of the open-ended items so that each item was worth between 1 and 4 points, rather than 1–100 or more. Because of the open-ended nature of the first question, for example, there was no highest "possible" score on the overall assessment because, theoretically, the students could have responded with an infinite number of pieces of information about penguins. The highest score on the assessment was, in fact, 19. Because 19 was the highest score achieved on the assessment, it will henceforth be used as the high score marker.

I did not score either incorrect information or what I think of as "noninformation." Because this is a study about knowledge gains, I thought that factoring in misconceptions would detract from the data about what the students learned. Furthermore, there were virtually no misconceptions on the posttest, so it did not look as though they were learning inaccurate information. Furthermore, because some of those early misconceptions were so far off base ("They [penguins] are born in a berry patch."), they indicated that the student really did not know anything about penguins. To give a negative point value for that answer would somehow imply that the student knew less than nothing, which seems inappropriate. Similarly, in the case of noninformation, I did not count answers such as "Penguins have eyes" as correct pieces of information. Yes, penguins do have eyes, of course, but that fact does not show that the student has learned anything.

To develop the scoring rubric, I went through each item and wrote down the answers to the questions based on the information in the film. Except for item #1, "Please tell me everything you know about penguins," the potential responses to the questions were finite. After I did all the assessments, pre-, post-, and retention, I began to compare the students' responses with mine. In one case, I found that the students almost universally understood a question differently than I intended it, so I modified the rubric accordingly. In response to the question "How do father penguins protect their eggs and babies from the cold?" I was looking for answers about how the male penguins huddle together against the winds. Nearly all the students, however, responded that the males hold the eggs and babies under a flap of skin in their bellies. Even though this was not the answer I intended when I wrote the assessment, it was a correct response so I included it in the scoring rubric.

After I scored the assessments, they underwent interreliability screening with another graduate student who was working on the larger study. We randomly selected 20% of the assessments to score for inter-rater reliability and this screening yielded 88.9% agreement.

The assessment scores were analyzed using independent t-tests between the pretest and posttest scores, pretest and retention test scores, and posttest and retention test scores and by calculating the effect size, d (Cohen, 1977), of viewing the film with Mrs. Evans. There was very little question, prior to showing the film, that the students would learn from it. As such, we were not as interested in testing for whether the treatment showed a statistically significant increase in scores; rather, we were interested in determining what that effect size actually was.

Findings

Content Knowledge

I found that, as expected, there were gains in knowledge about penguins from viewing the film *March of the Penguins*. What was startling, however, was the enormity of the gains. As shown in Table 1, the mean score on the pretest was 4.10 out of 19 and the mean score on the posttest, given immediately after the film was shown and before the penguin unit, was 12.95. The range of scores on the pretest was 1–7, on the posttest the range was 6–19. Put another way, the students' knowledge about penguins tripled as a result of watching the film with Mrs. Evans. As shown in Table 2, the effect size of 2.70 is astronomical; typically, an effect size < 0.3 is considered small, 0.4–0.6 is moderate, and > 0.7 is large (Ott & Longnecker, 2001). In fact, I checked to make sure that an effect size of 2.7 was even possible! Not only was the mean score so much higher, but it was also shown that every student made gains from the pretest to the posttest. In other words, every student learned at least something about

Table 1
Mean Scores

	Pretest	Posttest	Retention test
Mean	4.10	12.95	12.28
SD	1.71	4.31	4.24
N	9	20	19

Table 2
Effect Size on Post and Retention Tests

Effect size on posttest	Effect size on retention test
2.70	2.53

penguins from watching this film. Here are some examples of the responses given on the pretest:

- "Penguins are black and have beaks."
- "They have sticky feet so they can walk up mountains."
- "I know the penguins don't drive cars."

Incidentally, the first of those responses received 1 point, half a point each for knowing that penguins are black and have beaks (indicating that the student also knows that penguins are birds). The second two answers were not awarded points. By contrast, here are some examples from the posttest:

- "Their feet are the nest, and they use their bellies to keep the egg tucked in."
- "They have to stay away from predators. They eat fish, krill, and squid."
- "They live in a big family called a colony."

Even *more* surprising, however, than the results on the posttest are the results from the test administered four months later. As seen in Table 1, the mean score on the retention test was 12.28 (compared with 4.10 and 12.95 on the pre- and posttests) and the range of scores was 5.5–19. These data show not only that the students

learned a tremendous amount of information about penguins from watching the film and participating in the unit following the film but also that they retained the information four months after seeing it. Some sample responses from the retention test include the following:

- "The daddy penguin hatches the egg. A baby penguins cannot go outside for a second or it will die. Penguins like to eat fish."
- "They, baby penguins cannot when they're in their eggs, cannot stay on ice without keeping warm. They have predators. When they're five, they can swim."
- "The mom or dad, when they eat fish, they cough it up and give it to the baby."

These responses show that the students' knowledge about penguins was deeply enriched by Mrs. Evans's unit.

The penguin unit continued in the classroom for four weeks after the film, but the retention test occurred three months after the unit's completion. So, although the students had the benefit of the entire penguin unit to explain the results of the retention test, they also had three months to forget what they had learned. Some of the students did forget some of what they learned, as we can see in the scores on the retention test (5.5 was the lowest score on the retention test, while 6 was the lowest on the posttest). Overall, however, it appears that their knowledge gains remained high; the mean score on the retention test was nearly as high as it was on the posttest. To make sense of the results from the assessments, we need to look closely at the results of the classroom observations.

Pedagogy and Instruction

Possibly one of the most important initial findings from the observations was the way Mrs. Evans showed the film to the class. In short, she did not merely press "play" and let the students watch. Instead, she showed it in sections of about 20 minutes each day so that it took a full week to watch. This was in part because the kindergarten school day is only two and a half hours and Mrs. Evans had many other things to cover each day, but it was also because she thought the students would learn more from absorbing a little bit of it at a time, rather than seeing it all at once. Even though she showed approximately 20 minutes of the film each day, she actually took approximately 40 minutes to view it with the students. She stopped to explain new vocabulary words with them such as *regurgitate*, *famished*, or *petrel* (Jacquet, 2006) and also to discuss what was happening in the film and to ask the students to make predictions. After the day's segment was finished, she had a discussion with the students about what they had learned about penguins, their habitat, predators and prey, and survival skills, as well as the students' impressions about these things. In short, she showed the movie the way she would have read a new information text with them, by engaging them in making meaning and scaffolding their comprehension (Keene & Zimmermann, 1997; Pressley, 2006).

In addition to showing the film, Mrs. Evans made the *March of the Penguins* book available to the students to read during free choice and other times. This was the unabridged version of the book; the text is the verbatim narration and the pictures are stills from the film. The students were very interested in this book and spent a lot of time looking at it together. Most of the time it seemed as though the students looked at the pictures and picked out words they knew from the text, rather than reading it word for word and page for page. They would find their favorite parts from the film in the book, look at the pictures, follow along with some of the text, and then flip to another favorite section. Often the students did this in pairs, showing each other the sections they liked best. The "scary" parts, including attacks on the penguins from predators, were probably looked at more than any others. Mrs. Evans did not read the book to the class, formally or otherwise, but she reminded them frequently that it was available to them. There were also other books about penguins featured in the classroom library at this time and the students looked at those as well.

After Mrs. Evans finished showing the film and I gave the posttests to the students, Mrs. Evans continued with the unit on penguins. Most of my classroom observations occurred during this time, so I was able to see the ways she integrated the film into her unit. There were numerous ways Mrs. Evans used the film as a launching point for different activities about penguins. Mrs. Evans brought in a penguin suit and the students took turns wearing it and waddling around the classroom. Then they practiced huddling together against freezing Antarctic winds and moving in and out of the center of the huddle. They also practiced transferring a "baby penguin" (actually a rather large stuffed penguin doll) to each others' feet like the penguins in the film and they learned—and frequently remarked upon—how difficult it is to do so. It is important to point out that these were not just "fun" activities or, worse, busy work; the students did indeed have fun doing these exercises, but the exercises also contained meaningful content about the penguins' survival skills in a harsh climate. Furthermore, Mrs. Evans did not manufacture penguin activities that did not have content so, for example, there were no construction paper penguin projects. Instead, Mrs. Evans was consistently cognizant and deliberate about what she wanted the students to learn about penguins and so she developed her lessons and activities accordingly.

In addition to these kinesthetic activities, Mrs. Evans and the students decided to write their own book about penguins because the *March of the Penguins* text had become the runaway favorite in the classroom. Each student wrote and illustrated a page, and Mrs. Evans bound it together. When it was complete, Mrs. Evans put *Penguin Facts* in the classroom library and it soon rivaled *March of the Penguins* in popularity. Here are some excerpts from the text with the students' original invented spelling:

- "Wen a mom givs the dad the egg it has to be quik."
- "The dad hahes [hatches] the egg and empure penguin hest to go weth out food for four munts."
- "The mom choks up food and givs it to the chik."
- "The mom and the dad keep the baby penguins warm under the belly."
- "If a moms chik dis, she tris to stel another babe."

One of the most interesting things I observed during my time in the classroom was the students "playing penguin" during centers and free time. It seemed as though the penguins captured their imaginations in a way that reached well beyond Mrs. Evans or the curriculum. During these play sessions, the students would take turns staying with the eggs or babies and going for food. Some would be predators and attack the penguins, with mixed results, and the moment when the parent regurgitates food for the chick was reenacted every time. It was obvious that many of the students were big fans of the film, and some of them told me that they had the movie at home and watched it frequently.

Discussion

Looking at the data, it is probably safe to assert that the film was responsible for the students' initial knowledge gains—after all, the post-test was administered before Mrs. Evans began the penguin unit—but Mrs. Evans's instruction likely played a major role in enabling the students to retain the information as well as they did. The lesson here is not simply that we should use high-quality documentary films and books in classrooms but that high-quality documentary films and books may be an effective way to generate interest and build a knowledge base on a topic. Building this knowledge base so that it can become schema for students to access as they read new materials is, of course, valuable to students' development and education in a number of ways. In some ways, it is the students' retention of their knowledge about penguins that makes these data so impressive, so it is important to identify what exactly Mrs. Evans did to enable the students to become so engaged with their topic. For a summary of Mrs. Evans's strategies, see Table 3.

Mrs. Evans did a terrific job of defining new vocabulary, including kinesthetic recreations of the penguins' journey, giving her students several opportunities to read and write about penguins, and avoiding worksheet activities. These are all hallmarks of effective instruction and are valuable in their own right. What Mrs. Evans also did, however, was repeatedly engage her students with the penguins' overwhelmingly difficult tasks in a way that made the students care deeply about the penguins. Mrs. Evans did not merely describe or give facts about the penguins' strategies for staying warm in the Antarctic winter.

Table 3
Summary of Strategies
From Mrs. Evans's Classroom

- Show the film in small increments with lots of scaffolding and discussion about new vocabulary and concepts.
- Choose key concepts from the film to teach in your unit.
- Design kinesthetic activities to help children, particularly young children, connect with the concepts.
- Integrate reading and writing into the unit.
- Have the children create their own text.

Instead, she had the students enact the penguins' huddle technique so that they could directly relate to the difficulty of keeping warm. Similarly, she did not merely tell her students how fragile the penguins' eggs are and how challenging it is for a female to transfer an egg to a male; she showed them how unwieldy it is by having them try for themselves. Interestingly, I think that Mrs. Evans used the same elements of the film that made it so wildly successful commercially to make it wildly successful as a teaching tool. In other words, we, as a nation, were captivated by this unlikely subject because the filmmakers did a superb job of showing us the penguins' plight. Mrs. Evans, whether deliberately or not, also used those extraordinary moments to capture her students' engagement and motivate them to learn as much as possible about penguins.

Of course, this is only one study in one classroom with one exceptionally good teacher. Although the data are compelling, it reflects the occurrences in only one case and is not meant to generalize a greater population. On the other hand, the data may be compelling enough to pursue for further research and, eventually, instructional interventions. Table 4 offers questions to help you make connections to teaching content area units in your classroom. In the meantime, and at the very least, it has prompted me to think harder about my practice by thinking of ways to engage my students—whether through high-quality books, films, websites, or other media—while also enriching their knowledge. More important than the medium, I suspect that it may be a set of problems, dilemmas, or challenges—How on earth can these penguins survive and procreate during such a brutal winter? or How on earth will I teach 30 students at different levels how to read while also managing their behavior?—that engage and motivate them to learn.

References

Anderson, R.C. (1984). Role of the reader's schema in comprehension, learning, and memory. In R.C. Anderson, J. Osborn, & R.J. Tierney (Eds.), *Learning to read in American schools: Basal readers and content texts* (pp. 243–257). Hillsdale, NJ: Erlbaum.

Anderson, R.C., & Pearson, P.D. (1984). A schema-theoretic view of basic processes in reading comprehension. In P.D. Pearson, R. Barr, M.L. Kamil, & P.B. Mosenthal (Eds.), *Handbook of reading research* (pp. 255–291). New York: Longman.

Casteel, C., & Isom, B. (1994). Reciprocal processes in science and literacy learning. *The Reading Teacher, 47*(7), 538–545.

Cohen, J. (1977). *Statistical power analysis for the behavioral sciences* (Rev. ed.). New York: Academic.

Duke, N.K., Pressley, M., & Hilden, K.A. (2004). Difficulties with reading comprehension. In C.A. Stone, E.R. Silliman, B.J. Ehren, & K. Apel (Eds.), *Handbook of language and literacy: Development and disorders* (pp. 501–520). New York: Guilford.

El-Hindi, A. (2003). Integrating literacy and science in the classroom: From ecomysteries to Readers Theatre. *The Reading Teacher, 56*(6), 536–538.

Table 4
Connections-to-Your-Classroom Questions

- The author concludes that the students became—and remained—so interested in penguins in part because Mrs. Evans had them enact and interact with the penguins' harsh habitat. By identifying with the penguins, the students developed massive intrinsic motivation to learn about the topic. Think of some ways you could engage your students with the problems or challenges inherent in one of the science or social studies topics you teach.

- As we know, there are not outstanding documentary films available for every subject we cover. What are some other ways to mix media to promote content learning?

- Mrs. Evans is known to be a master teacher. Did she do anything *really* special to make this unit so effective or was she "merely" using the strategies that are the hallmark of effective teachers? Think of one of your successful units; what kinds of strategies were similar to Mrs. Evans's practice? What strategies were different? After reading the article, can you think of any things you could have done to make the unit even more successful?

Fisher, D., Flood, J., Lapp, D., & Frey, N. (2004). Interactive read-alouds: Is there a common set of implementation practices? *The Reading Teacher, 58*(1), 8–17. doi:10.1598/RT.58.1.1

Jacquet, L. (Director). (2005). *March of the penguins* [Motion picture]. United States: Warner Independent Pictures.

Jacquet, L. (2006). *March of the penguins*. Washington, DC: National Geographic Society.

Keene, E.O., & Zimmermann, S. (1997). *Mosaic of thought: Teaching comprehension in a reader's workshop*. Portsmouth, NH: Heinemann.

Kintsch, W. (1998). *Comprehension: A paradigm for cognition*. Cambridge, UK: Cambridge University Press.

McKoon, G., & Ratcliff, R. (1992). Inference during reading. *Psychological Review, 99*(3), 440–466. doi:10.1037/0033-295X.99.3.440

Ott, R., & Longnecker, M. (2001). *An introduction to statistical methods and data analysis* (5th ed.). Pacific Grove, CA: Duxbury.

Pressley, M. (2006). *Reading instruction that works: The case for balanced teaching* (3rd ed.). New York: Guilford.

Pressley, M., Mohan, L., Raphael, L., & Fingeret, L. (2007). How does Bennett Woods Elementary School produce such high reading and writing achievement? *Journal of Educational Psychology, 99*(2), 221–240. doi:10.1037/0022-0663.99.2.221

Pressley, M., Raphael, L., Gallagher, J.D., & DiBella, J. (2004). Provident-St. Mel School: How a school that works for African-American students works. *Journal of Educational Psychology, 96*(2), 216–235.

Pressley, M., Wharton-McDonald, R., Allington, R., Block, C.C., Morrow, L., Tracey, D., et al. (2001). A study of effective first-grade literacy instruction. *Scientific Studies of Reading, 5*(1), 35–58. doi:10.1207/S1532799XSSR0501_2

Shepard, L. (1994). The challenges of assessing young children appropriately. *Phi Delta Kappan, 76*(3), 206–212.

Short, K.G., & Armstrong, J. (1993). Moving toward inquiry: Integrating literature into the science curriculum. *New Advocate, 6*(3), 183–200.

van den Broek, P. (1994). Comprehension and memory of narrative texts: Inferences and coherence. In M.A. Gernsbacher (Ed.), *Handbook of psycholinguistics* (pp. 539–588). San Diego: Academic.

Questions for Reflection

• In addition to the questions listed in Table 4, think about Mrs. Evans's use of a film as text in her classroom. Today's children are exposed at a young age to information presented in sound, images, and multimedia, along with traditional print. In your literacy instruction, what role do digital, visual, oral, and other nonprint media play? How can you ensure that children become familiar with and grow as readers and writers of both traditional texts and multimedia?

Helping Students Become Accurate, Expressive Readers: Fluency Instruction for Small Groups

Melanie Kuhn

Ensuring that students become fluent readers is one of the major goals of reading instruction (Kuhn & Stahl, 2003; National Institute of Child Health and Human Development, 2000). One reason for its importance is that fluent readers no longer have to intentionally decode the majority of words they encounter in a text. Instead, they can recognize words both automatically and accurately. A second, and equally important, reason is that fluent readers are able to read texts with expression or prosody. It is this combination of accuracy, automaticity, and prosody that makes oral reading sound like spoken language. Finally, it is becoming increasingly apparent that fluency plays an important role in terms of a reader's ability to construct meaning from text, the ultimate goal of reading instruction.

Although recently the subject has begun to receive greater amounts of attention (Kuhn & Stahl, 2003; National Institute of Child Health and Human Development, 2000), fluency has often been overlooked within the literacy curriculum. There are several reasons why fluency has failed to receive greater emphasis in terms of reading instruction to date. Among these are the prevalence of strategies designed for individual instruction (Kuhn, 2003), an assumption that increased amounts of decoding instruction would automatically lead to improved fluency (Allington, 1983; Fleisher, Jenkins, & Pany, 1979/1980), and reliance on round-robin reading as one of the primary approaches for oral reading instruction (Ash, Kuhn, & Walpole, 2003).

Fluency's Role in the Reading Process

Before deciding to devote any of the limited time available for reading instruction to improving fluency, it is important to understand the ways in which fluent reading contributes to skilled reading in general and comprehension in particular. There are two primary ways in which fluency plays a part in learners' reading development (Kuhn & Stahl, 2003; National Institute of Child Health and Human Development, 2000; Samuels, 1979; Schreiber, 1991). The first involves the development of automatic word recognition, while the second deals with prosody, or those elements of fluency that allow oral reading to sound like spoken language.

Contribution of Automatic Word Recognition to Comprehension

Skilled readers share certain attributes. For example, they are able not only to identify words accurately but also to recognize them instantly. This is important because readers who need to spend a significant portion of their time identifying individual words rarely have enough attention left over to focus on a text's meaning (Adams, 1990; LaBerge & Samuels, 1974; Perfetti, 1985; Stanovich, 1980). It is also

Reprinted from Kuhn, M. (2004). Helping students become accurate, expressive readers: Fluency instruction for small groups. *The Reading Teacher, 58*(4), 338-344.

important to note that, in order to ensure adequate comprehension, learners must develop automatic word recognition through the extensive reading of connected text (e.g., Chomsky, 1976; Fleisher et al., 1979/1980) rather than simply developing the ability to recognize words in isolation.

Contribution of Prosody

While automatic word recognition ensures that fluent readers can accurately and effortlessly decode text, it does not account for their ability to make oral reading sound like spoken language (Stahl & Kuhn, 2002). There is an implicit understanding that fluency involves reading with expression or prosody. In other words, fluent reading incorporates prosodic features such as pitch, stress, and the use of appropriate phrasing (Dowhower, 1991; Schreiber, 1991). As with automaticity, it is also important to look at the ways in which prosody relates to comprehension.

Learners who have not achieved fluency read either in a word-by-word manner or by grouping words in ways that do not parallel spoken language (Dowhower, 1991; Reutzel, 1996; Schreiber, 1991). It is often the case that their reading is monotonous as well. These qualities reflect their inability to transfer prosodic elements that occur naturally in speech onto written text. Fluent readers, on the other hand, make appropriate use of phrasing, pitch, and emphasis in their reading (Chall, 1996; Dowhower; Schreiber). In so doing, they manage to make their oral reading sound like spoken language (Stahl & Kuhn, 2002). However, readers are able to employ prosody correctly only as they become aware of the connection between written and oral language. Conversely, the correct use of prosody serves as an indicator of a reader's understanding of the material because without such an understanding it would be impossible to apply these elements appropriately. It is important to note that this ability develops as learners listen to and read along with skilled models of expressive reading. Given this understanding of the role automaticity and prosody play in the ability to construct meaning from text, it seems likely that instruction designed to develop learners' fluency will lead to improvements in their comprehension as well.

Promoting Fluent Reading Through Flexible Grouping

In order to ensure that fluency instruction is included in the curriculum, it is necessary to create strategies that are classroom-friendly and that can be easily integrated within current literacy practice. One such example of effective literacy instruction is that of flexible grouping. Flexible grouping consists of temporary groups that vary in membership and can be based upon either student interest or instructional needs (Reutzel, 2003). Because the groups are not permanent, small numbers of students can be brought together to receive instruction designed to meet their specific learning needs. Therefore, it seems that it would be beneficial to develop a strategy that combines effective fluency instruction within a flexible grouping format. Such a strategy can target those learners who are experiencing difficulty making the transition from purposeful decoding to fluent reading.

With these requirements in mind, I decided to adapt a modification of the traditional repeated-reading strategy and a wide-reading strategy, in which students choral or echo read an equivalent amount of text without repetition, for use with small groups of struggling second-grade readers. I considered it important to further investigate these strategies for two reasons. First, several earlier studies found that repeated readings and wide-reading approaches led to equivalent gains in fluency development (Kuhn, 2000; Kuhn & Stahl, 2003). If it is the case that both procedures lead to equivalent growth, then it may be reasonable to make use of both forms of instruction as part of a fluency-oriented curriculum. Second, given the lack of attention to prosody in many previous studies, I felt it was important to focus on expressive oral reading as one of my goals. Again, it is hoped that such an emphasis will serve as a means of assisting students in the development of their own use of expression and, ultimately, their comprehension.

Subjects and Design

My project was designed to assess the effectiveness of a modified repeated-reading strategy, fluency-oriented oral reading (FOOR), and a wide-reading approach, in which students read equivalent amounts of nonrepetitive text, on the fluency development of struggling readers within a flexible grouping format. I looked at the two strategies in terms of promoting both accurate and automatic word recognition, as well as prosody, among the learners. I also wanted to see if the procedures led to growth in the students' comprehension because, as was noted above, gains in fluency appear to lead to improved comprehension.

Twenty-four second graders were selected to participate in this project. Second grade was selected because it is generally seen as the point at which students make the transition to fluent reading (Chall, 1996; Kuhn & Stahl, 2003; Rasinski, Padak, Linek, & Sturtevant, 1994). The students who took part in this project attended a low- to middle-socioeconomic–status public school (50–60% free or reduced cost lunch) in a small southeastern U.S. city. Of the 24 students, 19 were African American, 4 were European American, and 1 was Hispanic. There were 10 boys and 14 girls, and all the students spoke English as their primary language.

The participating students were reading at the first-grade level or below according to the Qualitative Reading Inventory (QRI, 1988) and Qualitative Reading Inventory–II (QRI–II, 1995), and their teachers indicated they were having difficulty moving beyond basic decoding skills. However, when their listening comprehension on second-grade passages of the QRI–II was assessed, the students were able to demonstrate understanding of the text. As a result, both the teachers and I considered it likely that the children would benefit from extra opportunities to develop their reading. It is also important to note that, although the students' groups remained intact for the six weeks of the intervention, they were not part of an existing subgroup within their classrooms and came together only for this short-term intervention.

The size of the reading groups was determined in consultation with the classroom teachers. We discussed what they considered to be a realistic number for small-group literacy instruction, with four to six students suggested as reasonable for such activities. After reflection, I decided to include six per group because of the possibility of attrition. The study itself consisted of three intervention groups: a fluency-oriented oral reading (FOOR) group, a wide-reading group, and a listening-only group. The listening-only group was included as a way to counter the Hawthorne effect, in which students show improvement simply as a result of their participation in a study. The groups were taken from their classrooms as a cohort and randomly assigned, without replacement, to an instructional intervention. In addition to these three groups, I included a control group. The control group consisted of two students from each of the participating classrooms. These students did not receive any reading instruction beyond what was occurring in their own class. Because the students in each of the other groups were taken as a cohort from a particular classroom, I felt the students in the control group would represent a balance of the instructional approaches used by the classroom teachers. The intervention involved 18 sessions over a six-week period. These occurred three times a week for 15 to 20 minutes each.

Reading Material

The students who participated were exposed to a variety of literacy materials. A series of 18 trade books were identified using either Fountas and Pinnell (1999) or the FEP/Booksource guide (1998) as ranging from the late first- through the second-grade instructional level [Table 1]. These levels were confirmed by a second-grade teacher with over 20 years' experience as an elementary and a Reading Recovery instructor. By presenting readers with a range of texts, including passages at the upper end of their instructional level, the treatment was designed to promote growth in what Vygotsky (1978) referred to as the Zone of Proximal Development, or that range in which learners can achieve with assistance what they

Table 1
Books Selected for Intervention

Amelia Bedelia (1992) by Peggy Parish. New York: HarperCollins.

Arthur's Funny Money (1981) by Lillian Hoban. New York: HarperCollins.

Arthur's Prize Reader (1979) by Lillian Hoban. New York: HarperCollins.

Aunt Eater Loves a Mystery (1987) by Doug Cushman. New York: HarperCollins.

Aunt Eater's Mystery Vacation (1993) by Doug Cushman. New York: HarperCollins.

Bedtime for Frances (1995) by Russell Hoban. New York: HarperCollins.

Big Max (1992) by Kin Platt. New York: HarperCollins.*

The Case of the Cat's Meow (1978) by Crosby Bonsall. New York: HarperCollins.

The Case of the Dumb Bells (1982) by Crosby Bonsall. New York: HarperCollins.*

The Case of the Two Masked Robbers (1988) by Lillian Hoban. New York: HarperCollins.

Come Back, Amelia Bedelia (1995) by Peggy Parish. New York: HarperCollins.*

The Fire Cat (1988) by Esther Averill. New York: HarperCollins.

Frog and Toad Are Friends (1970) by Arnold Lobel. New York: HarperCollins.

Frog and Toad Together (1979) by Arnold Lobel. New York: HarperCollins.*

The Golly Sisters Go West (1985) by Betsy Byars. New York: HarperCollins.*

Harry the Dirty Dog (1956) by Gene Zion. New York: HarperCollins.

Hooray for the Golly Sisters (1990) by Betsy Byars. New York: HarperCollins.

Whistle for Willie (1964) by Jack Ezra Keats. New York: Puffin.*

* indicates a book read by the fluency-oriented oral reading group.

are unable to accomplish on their own. The books used for the project included *Harry the Dirty Dog* (1956) by Gene Zion, *Whistle for Willie* (1964) by Ezra Jack Keats, and *The Golly Sisters Go West* (1985) by Betsy Byars.

Procedures

As was mentioned earlier in the article, many of the strategies developed to assist learners in becoming fluent readers are designed for individuals. The best known of these approaches is

that of repeated readings. This method requires students to read a "short, meaningful passage several times until a satisfactory level of fluency is reached" (Samuels, 1979, p. 404). In a review of this method, Dowhower (1989) indicated that passages should be short, ranging from 50–300 words; that students should have about an 85% accuracy rate on their initial reading of the passage; and that the optimal number of repetitions of a passage is between three and five.

However, because one goal of this study was to determine whether repeatedly reading text and reading equivalent amounts of nonrepeated text led to comparable growth in reading fluency, I felt that the use of complete stories would provide a closer parallel to the other conditions. Therefore, I modified the original repeated readings approach outlined above so that students repeatedly read a story three to four times over the course of the three weekly sessions, a method similar to other modifications of repeated readings (e.g., Hoffman & Crone, 1985; Stahl, Heubach, & Cramond, 1997).

The fluency-oriented oral reading strategy (FOOR) made use of several elements that have proved successful in earlier fluency studies (Hoffman & Crone, 1985; Koskinen & Blum, 1986; Morris & Nelson, 1992) including modeling, repetition, positive feedback from instructors or peers, and opportunity for oral rendition of practiced texts. This intervention occurred over a three-day cycle. On Day 1, I introduced a story and echo read the text with the students. Depending upon the length of the text, the students then had the opportunity to chorally read part or all of the text along with me. On Day 2, the students broke into pairs and, reading alternate pages, reread the entire text with a partner. After completing the text once, if time permitted, the students had the opportunity either to practice a section of text with their partners or to repeat the entire story a second time reading alternate pages. On Day 3, the students had the opportunity to participate in a final choral reading of the text and were invited to perform a portion of the selection before the group if they so wished.

Wide reading was selected as the second approach in order to determine the effectiveness of scaffolded, but nonrepeated, reading in the development of students' fluency. Previous studies have indicated that when students read significant amounts of connected text with teacher support, such as is available in echo or choral readings of a story, they are as likely to demonstrate growth in their reading fluency as their peers who repeatedly read fewer texts over the same period (Kuhn & Stahl, 2003). Therefore, the wide-reading component incorporated the echo or choral reading of a given text in order to support the students in their development of accurate and automatic word recognition along with prosody. Again, students participated in three sessions per week. These sessions involved a single scaffolded reading of a different story at each meeting. The same six books used with the fluency-oriented oral reading group were used here; however, 12 additional selections were included in order to ensure that the participating students were reading new material at each sitting. Each child in both the FOOR and the wide-reading condition was provided with an individual copy of the texts.

The third condition consisted of a listening-only component in which the same 18 stories read in the wide-reading sessions were covered. However, rather than having students read the stories themselves, I provided an expressive rendition. This ensured that the students were exposed to the same amount of literature as their peers in the wide-reading condition. As was mentioned above, the control group did not participate in any literacy activities outside of the regular curriculum.

Assessment Materials

In addition to the time spent working with the trade books, there was a period of individual pre- and posttesting. The students' comprehension, as well as their accurate and automatic word recognition within text, was assessed using the QRI and the QRI–II, which are informal reading inventories. Word recognition in isolation was assessed using the Test of Word Recognition Efficiency (TOWRE), a standardized measure. In addition, the National Assessment of Educational Progress's (NAEP) Oral Reading Fluency Scale was used to evaluate the students' oral reading.

Results and Discussion

After the assessment measures were readministered at the end of the intervention, certain differences emerged between the groups (Kuhn, 2000). To begin with, the wide-reading and FOOR groups were able to identify a greater number of words in isolation than did the listening-only or control groups on the TOWRE. Similarly, the FOOR and wide-reading groups demonstrated greater growth in terms of the number of correct words read per minute on the QRI and QRI–II passages at their independent and instructional levels than did either the students in the listening-only group or the controls. Next, two raters independently assessed the students' oral reading of the QRI passages using the NAEP Oral Reading Fluency Scale. According to both raters, the reading of the students in the FOOR and wide-reading groups was more fluent than that of the students in the listening-only and control groups. However, according to their responses to the questions that correspond with the passages on the QRI and QRI–II, only the students in the wide-reading group showed improved comprehension.

Given that the FOOR and the wide-reading interventions incorporated extensive opportunities to read connected text, provided models of expressive reading, and used both challenging materials and student accountability, it is not surprising that the students who participated in these groups made gains in word recognition and prosody, whereas the students in the control group did not. However, it is worth noting that the students who were exposed to the stories through the listening-only condition did not make similar growth. This lends weight to the argument that, while reading aloud to students is important in fostering a love of reading, learners must actively engage in the reading of connected text if they are to become skilled readers.

Further, while the FOOR and the wide-reading groups both showed improvements in terms of prosody and word recognition, only the wide-reading group showed greater growth in terms of comprehension. One possible explanation of these findings involves what students may have considered to be the implicit focus of the sessions. Because the amount of time available for working with the students was limited, I chose to focus primarily on smooth, expressive reading. As a result, comprehension and vocabulary were dealt with implicitly rather than explicitly. Because the FOOR approach incorporated significant amounts of repetition, students may have seen word recognition and expression as the dominant focus. While the students enjoyed the stories selected, each story, or portion of a story, was reread several times. Given this pattern, it is possible that, after the initial reading, the students focused their attention on expression and accurate word recognition rather than on the text's meaning. It is also possible that they brought this understanding to their posttests, resulting in gains in prosody and word recognition but not in comprehension.

The wide-reading group, on the other hand, read a new book at each session. As a result, comprehension, expression, and word recognition may have been viewed as having equivalent importance. It could be that the students developed a broader implicit focus, one that included the understanding and enjoyment of the stories as well as the accurate and expressive reading of the text. It is equally possible that this focus carried over to the posttesting and led to the wide-reading group's growth in comprehension as well as in word recognition and prosody.

Similar findings were noted in two previous studies designed to assist readers in their fluency development (O'Shea, Sindelar, & O'Shea, 1985, 1987). O'Shea et al. argued that while repeated readings led to improved levels of fluency, learners did not automatically shift their attention to the comprehension of text. Instead, they felt it might be necessary to actively focus the readers' attention on the content of a passage in order to show improvements in their comprehension. Their research indicated that such a focus did indeed lead to improvements in the students' ability to construct meaning from text. Anderson, Wilkinson, and Mason (1991) also reported similar findings when working with small groups of third graders using a guided reading lesson. They found that when the focus of a lesson was on meaning, students made greater gains in comprehension than when the focus was on word analysis and accurate reading. These findings were stronger for the low and average readers than for their more skilled peers. Therefore, it seems a reasonable possibility that learners may look toward whatever cues exist, whether implicit or explicit, to decide where to focus their attention during reading.

An alternative explanation for the wide-reading group's growth in comprehension is based upon the fact that learners' ability to construct meaning may improve as a result of increasing the amount of connected text they are responsible for reading (Anderson, Wilson, & Fielding, 1988; Guthrie, 1982; Leinhardt, Zigmond, & Cooley, 1981). In the current study, the students in the wide-reading group read 18 texts beyond those they encountered in the classroom, whereas the FOOR group read only 6. And, while the listening-only group was also exposed to 18 stories, the students did not read the books themselves. Because the posttest measure required that the students not only respond to a series of stories but also read the passages themselves, it seems reasonable that the differing requirements in each group led to different outcomes and that improvements in comprehension may have occurred as the result of the students actively reading a wide range of texts.

Implications for the Classroom

Despite the differences in results, both the FOOR and the wide-reading approaches used in flexible grouping formats seem to provide effective fluency-oriented instruction. These approaches ensure that students have increased opportunities to read connected text and create an expectation of student accountability for the material. Further, both approaches provide a model of expressive reading, are relatively easy to implement, and can be used with a variety of texts, from basal readers to the more challenging types of trade books that were used in this study. At the same time, the differing results from the two strategies indicate that the FOOR strategy might be more effective for students who need to work primarily on the mechanics of their reading, or automaticity and prosody, whereas the wide-reading approach could be used with students who need to work on improving not only their word recognition and expression but also their comprehension. However, given the importance of reading fluency in the overall reading process, both approaches appear to be effective means of integrating fluency instruction with the literacy curriculum.

References

Adams, M.J. (1990). *Beginning to read: Thinking and learning about print.* Cambridge, MA: MIT Press.

Allington, R.L. (1983). Fluency: The neglected reading goal. *The Reading Teacher, 36,* 556–561.

Anderson, R.C., Wilkinson, I.A.G., & Mason, J.M. (1991). A microanalysis of the small-group, guided reading lesson: Effects of an emphasis on global story meaning. *Reading Research Quarterly, 26,* 417–441.

Anderson, R.C., Wilson, P.T., & Fielding, L.G. (1988). Growth in reading and how children spend their time outside of school. *Reading Research Quarterly, 23,* 285–303. doi: 10.1598/RRQ.23.3.2

Ash, G.E., Kuhn, M.R., & Walpole, S. (2003, December). *Flying in the face of research: Inservice teachers' use of round robin reading (research in progress).* Paper presented at the National Reading Conference, Scottsdale, AZ.

Chall, J.S. (1996). *Stages of reading development* (2nd ed.). Fort Worth, TX: Harcourt-Brace.

Chomsky, C. (1976). After decoding: What? *Language Arts, 53,* 288–296.

Dowhower, S. (1989). Repeated reading: Research into practice. *The Reading Teacher, 42,* 502–507.

Dowhower, S.L. (1991). Speaking of prosody: Fluency's unattended bedfellow. *Theory Into Practice, 30,* 158–164.

FEP/Booksource. (1998). *1998 books for early childhood to adult.* St. Louis, MO: The Booksource.

Fleisher, L.S., Jenkins, J.R., & Pany, D. (1979/1980). Effects on poor readers' comprehension of training in rapid decoding. *Reading Research Quarterly, 15,* 30–48.

Fountas, I.C., & Pinnell, G.S. (1999). *Guided reading: Good first teaching for all children.* Portsmouth, NH: Heinemann.

Guthrie, J.T. (1982). The book flood. *Journal of Reading, 26,* 286–288.

Hoffman, J.V., & Crone, S. (1985). The oral recitation lesson: A research-derived strategy for reading basal texts. In J.A. Niles & R.V. Lalik (Eds.), *Issues in literacy: A research perspective, 34th yearbook of the National Reading Conference* (pp. 76–83). Rochester, NY: National Reading Conference.

Koskinen, P.S., & Blum, I.H. (1986). Paired repeated reading: A classroom strategy for developing fluent reading. *The Reading Teacher, 40,* 70–75.

Kuhn, M.R. (2000). *A comparative study of small group fluency instruction.* Unpublished doctoral dissertation, University of Georgia, Athens.

Kuhn, M.R. (2003). Fluency in the classroom: Strategies for whole-class and group work. In L.M. Morrow, L.B. Gambrell, & M. Pressley (Eds.), *Best practices in literacy instruction* (pp. 127–142). New York: Guilford.

Kuhn, M.R., & Stahl, S. (2003). Fluency: A review of developmental and remedial strategies. *The Journal of Educational Psychology, 95,* 1–19.

LaBerge, D., & Samuels, S.J. (1974). Toward a theory of automatic information processing in reading. *Cognitive Psychology, 6,* 293–323.

Leinhardt, G., Zigmond, N., & Cooley, W.W. (1981). Reading instruction and its effects. *American Educational Research Journal, 18,* 343–361.

Morris, D., & Nelson, L. (1992). Supported oral reading with low-achieving second graders. *Reading Research and Instruction, 31,* 49–63.

National Institute of Child Health and Human Development. (2000). *Report of the National Reading Panel. Teaching children to read: An evidence-based assessment of the scientific research literature on reading and its implications for reading instruction. Reports of the subgroups* (NIH Publication No. 00-4769). Washington, DC: U.S. Government Printing Office. Retrieved May 12, 2003, from http://www.nichd.nih.gov/publications/nrp

O'Shea, L.J., Sindelar, P.T., & O'Shea, D.J. (1985). The effects of repeated readings and attentional cues on reading fluency and comprehension. *Journal of Reading Behavior, 17,* 129–142.

O'Shea, L.J., Sindelar, P.T., & O'Shea, D.J. (1987). The effects of repeated readings and attentional cues on the reading fluency and comprehension of learning disabled readers. *Learning Disabilities Research, 2,* 103–109.

Perfetti, C.A. (1985). *Reading ability.* New York: Oxford University Press.

Rasinski, T.V., Padak, N., Linek, W., & Sturtevant, E. (1994). Effects of fluency development on urban second-grade readers. *Journal of Educational Research, 87,* 158–165.

Reutzel, D.R. (1996). Developing at-risk readers' oral reading fluency. In L.R. Putnam (Ed.), *How to become a better reading teacher* (pp. 241–254). Englewood Cliffs, NJ: Merrill.

Reutzel, D.R. (2003). Organizing effective literacy instruction: Grouping strategies and instructional routines. In L.M. Morrow, L.B. Gambrell, & M. Pressley (Eds.),

Best practices in literacy instruction (2nd ed., pp. 241–267). New York: Guilford.

Samuels, S.J. (1979). The method of repeated readings. *The Reading Teacher, 32*, 403–408.

Schreiber, P.A. (1991). Understanding prosody's role in reading acquisition. *Theory Into Practice, 30*, 158–164.

Stahl, S.A., Heubach, K., & Cramond, B. (1997). *Fluency-oriented reading instruction* (Reading Research Rep. No. 79). Athens, GA: National Reading Research Center.

Stahl, S.A., & Kuhn, M.R. (2002). Making it sound like language: Developing fluency. *The Reading Teacher, 55*, 582–584.

Stanovich, K.E. (1980). Toward an interactive-compensatory model of individual differences in the development of reading fluency. *Reading Research Quarterly, 16*, 32–71.

Vygotsky, L.S. (1978). *Mind in society: The development of higher psychological processes* (M. Cole, V. John-Steiner, S. Scribner, & E. Souberman, Eds. & Trans.). Cambridge, MA: Harvard University Press. (Original work published 1934)

Questions for Reflection

• Think about the fluency instruction in your classroom. Does it emphasize automaticity, accuracy, *and* prosody? Does it make the connection from fluency to comprehension? How are the approaches described in this article similar or different from those you currently use in your instruction? What aspects of FOOR and wide reading could you incorporate in order to improve your classroom practice?

• What types of instructional grouping have you found most effective? How do you manage small-group work in your classroom? Can you see ways that peer coaching could be incorporated in fluency instruction with your students?

• How do you assess reading fluency among your students? Do your assessment methods take into account *all* the components that go into making a fluent reader?

Making the *Very* Most of Classroom Read-Alouds to Promote Comprehension and Vocabulary

Lana Edwards Santoro, David J. Chard, Lisa Howard, and Scott K. Baker

Melissa Duarte (all names are pseudonyms), an experienced first-grade teacher at Kennedy Elementary School, started the school year with the important goal of teaching her 24 students the decoding skills needed to become independent readers. Evidence from her progress monitoring throughout the year suggests that she is likely to accomplish this goal. However, Melissa and her fellow first-grade teachers are frustrated because their comprehensive reading program (with small-group instruction and intervention for English-language learners) is time consuming and leaves little opportunity to address important content areas such as science and social studies, or to teach students how to think about the ideas they read.

Melissa considered using more read-aloud opportunities to teach vocabulary and comprehension. Her literacy coach was supportive but requested that she identify specific studies documenting the effectiveness of read-aloud instruction for teaching vocabulary and comprehension. Melissa could not find support for such practices in the professional journals to which she had access.

Because many teachers share Melissa's frustrations, we studied the daily use of read-alouds to introduce content not addressed in core reading material and to explicitly teach comprehension skills and vocabulary in first grade. We recognize that there are different approaches to classroom read-alouds. Sometimes read-alouds are used without instructional interruption for the purpose of enjoying and listening to a story. Although there certainly isn't anything inherently wrong with using read-alouds for student enjoyment, like Melissa, we wanted to find ways to use read-alouds to make the most of precious instructional time. Would there be ways to maintain enjoyment while instruction was purposefully incorporated with read-alouds?

There is considerable interest in this topic despite the few specific studies on read-aloud practices. Recent research has established that effective read-alouds contribute to students' comprehension development (Fisher, Flood, Lapp, & Frey, 2004; Hickman, Pollard-Durodola, & Vaughn, 2004). Beck and McKeown (2001) also describe read-aloud activities that build background knowledge, language, and listening comprehension skills. For many students who struggle with decoding skills or who are just learning to read fluently, it would seem reasonable that comprehension strategies be taught through oral language opportunities (e.g., read-alouds).

Hickman et al. (2004), Fisher et al. (2004), and Beck and McKeown (2001) provided support for reading aloud as an important part of early reading instruction. Extending previous research, we developed and empirically evaluated the effectiveness of specific read-aloud practices with first-grade children. We wanted to incorporate instruction to improve comprehension skills and strategies, enhance vocabulary knowledge,

Reprinted from Santoro, L.E., Chard, D.J., Howard, L., & Baker, S.K. (2008). Making the *very* most of classroom read-alouds to promote comprehension and vocabulary. *The Reading Teacher, 61*(5), 396–408.

and introduce content that addresses standards in science and social studies. A more extensive description of the analysis of the study's data is available from the lead author (Santoro).

This article describes the curriculum used in our research and discusses general strategies for building comprehension when reading aloud to children. We used existing research to help us enhance daily classroom read-alouds for more powerful instruction. Text structure, text-focused discussions, and vocabulary are three primary areas where the research demonstrates links between instruction and student comprehension. Specific principles that guided our work are presented in Table 1.

Text Structure

"Text structures" are frames that identify important information and connections between ideas (Dickson, Simmons, & Kame'enui, 1998; Englert & Mariage, 1991, 1992; Goldman & Rakestraw, 2000; Pearson & Fielding, 1991; Williams, 2005). The early elementary grades are an ideal time to teach text structure (Adams, 1990). Familiarity with narrative text structure gives students a framework for discussing stories and retelling. As a story is read, the teacher can help students discuss *who* the story is about, *what* happened first, *what* happened next, and *what* happened at the end. If these same target elements are routinely used to identify critical features of a story, students have repeated opportunities to discuss them and make text-to-text connections. For example, not only could students identify story elements in Jan Brett's *The Mitten* (1990, Scholastic), but also they could compare characters and story sequence using the same set of story elements for Brett's *The Hat* (1998, Hodder) or Karma Wilson's *Bear Snores On* (2003, Simon and Schuster). Students could also base a retelling on the same set of target story elements.

Read-alouds also provide an ideal opportunity to teach expository, or information, text structure. Expository texts' use of complex organizational patterns, like compare and contrast, cause and effect, and problem and solution, appears to result in knowledge of text structure and book language that must not be disregarded (Duke & Kays, 1998). At the very least, young children can be taught that reading information texts often involves dual purposes of reading to locate particular information (Dreher, 1993; Guthrie & Kirsch, 1987) and to learn something new. The research on text structure provided a general format for our read-alouds. Students would need to listen for and apply a different text structure or framework depending on whether the read-aloud was a story book or information book.

Text-Focused Discussions

Despite the general support for using read-alouds, the ideal format for conducting them is not clear (Fisher et al., 2004). Most recently, Beck and McKeown (2001) explored the use of "text talk" in first-grade classrooms. Their findings suggested that text-based discussions as part of read-alouds may increase vocabulary acquisition and

---

Table 1
Principles That Guided the Read-Aloud Project

We wanted to...

- Challenge students to develop more complex comprehension strategies than would be necessary for the relatively simple narrative and information texts typically used in first grade
- Use both narrative and information text with lessons to explicitly make text-to-text connections
- Deepen student comprehension and facilitate dialogic interactions both between students and among students
- Use independent student retellings of texts as the primary outcome

comprehension (Beck, McKeown, Hamilton, & Kucan, 1997).

Our read-alouds incorporated structured, interactive teacher and student text-based discussions. Rather than simply reading aloud without discussion, we hoped to create opportunities for children to reflect on the storyline (or the text's language) to promote comprehension. For example, a teacher might pause to have students identify the main character, then expand the discussion by asking about specific character clues. In addition to asking students to predict, a teacher could ask *why* students made a particular prediction, then ask them to explain whether the prediction was correct after reading the story. In this way, students become true partners in discussions about the text.

Vocabulary

The importance of vocabulary to comprehension is widely documented (Anderson & Freebody, 1981; Anderson & Nagy, 1991; Baker, Simmons, & Kame'enui, 1998). Read-alouds can provide an ideal "teacher-centered" approach for introducing and talking about new words (Dickinson & Smith, 1994; Elley, 1989; Robbins & Ehri, 1994; Sénéchal, 1997). Reading aloud and facilitating text-based discussions about words provide contexts and opportunities for children to learn new words before they have the reading skills necessary to acquire vocabulary independently (Biemiller, 2001). In addition to generally discussing vocabulary within the context of a read-aloud text, vocabulary must also be taught directly (Biemiller, 2001). Before reading Carle's *The Grouchy Ladybug* (1996, HarperTrophy), the word *grouchy* could be explicitly defined and discussed in context, by saying something like the following.

> The title of this book is *The Grouchy Ladybug*. Grouchy means grumpy or angry. Someone who is grouchy is not happy. What does grouchy mean? Show me, with your face, what grouchy looks like. Look at the book cover again. How would you describe the ladybug on the cover?

When later discussing story elements, like main character, grouchy would be used to describe the ladybug. "The grouchy ladybug is grouchy, mean, and not polite." Finally, to promote additional discussion and interaction, prompts can be used to extend student word knowledge (Beck, McKeown, & Kucan, 2002), such as "Who can tell me a time when you felt grouchy?" "When you're grouchy you're really unhappy. Tell me how that feels." or "If someone is grouchy, how are they acting, what do they do?"

Read-Aloud Project Overview

Our federally funded project was to design and evaluate a framework for teaching comprehension of complex narrative and information texts to first-grade students in general education classrooms during read-aloud time (Baker, Chard, & Edwards, 2002). Table 1 outlines the principles guiding our curriculum development. To determine whether our instruction affected comprehension, we assessed the performance of those students who were *most* at risk for overall reading and comprehension difficulties, as well as students who were on track for successful reading development. We compared the performance of students who participated in the read-aloud curriculum with students from classrooms where teachers used their own read-aloud texts and procedures. Our results indicated that enhancing read-alouds with comprehension strategies and text-based discussions made a positive difference in student performance. Students from classrooms using the read-aloud curriculum demonstrated higher levels of comprehension and vocabulary knowledge and included more accurate, higher quality information in retellings. Participating students could also speak with more depth and metacognitive awareness about comprehension (e.g., articulate why it would help you understand better if you identified the type of book that you would be reading). We found no differences in comprehension and vocabulary between the at-risk and average-achieving students in classrooms that used the read-aloud curriculum (Baker, Chard, & Edwards, 2004; Baker, Chard, Santoro, Otterstedt, & Gau, 2006;

Santoro, Baker, Chard, & Howard, in press; Santoro, Chard, & Baker, 2005).

Read-Aloud Curriculum Organization and Structure

We considered several issues when deciding how to structure read-alouds and incorporate comprehension instruction with a series of lessons. To maintain the integrity of a read-aloud experience, optimize instructional time, and make the lessons feasible, we tried to keep daily lessons to between 20 and 30 minutes.

We began our project by reviewing national guidelines such as the National Research Council standards (Snow, Burns, & Griffith,1998) and state standards to identify skills and strategies for read-aloud focus. For example, the National Research Council lists "connecting information and events in text-to-life and life-to-text experiences, predicting and justifying what will happen next in stories, and describing new information gained from text in your own words" (pp. 80–81) as instructional priorities in kindergarten and first grade. Because both state standards and the National Research Council emphasize the importance of expository text in K–3 instruction, we recommend using information and narrative texts together to address early elementary comprehension goals. We incorporated state standards for first-grade science and social studies into our lessons and selected books that would address standards for content knowledge. We integrated language arts and comprehension standards—along with specific content area standards—with our instruction.

We next considered curriculum structure, constructing lessons around a set of week-long "units" consisting of one narrative text and one information text on a common science or social studies theme or topic. The curriculum alternated between a series of science units and a series of social studies units. We designed the curriculum to correspond to holidays often discussed in elementary school curricula. Despite slight differences in the alternating sequence between science and social studies (to align with holidays), our goal was to build connections between texts, themes, other curricula sources, and common activities and events.

Science units were grouped into three-week themes focusing on animals. An example of a theme from the curriculum was "insects." The first week and unit focused on the general animal category and included an information book about insects and a narrative book featuring many different kinds of insects as story characters. The next two weeks and units in that theme contained specific examples from the general animal category, in this case butterflies and ladybugs. Planning thematic connections created opportunities to build background knowledge and make intertextual connections.

We organized our social studies units into two-week themes focusing on famous people and holidays. For example, the first week of the Presidents' Day theme was about George Washington, and included an information book about George Washington and a narrative book about a character that reflected some of the traits or issues discussed in the information book. The second week of the Presidents' Day theme focused on Abraham Lincoln. We created a total of 15 science and social studies units for our read-aloud intervention (see Table 2).

We also wanted to scaffold instruction from more teacher-directed classroom discussions to more independent student responses. In units 1–5, the lessons emphasized teacher demonstration of comprehension tasks using think-alouds, models, and explanations. In units 6–10 the emphasis was on guiding student responses. Teachers asked questions and elicited answers with prompts and support as necessary. Units 11–15 emphasized guided and more independent student responses with less teacher support and prompting. For example, students did retellings with minimal prompting from teachers.

We included four lessons in each unit, two featuring the narrative text and two featuring the information text. This system provided flexibility to implement the curriculum each week and review content, especially given that school calendars are often disrupted with holidays, assemblies, testing, and snow days. On the "extra" or fifth day of instruction, teachers were encouraged

Table 2
Scope and Sequence of the Read-Aloud Curriculum Units and Texts

Unit	Content	Theme	Topic	Information text	Narrative text	Vocabulary
1	Science	Mammals	Mammals	*A True Book: Mammals* (Stewart, 2000, Children's Press)	*Bear Snores On* (Wilson, 2003, Simon and Schuster)	snores, nibble, slumbering, mammal
2	Science	Mammals	Bats	*Bats* (Gibbons, 2000, Holiday House)	*Stellaluna* (Cannon, 1999, Chrysalis)	nocturnal, migrate, hibernate, clutch, dodging
3	Science	Mammals	Elephants	*What Is an Elephant?* (Crossingham & Kalman, 1997, Crabtree)	*How the Elephant Got Its Trunk: A Retelling of the Rudyard Kipling Tale* (Richards, 2003, Henry Holt)	species, habitat, herbivore, curious, continued, trickle
4	Social studies	Thanksgiving	Thanksgiving	*The Pilgrims' First Thanksgiving* (McGovern, 1993, Scholastic)	*Gracias, the Thanksgiving Turkey* (Cowley, 2005, Scholastic)	gracias, amigos, fragrant, Pilgrims, voyage
5	Social studies	Thanksgiving	Native Americans	*Pocahontas* (Hudson, 2001, Heinemann Library)	*The Rough-Face Girl* (Martin, 1998, Putnam)	biography, settlers, portrait, invisible, cruel, swift
6	Science	Reptiles	Reptiles	*What Is a Reptile?* (Kalman, 1998, Crabtree)	*Lizard's Home* (Shannon, 1999, Greenwillow)	fairness, grinning, predator, molt, scaly
7	Science	Reptiles	Crocodiles	*The Crocodile: Ruler of the River* (Tracqui, 1997, Charlesbridge)	*Bill and Pete* (dePaola, 1996, Putnam)	competition, independent, territory, nickname, famous, adventure
8	Science	Reptiles	Sea turtles	*A True Book: Sea Turtles* (Lepthien, 1997, Children's Press)	*Albert's Impossible Toothache* (Williams, 2004, Walker)	protection, extinct, impossible, worry, announced, moaned
9	Social studies	African American leaders	Martin Luther King, Jr.	*Martin's Big Words* (Rappaport, 2007, Jump at the Sun)	*Night Golf* (Miller, 2002, Lee & Low)	protest, segregation, golf, caddy
10	Social studies	African American leaders	Rosa Parks	*I Am Rosa Parks* (Parks & Haskins, 1999, Puffin)	*Daisy and the Doll* (Medearis & Medearis, 2005, University Press of New England)	autobiography, contest, ashamed, recite, variety

(continued)

Table 2
Scope and Sequence of the Read-Aloud Curriculum Units and Texts (Continued)

Unit	Content	Theme	Topic	Information text	Narrative text	Vocabulary
11	Social studies	Presidents	George Washington	*A Picture Book of George Washington* (Adler, 1990, Holiday House)	*Liar, Liar, Pants on Fire* (deGroat, 2003, SeaStar)	*survey, play, notice, reply*
12	Social studies	Presidents	Abraham Lincoln	*Honest Abe* (Kunhardt, 1998, HarperTrophy)	*A. Lincoln and Me* (Borden, 2001, Scholastic)	*slavery, lanky, clumsy*
13	Science	Insects	Insects	*A True Book: Insects* (Stewart, 2000, Children's Press)	*The Bugliest Bug* (Shields, 2005, Candlewick)	*antennae, arachnid, pair, bugliest, applauded, clever*
14	Science	Insects	Butterflies	*Monarch Butterflies* (Waxman, 2003, Lerner)	*Butterfly Boy* (Kroll, 2002, Boyds Mills)	*nectar, chrysalis, crimson, sweltering*
15	Science	Insects	Ladybugs	*Ladybugs* (Llewellyn & Watts, 2003, Franklin Watts)	*The Grouchy Ladybug* (Carle, 1996, HarperTrophy)	*oozes, grouchy, encountered*

to reread one of the texts, do writing-based retelling activities, complete an unfinished lesson, or conduct a review by comparing and contrasting texts used in prior weeks.

Book Selection

Criteria we considered when selecting books and determining the themes for read-aloud instruction included the book's topic, target audience, length, cost, availability, representation of diversity, text coherence, and potential for connections with other texts and topics addressed in first-grade curricula. Table 3 summarizes book selection considerations.

Texts can be selected based on topics that interest young children. For example, we selected several different types of animals for our science units because of the relative ease in comparing and contrasting critical features of general animal categories—it would be fairly easy to compare and contrast what makes an animal a mammal versus what makes an animal a reptile. We also selected books about specific types of animals within each category. Within the general category of reptiles, for example, we sought books about lizards, snakes, and crocodiles. For the social studies units, we focused on books about holidays and famous people because holidays are often introduced in the early grades in the United States as anchors for thematic topics within the curriculum, and because "famous people" was included in state standards for both states where our read-aloud intervention was implemented. We considered books on topics including Thanksgiving, Pocahontas, Martin Luther King, Rosa Parks, George Washington, and Abraham Lincoln.

We also selected books based on the target audience, 6- to 8-year-old children. We intentionally avoided overly simplistic books in favor of those that included rich context for compre-

Table 3
Book Selection Criteria

Criterion	Considerations
Topics	• High interest for young children (e.g., animals) • Ability to compare and contrast topics across books • Connected to district, school, and curricula themes • Connected to state and district standards
Target audience	• Grade level of students • Interests of students • Length of books
Diversity and multicultural connections	• Male and female characters • Different cultures and ethnicity groups represented • Different settings and geographical locations
Text coherence	• Clear story structure • Expository information presented with clarity and accuracy
Text-to-text author and illustrator connections	• Some books written by the same author • Some books illustrated by the same illustrator

hension and vocabulary instruction. A length of approximately 32 pages was about right for our planned read-aloud and lesson timeframe of 20 to 30 minutes. We also looked for books that included diverse characters and settings.

Finally, we considered text coherence. We wanted to ensure that narrative texts didn't include a confusing story structure with multiple plot episodes, and that content in information texts was presented accurately and clearly. The books we selected facilitated connections between topics and other texts. We looked for well-known authors and illustrators so we could make comparisons across units about different books by the same author. We chose books by well-known authors who would likely be familiar to children participating in the project (see Table 2 for a list of texts and how they were paired).

Vocabulary Selection

When selecting words, we chose those that were

• Functional and meaningful

• Rich, varied, and interesting without comprising the text's overall meaning

• Important to understanding the story (Kuhn & Stahl, 1998)

We selected two to four words from each text to explicitly teach and discuss. For example, for the book *Bear Snores On*, we selected *snores* as target vocabulary because we felt *snores* was central to understanding the meaning of the story and an important word from the story's title. If students didn't know the word *snores* it would be very difficult to understand the story. We used Beck et al.'s (2002) tier selection criteria, selecting tier two and tier three words for our target vocabulary. We looked for high-frequency tier two words that would help students expand their vocabulary knowledge (e.g., *curious*, *sweltering*, and *protect*). The tier three words occurred with less frequency but were important within a particular content domain. In many cases, our tier three words (such as *mammal*, *habitat*, and *predator*) were selected from information texts and were science related.

Pulling It All Together in Read-Aloud Lessons

We included before, during, and after components in all lessons (Table 4). In the before reading portion of the lesson we identified the book type (narrative or information) and prepared students for either listening to a story or learning from an expository text. For example, a teacher might provide the following introduction, "When we start any new book we want to identify our purpose for reading, so there is an important question we always want to ask before we start. That question is, 'Is this an information book or a story book?'" For narrative books, students made predictions about whom or what the story was about and what they thought would happen. For information books, students were asked to identify "what they knew" and "what they wanted to know" about the topic using a K-W-L chart (What I *K*now, What I *W*ant to Know, What I *L*earned) (Ogle, 1986). For example, before reading Crossingham and Kalman's *What Is an Elephant?* (1997), a teacher might say something like the following:

> Let's start with the *K* part of the chart, "what I know." We'll write down a couple of things we think we know about elephants. We don't need to think of or write everything we might know, just one or two things to get our brains thinking. I remember from our book on mammals that elephants are mammals, so I'll write that down. Does anybody else think they know something about elephants? I'll write two more things.

Concept vocabulary necessary to understand the story was directly taught with "student-friendly" definitions prior to reading the book (Beck et al., 2002).

During reading, the lessons focused on text structure in the narrative texts, such as whom the story was about, what happened first, what happened next, and what happened at the end of the story. When reading about the first main thing that happened in a story, teachers would help students recognize and explain that the first important event happens at the beginning of the story and it gets the story started. In the book *How the Elephant Got Its Trunk: A Retelling of the Rudyard Kipling Tale* (Richards, 2003), a teacher would pause to discuss how the little elephant tries to ask members of her family (her mother, father, sister, brother) and some other animals (the giraffe, the hippopotamus) what the crocodile eats for dinner, but no one will answer her.

K-W-L components were also discussed during reading of information texts. When reading *What Is an Elephant?*, a teacher might pause to make the following comments:

Table 4
Comprehension Strategy Focus for the Before, During, and After Lesson Components

Before reading	During reading	After reading
• Identifying the purpose for reading (e.g., information or story) • Previewing (title, author, illustrator) • Predicting/priming • Defining critical vocabulary	• Using a consistent framework to discuss the text (e.g., story elements, K-W-L with focus questions) • Using question-asking strategies • Making connections (text-to-text, • text-to-self, text-to-world) • Making inferences • Self-monitoring • Vocabulary	• Retelling • Introducing, reviewing, and extending vocabulary

This paragraph contained a lot of information. Let's review what it said and put some facts about elephants on the *L* part of our K-W-L Chart. One of the first things it said was that elephants are mammals. On our K-W-L Chart, we had that as something we thought we knew. Now we can add it to the *L* part of the chart. The book said that because they are mammals, elephants are warm-blooded. What else do we know about elephants because they are mammals?

Questioning during reading also included higher level thinking skills (making predictions with text-based confirmations and drawing inferences). For example, when reading *The Bugliest Bug* (Shields, 2005), a teacher might pause to remind students that authors don't always tell us everything, as in the following excerpt.

> You know, authors don't always say things directly. This part of the story is talking about the stage where the contest is taking place. It says that "A lacy white curtain hung from the trees" (p. 7). Knowing what you know now, what do you think the lacy white curtain is?

We also provided structured opportunities for students to talk about the text in "book clubs" of two or four students. Book clubs consisted of a small group of students, typically student pairs or "book club partners," matched by the teacher. During read-alouds, teachers would pause and ask students to discuss a particular comprehension question. A focus question was always used to direct the student-to-student discussions. For example, a teacher might ask students to turn to their book club partner to share thoughts about who the main character is in the story. Finally, vocabulary was taught or reviewed if it occurred in the text.

After reading, teachers would model a story or information book retelling using a common text structure framework. With a story, for example, teachers used a visual prompt sheet that included icons for the main character, what happened first, what happened next, and what happened at the end. Figure 1 and Figure 2 show examples of a story retelling prompt sheet used with the book *Butterfly Boy* (Kroll, 2002). The

framework used in this example includes who, problem, solution, and end. In addition to using the retelling sheets to model and help prompt student retellings, many teachers had students write notes or draw simple pictures on their prompt sheets. Figure 1 is an example of a first-grade student's story retelling prompt sheet from the beginning of the year. Figure 2 shows that by the end of the year, students were able to write more story information on the prompt sheets. When students practiced retellings, they used their own story retelling sheets to prompt them. The K-W-L chart provided the framework for information book retellings. As with the narrative retellings, students practiced as a small group or in pairs.

Vocabulary was discussed and reviewed after reading. When discussing the word *worry* from *Albert's Impossible Toothache* (Williams, 2004), teachers would ask students to practice

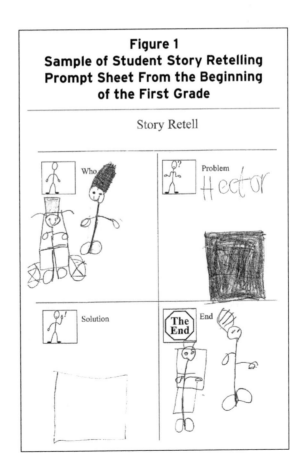

Figure 1
Sample of Student Story Retelling Prompt Sheet From the Beginning of the First Grade

Story Retell

Who

Problem
Hector

Solution

The End   End

Figure 2
Sample of Student Story Retelling Prompt Sheet From the End of First Grade

Story Retell

Tisha   5-6-03

Who
Amilow and Abralow.

Problem
The Dad painted grage door blue.

Solution
Amilow put his white shirt on and the b···· ···e

End
Amilow was happy agin and then Dad inportin new it to Amilow he painted. hi how u· so

---

saying the word, define the word, and then discuss a text-based example of it. For example, consider the following:

> One of the other words we learned is worry. Everyone, say "worry." What does worry mean? Why is Albert's mother worried about him? Why is she concerned about him?

If class time permitted, discussions after reading also included vocabulary extension activities with opportunities for students to expand their knowledge and use of target words. For the vocabulary words *slumbering* and *nibbling*, the following questions guided discussions. Students were asked to justify and explain their answers.

- If you are running, are you slumbering? How do you know?

- If you are taking a nap with your eyes closed, are you slumbering? How do you know?

- If you are biting off small bits of cookie, are you nibbling or slumbering? How do you know?

- If you fall asleep during a movie, are you nibbling or slumbering? How do you know?

Overall, read-aloud lessons included making text-to-text and text-to-life connections before, during, and after reading, which were integrated with the lessons and later became connections between books both within and across units. Lessons also addressed literal and inferential comprehension and a range of comprehension strategies. Table 4 highlights the comprehension strategy focus that was targeted in the before, during, and after reading components of lessons.

Narrative Lessons

The first narrative lesson always included a 5-minute introduction of the book, a discussion about whether the text was a story or an information book, and predictions. During the 10- to 15-minute read-aloud teachers would pause to confirm predictions about the text, use think-alouds to clarify story events or vocabulary, and make connections to other texts. In sum, the read-aloud for the first narrative lesson was centered on story structure and the information students would need for retellings. After the read-aloud, teachers would use a large story retelling chart, or a transparency for an overhead projector, to model a story retelling. Students would each have copies of the retelling prompt sheet. The following lesson excerpt illustrates how a teacher might discuss retelling components and model a retelling by guiding student responses.

> Now that we've discussed our book we're going to do a retelling of *Albert's Impossible Toothache* as a class. Look at the overhead (or your retelling sheet). Let's see how clear we can make our retelling. Our goal should be that someone listening to our retell-

ing would have a good understanding of the story. OK, let's see what we can do.

What are the first two things we tell? We describe the book type and its title. So, we might say something like..."We read a story book called *Albert's Impossible Toothache*."

Remember, the next thing we tell is who is the main character, and something about that character. We could say "This story is about, or the main character in this story is Albert Turtle. He is a young land turtle who doesn't like it that no one ever believes him."

Then what do we tell? We talk about what happens first, by describing the first important thing that happens in the story. For example, with this story we would want to say something like, "In *Albert's Impossible Toothache*, the first important thing that happens is that Albert complains, or announces, tells, that he has a toothache. But no one in his family believes him. They say it's impossible, it couldn't happen."

Now what do we tell? We have to talk about what happens next. Because a lot of things usually happen in a story, when we tell what happens next in a story, we pick out just the important things. And sometimes we have come up with one sentence that summarizes or describes many events. So, we might say, "Next, Albert's mother tries a lot of different things to get him to get out of bed. But nothing works, so Albert's mother worries and worries—she is very concerned about him." If we have time or want to tell all the details of what Albert's mother tried, we could say, "Albert's mother fixes him a special breakfast, asks him to play catch with her, and has Albert look at pictures of the family in Disneyland."

The next thing in a retelling is what happens at the end—including describing how the main character feels. So, for this story we could say, "At the end of this story, Albert's grandmother comes to Albert's house. The family tells her about Albert and his impossible toothache. Instead of telling Albert his toothache is impossible, Grandmother Turtle believes him and asks Albert where his toothache is. Albert shows her his toe, where a gopher bit him. Albert's toothache is an ache caused by a tooth! Grandmother Turtle fixes Albert's "toothache" by wrapping his toe with her handkerchief. Albert is happy. He smiles a big smile—he beams—and gets out of bed."

The very last part of a good story retelling is giving a personal response. We tell whether we liked or didn't like the story *and* tell why. For this story, I would say, "I liked this book. One of the main reasons is that I thought it was neat that Grandmother Turtle believed Albert when no one else did."

During this first narrative lesson, vocabulary was also discussed and reviewed. The modeled retelling and vocabulary activities took approximately 10 minutes.

The second narrative lesson in a unit began with a brief review of the title, author, and illustrator. Students were asked to identify whether the book was a story or information book and to describe the text features that helped them decide. Students reviewed the retelling chart from the first narrative lesson before the text was read a second time. During the second reading of the narrative text there were more pauses for teacher–student discussion and increased emphasis on inferential understanding. Lessons also featured more book club opportunities during pauses in the read-aloud. The second read-aloud took approximately 15 to 20 minutes because of the increased teacher–student discussions. The after-reading component included a teacher-guided retelling using a chart or overhead projector, and concluded by having students work with a book club partner to practice story retelling using prompt sheets.

First let's do a quick story retelling for *Albert's Impossible Toothache* as a class. Look at the overhead or your retelling sheet. The first two things we tell are book type and book title. We read a story book called *Albert's Impossible Toothache*. The next thing we tell is who the main character is and something about that character. The main character in this story is Albert Turtle. He is a young land turtle who doesn't like it that no one ever believes him.

Once we've told about the main character, we start telling the important things that happen in the story—starting with what happens first. In *Albert's Impossible Toothache*, the first important thing that happens is that Albert complains or announces to, tells, his family he has a toothache and he won't get out of bed. No one in his family believes him. Then we tell what happens next. Albert's mother tries a lot of different things to get him to get out of bed. She fixes him a special breakfast, asks him to play catch with her, and asks him to look at pictures of the family in Disneyland. Nothing works, and Albert's mother worries and worries—she is very concerned about him.

Then we tell what happens at the end, including how the main character feels. At the end of *Albert's Impossible Toothache*, Albert's grandmother comes to Albert's house. Instead of telling Albert his toothache is impossible, Grandmother Turtle believes him and asks him where his toothache is. Albert shows her his toe, where a gopher bit him. Albert's toothache is an ache caused by a tooth! Grandmother Turtle fixes Albert's "toothache" by wrapping his toe with her handkerchief. Albert is happy. He smiles a big smile—he beams—and gets out of bed. The very last part of a good story retelling is giving a personal response—I liked this book because I liked how Grandmother Turtle believed Albert.

Now each of you is going to take a turn doing a complete story retelling for *Albert's Impossible Toothache* with your book club partner. When it's your turn, use the words and pictures on the Story Retelling Sheet to help you remember all the parts you need to include, and use the words and pictures you put on the sheet to help you remember what you want to tell about this particular story. Don't forget to end your retelling with whether you liked the story or didn't like it and why. Each person will have about one and a half minutes, and I will tell you when it's time to switch. Those who want to start first, raise your hand. Those who will be listeners, remember to listen closely to your partner so you can give them feedback when they are done. OK, get ready to start.

Information Lessons

The first information lesson in a unit began with a 5- to 10-minute topic introduction, identification of the title and author, and a discussion about whether the text was a story or information book. A modified K-W-L chart (Ogle, 1986) helped students prepare and activate background knowledge. Teachers guided students through a brainstorm about what they thought they knew about the text's topic and wrote student responses in the "what I think I know" section of the K-W-L chart. Next, teachers asked students to think about what they wanted to learn about the topic. To help students make connections

across multiple texts, we asked that teachers always use predetermined focus questions for "what you want to know" in addition to soliciting one or two student-generated questions. For example, when reading texts on specific animal types like crocodiles, teachers would always ask the following questions. "What does a crocodile look like?" "What does a crocodile eat?" (see Figure 3).

Reading the information text in the first lesson took approximately 10 to 15 minutes. We selected excerpts focusing on the information in the "what you want to know" component of the K-W-L chart that were of interest to students. The read-aloud focused on confirming student predictions, drawing conclusions, making connections, and learning vocabulary. Unlike the repeated reading format used for narrative book lessons, the information book was read in two parts across two lessons. After the read-aloud in the first lesson, teachers guided students through a retelling and summary of that lesson's excerpts. The classroom K-W-L chart facilitated a teacher-directed retelling focusing on "what you learned." Teachers would spend approximately 5 to 10 minutes concluding the lesson with the retelling and text summary.

The second information lesson began with a 5- to 10-minute review of the topic, purpose for reading, and the K-W-L chart from the previous lesson. Students were instructed to listen for new information to add to the "what you learned" section of the chart. The read-aloud began where the previous lesson ended and again focused on making and confirming predictions, drawing conclusions, and making connections to personal experiences and other texts. Like the first information text lesson, the second also directed teachers to spend approximately 10 to 15 minutes on the read-aloud and conclude with a teacher-directed review of the completed K-W-L chart. Next, students met in book clubs to talk about what they learned by practicing retellings with a fact sheet. The fact sheet highlighted content details from the focus questions that were used in the K-W-L chart's "what you want to know" section. Figure 4 shows an example of the fact sheet that was used for the book *Sea Turtles* (Lepthien, 1997).

Fact sheets were used as prompts to help students with retellings. The final teacher-directed summary of the K-W-L chart and the student retelling with fact sheets took approximately 5 to 10 minutes.

Beyond the Read-Aloud Project

Recall the opening example of Melissa Duarte and her colleagues on the first-grade team. These teachers struggled to find time to fit everything into classroom schedules, and were frustrated because their comprehensive reading program was extremely time consuming. Melissa and her colleagues felt they were unable to fully cover reading, mathematics, and other content areas such as science and social studies, and wanted additional time to teach students how to apply comprehension strategies to what they read. Our project demonstrated that read-aloud time is an ideal opportunity to build comprehension through the use of oral language activities, listening comprehension, and text-based discussion.

Our research showed that read-alouds, with explicit comprehension instruction and active, engaging discussions about text, can promote comprehension and vocabulary even as students are learning to read (Baker et al., 2004; Baker et al., 2006; Santoro et al., in press; Santoro et al., 2005). In terms of overall comprehension, as measured by a composite of all the comprehension measures used in our study, the study benefited the read-aloud project students. In terms of narrative text specifically, students in read-aloud classrooms had longer retellings than students from classrooms that did not follow read-aloud lessons and procedures. Students in read-aloud classrooms also had retellings that reflected a depth of text comprehension. For example, students who received the read-aloud curriculum produced retellings with more text-based examples and elaborate, rich statements. Increased quality and depth was documented when retellings were scored. Components of the read-aloud curriculum that may have contributed to this outcome include the intentional emphasis on text structure throughout lessons, the use of visual prompt sheets to facilitate retellings, daily

Figure 3
K-W-L Chart With Focus Questions Added to the "What Do You Want to Know?" Column

K-W-L

What You Think You **K**now	What You **W**ant to Know	What You **L**earned
	• What does a crocodile look like? • What does a crocodile eat?	

Figure 4
Student Fact Sheet for Prompting *Sea Turtles* Information Retell

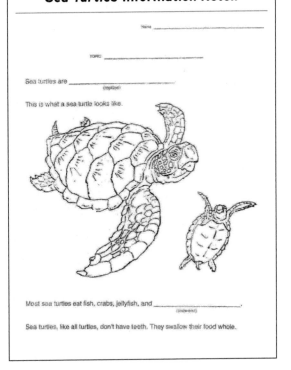

practice of student retellings, and text-focused discussions.

Incorporating comprehension instruction and read-alouds appears to be a promising way to boost student comprehension. There are certainly times when read-alouds can simply focus on the enjoyment of books; however, read-alouds must be carefully planned if they are to affect students' comprehension. Making the *very* most of read-aloud time requires teaching students to recognize the differences between narrative and information text structure, to know the meanings of target vocabulary, and to become active participants in purposeful discussions about texts.

Note

Research on the read-aloud curriculum was supported by the U.S. Department of Education, Institute of Education Sciences, Grant number CFDA 84.305G.

References

Adams, M.J. (1990). *Beginning to read: Thinking and learning about print.* Cambridge, MA: MIT.

Anderson, R.C., & Freebody, P. (1981). Vocabulary knowledge. In J.T. Guthrie (Ed.), *Comprehension and teaching: Research reviews* (pp. 77–117). Newark, DE: International Reading Association.

Anderson, R.C., & Nagy, W.E. (1991). Word meanings. In R. Barr, M.L. Kamil, P. Mosenthal, & P.D. Pearson (Eds.), *Handbook of reading research* (Vol. 2, pp. 690–724). White Plains, NY: Longman.

Baker, S., Chard, D.J., & Edwards, L. (2002). *The story readaloud project: The development of an innovative instructional approach to promote comprehension and vocabulary in first grade classrooms.* Research funded by the U.S. Department of Education, Institute of Education Sciences (CFDA 84.305G). Washington, DC: U.S. Department of Education, Institute of Education Sciences.

Baker, S., Chard, D.J., & Edwards, L. (2004, June). *Teaching first grade students to listen attentively to narrative and expository text: Results from an experimental study.* Paper presented at the 11th annual meeting of the Society for the Scientific Study of Reading, Amsterdam.

Baker, S., Chard, D.J., Santoro, L.E., Otterstedt, J., & Gau, J. (2006). *Reading aloud to students: The development of an intervention to improve comprehension and vocabulary of first graders.* Manuscript submitted for publication.

Baker, S.K., Simmons, D.C., & Kame'enui, E.J. (1998). Vocabulary acquisition: Research bases. In D.C. Simmons & E.J. Kame'enui (Eds.), *What reading research tells us about children with diverse learning needs: Bases and basics* (pp. 183–218). Mahwah, NJ: Erlbaum.

Beck, I.L., & McKeown, M.G. (2001). Text talk: Capturing the benefits of read-aloud experiences for young children. *The Reading Teacher, 55,* 10–20.

Beck, I.L., McKeown, M.G., Hamilton, R.L., & Kucan, L. (1997). *Questioning the author: An approach for enhancing student engagement with text.* Newark, DE: International Reading Association.

Beck, I.L., McKeown, M.G., & Kucan, L. (2002). *Bringing words to life: Robust vocabulary instruction.* New York: Guilford.

Biemiller, A. (2001, Spring). Teaching vocabulary: Early, direct, and sequential. *American Educator, 25* 24–28, 47.

Dickson, S.V., Simmons, D.C., & Kame'enui, E.J. (1998). Text organization: Research bases. In D.C. Simmons & E.J. Kame'enui (Eds.), *What the research tells us about children with diverse learning needs: Basis and basics* (pp. 239–278). New York: Erlbaum.

Dickinson, D.K., & Smith, M.W. (1994). Long-term effects of preschool teachers' book readings on low-income children's vocabulary and story comprehension. *Reading Research Quarterly, 29,* 104–122.

Dreher, M.J. (1993). Reading to locate information: Societal and educational perspectives. *Contemporary Educational Psychology, 18,* 129–138.

Duke, N., & Kays, J. (1998). "Can I say 'Once upon a time'?": Kindergarten children developing knowledge of information book language. *Early Childhood Research Quarterly, 13,* 295–318.

Elley, W.B. (1989). Vocabulary acquisition from listening to stories. *Reading Research Quarterly, 24,* 174–187.

Englert, C.S., & Mariage, T.V. (1991). Shared understandings: Structuring the writing experience through dialogue. *Journal of Learning Disabilities, 24,* 330–342.

Englert, C.S., & Mariage, T.V. (1992). Shared understandings: Structuring the writing experience through dialogue. In D. Carnine & E. Kame'enui (Eds.), *Higher order thinking: Designing curriculum for mainstreamed students* (pp. 107–136). Austin, TX: Pro-Ed.

Fisher, D., Flood, J., Lapp, D., & Frey, N. (2004). Interactive read-alouds: Is there a common set of implementation practices. *The Reading Teacher, 58,* 8–17.

Goldman, S.R., & Rakestraw, J.A. (2000). Structual aspects of constructing meaning from text. In M.L. Kamil, P. Mosenthal, P.D. Pearson, & R. Barr (Eds.), *Handbook of reading research* (Vol. 3, pp. 311–336). Mahwah, NJ: Erlbaum.

Guthrie, J.T., & Kirsch, I.S. (1987). Distinctions between reading comprehension and locating information in text. *Journal of Educational Psychology, 79,* 220–227.

Hickman, P., Pollard-Durodola, S., & Vaughn, S. (2004). Storybook reading: Improving vocabulary and comprehension for English-language learners. *The Reading Teacher, 57,* 720–730.

Kuhn, M.R., & Stahl, S.A. (1998). Teaching children to learn word meanings from context: A synthesis and some questions. *Journal of Literacy Research, 30*, 119–138.

Ogle, D. (1986). K-W-L: A teaching model that develops active reading of expository text. *The Reading Teacher, 39*, 564–570.

Pearson, P.D., & Fielding, L. (1991). Comprehension instruction. In R. Barr, M.L. Kamil, P. Mosenthal, & P.D. Pearson (Eds.), *Handbook of reading research* (Vol. 2, pp. 815–860). White Plains, NY: Longman.

Robbins, C., & Ehri, L.C. (1994). Reading storybooks to kindergartners helps them learn new vocabulary words. *Journal of Educational Psychology, 86*, 54–64.

Santoro, L.E., Baker, S.K., Chard, D.J., & Howard, L. (in press). The comprehension conversation: Using intentional and purposeful text-based discourse during read-alouds to promote student comprehension and vocabulary. In B. Taylor & J. Ysseldyke (Eds.), *Educational interventions for struggling readers*. New York: Teachers College.

Santoro, L.E., Chard, D.J., & Baker, S.K. (2005, April). *Optimizing first grade read-aloud instruction*. Paper presented at the annual meeting of the American Educational Research Association, Montreal, Canada.

Sénéchal, M. (1997). The differential effect of storybook reading on preschoolers' acquisition of expressive and receptive vocabulary. *Journal of Child Language, 24*, 123–138.

Snow, C.E., Burns, M.S., & Griffith, P. (Eds.). (1998). *Preventing reading difficulties in young children*. Washington, DC: National Academy Press.

Williams, J.P. (2005). Instruction in reading comprehension for primary-grade students: "A focus on text structure". *Journal of Special Education, 39*, 6–18.

Questions for Reflection

• When selecting books to read aloud, teachers and parents often gravitate toward narrative selections. How often do you use informational texts for read-alouds in your classroom? How well are informational books represented in your classroom library? What can you do to ensure that students gain experience with both fiction and nonfiction across the curriculum? What are the benefits of doing so?

• When students do retellings in small groups or pairs, the role of listener is as important as the role of speaker. How do you help children become good, active listeners—not only when they listen to you or another adult in class but also when they listen to their peers? How do you include and connect the language arts of speaking and listening in your classroom?

Vocabulary Visits: Virtual Field Trips for Content Vocabulary Development

Camille L.Z. Blachowicz and Connie Obrochta

At a meeting of a teacher study group on vocabulary learning, a group of primary teachers were sharing stories of surprises they encountered when reading with their students. "I had a whole group of kids who didn't know what an umbrella was," lamented one teacher. Another chimed in, "I took a wonderful running record of one child who was reading about the Olympics. He decoded everything perfectly, and when we discussed the selection, he didn't know the word *athlete*...and he had read it perfectly 11 times!" The grade team leader asserted, "Our students are smart, but they need more concept and vocabulary development. Every time we take a field trip they learn a lot. I wish we could take more field trips!" Many of the teachers in the room nodded affirmatively.

Discussions like this are echoed in schools around the United States. They reflect a significant body of research that suggests wide differences in concept and vocabulary knowledge exacerbate the achievement gap seen in so many schools, especially those with large numbers of children living in poverty (Hart & Risley, 1995). Educators sometimes attribute this difference to the Matthew effect—the sad reality that having a well-developed vocabulary allows you to learn new words more easily than classmates who have a smaller fund of word knowledge (Stanovich, 1986). This is especially significant in the content areas—not knowing what a circle is will make it a lot harder for students to understand and learn new terms like *diameter, radius,* and *circumference*. Students need "anchor" concepts and vocabulary to learn new words, which are then connected to the concepts they already know.

Similar experiences, knowledge, and thinking led a reading specialist and a group of teachers in a multiethnic urban school to develop Vocabulary Visits—virtual field trips using books to develop the content vocabulary of first-grade students.

Why a Vocabulary Field Trip?

Because school budgets are stretched to the limit, teachers are limited in the number of field trips they can take during the school year. The school in which this strategy was designed has 50% of its students receiving free lunch and a 13% mobility rate, leaving little discretionary family income to contribute extra funds. Yet the teachers all recognized that students came back from field outings with new ideas, new questions to pursue, and new vocabulary to use in talking and writing about their learning. The teachers wanted to capture some of the positive aspects of field-trip learning and integrate them with the instructional program. The specialist and teachers spent considerable time thinking about and discussing what made a good field trip and why their students seemed to come away from these experiences with such increased concept and vocabulary knowledge. After some discussion,

Reprinted from Blachowicz, C.L.Z., & Obrochta, C. (2005). Vocabulary Visits: Virtual field trips for content vocabulary development. *The Reading Teacher, 59*(3), 262-268. doi: 10.1598/RT.59.3.6

they decided that the following characteristics of field trips help students develop vocabulary:

- Field trips have a content focus. Good field trips connect to the curriculum and its content, which provide an integrated context for learning and a relational set of concepts and terms.
- Field trips engage the senses. Students are seeing, hearing, smelling, feeling, and sometimes tasting as they encounter new concepts and vocabulary.
- Field trips are preceded by preparation that helps "plow the soil" for planting the seeds of new learning. Students know what they are going to encounter and often teachers do a read-aloud to get them ready.
- Field trips involve the mediation of an adult. A docent, teacher, parent, or other chaperone is there to help explain, clarify, focus, or point out interesting things.
- Field trips involve exploration, talk, reading, and writing by the students.
- Field trips often involve a follow-up of new concepts and terms.

The teachers decided to structure read-aloud book experiences as virtual field trips for the classroom using scaffolded book read-alouds, active learning with visuals, and other activities that appeal to the senses while developing new concepts and vocabulary.

Grounding Vocabulary Visits in Theory and Research

Two areas of theory and research ground the Vocabulary Visit instructional process: vocabulary development through read-alouds and active learning.

Read-alouds

Reading aloud to children, sometimes also referred to as shared storybook reading, gives students the opportunity to develop new vocabulary. Because children's books present more advanced, less familiar vocabulary than everyday speech (Cunningham & Stanovich, 1998), listening to books read helps students go beyond their existing oral vocabularies and presents them with new concepts and vocabulary. Discussion after shared storybook reading also gives students opportunities to use new vocabulary in the more decontextualized setting of a book discussion (Snow, 1991).

Numerous studies have documented that young students can learn word meanings incidentally from read-aloud experiences (Eller, Pappas, & Brown, 1988; Elley, 1988; Robbins & Ehri, 1994). Involving students in discussions during and after listening to a book has also produced significant word learning, especially when the teacher scaffolded this learning by asking questions, adding information, or prompting students to describe what they heard. Whitehurst and his associates (Whitehurst et al., 1994; Whitehurst et al., 1999) called this process "dialogic reading."

Research also suggests that scaffolding may be more essential to those students who are less likely to learn new vocabulary easily. Children with small vocabularies initially are less likely to learn new words incidentally and need a thoughtful, well-designed, scaffolded approach to maximize learning from shared storybook reading (Robbins & Ehri, 1994; Sénéchal, Thomas, & Monker, 1995). Research points to teacher read-alouds as a positive way to develop the oral vocabularies of young learners.

Active Learning

The role of active learning in vocabulary development has been well established. Students who engage with words by hearing them, using them, manipulating them semantically, and playing with them are more likely to learn and retain new vocabulary (Beck, McKeown, & Kucan, 2002; Blachowicz & Fisher, 2005; Stahl & Fairbanks, 1986). Furthermore, relating new words to what is already known creates elaborated schemata and links between concepts that provide for enduring learning (Anderson & Nagy, 1991).

A series of studies by Sénéchal and her colleagues (Hargrave & Sénéchal, 2000; Sénéchal & Cornell, 1993; Sénéchal et al., 1995) found that students' engagement and active participation in storybook reading was more productive for vocabulary learning in storybook read-alouds than passive listening, even to the most dramatic "performance" of book reading. This has been confirmed by a growing number of studies that scaffolded young students' learning by focusing their attention on target words and engaging them in interactive discussion about books using specific vocabulary before, during, and after reading (Brett, Rothlein, & Hurley, 1996; Penno, Wilkinson, & Moore, 2002; Wasik & Bond, 2001). So the activity of the learners is an important component of learning from read-alouds.

Use of the senses, particularly of visualization, is an important activity for engagement and for focusing attention in learning. Sensory representation helps learners connect with new information and provides alternative codes for understanding and retention (Paivio, 1971; Sadoski, Goetz, Kealy, & Paivio, 1997). Classic, seminal work on concept mapping (Johnson, Pittelman, Toms-Bronowski, & Levin, 1984) has been extended to current strategies such as concept muraling (Farris & Downey, 2004), which represents words and their relations to a topic in a semantically organized graphic. All of these studies attest to the enduring power of visualization in word learning.

When the teachers in this study decided to couple the power of field-trip learning with the research and theory on vocabulary learning, it was agreed that the process would share books and new vocabulary and concepts through teacher read-alouds, that the teacher's role would be to scaffold word learning by focusing attention on specific vocabulary, and that questioning and probing would be used to make students use the new vocabulary and relate it to what they already knew. Each lesson would also be linked to the senses that are stimulated in a real trip, and students would also be called on to use the words though semantic grouping, manipulation, speaking, and writing.

Planning a Vocabulary Visit

The first step in planning was to identify focal topics for the Visit. The teachers in this study decided to use content area books. Much new research on primary-age students and their learning suggests that the primary curriculum is ripe for content learning and that many more resources for content reading now exist (Duke, Bennett-Armistead, & Roberts, 2003). The Vocabulary Visit team decided to use the standards for social studies and science to help them pick topics. They looked at first-grade standards and also at later years to develop vocabulary that would bootstrap students in following years and provide an appropriate learning challenge (Biemiller, 2001). The topics they chose for the first trials were the human body (skeletons), weather and climate, animal habitats, and recycling. All of these topics were relevant to their curricula.

The next step was to assemble a set of at least five texts that could be used for the Visits. Read-alouds are an important part of the process and an important research-based strategy for increasing vocabulary knowledge. Such primary books are now easy to find online and through references on literature for school-age children. Consulting school and local librarians and just rummaging through various classroom libraries quickly produced a starter set. Choosing books in a range of difficulty allows for scaffolded learning and provides for individual differences.

The third step was reviewing the books and choosing a basic vocabulary set that the teacher wanted to use during the discussions. For example, for the set of skeleton books, some core words were *bone*, *skull*, *leg*, *arm*, *wrist*, *ankle*, *foot*, *ribs*, *brain*, *spine*, *backbone*, and some functional words such as *protect* (the skull *protects* the brain).

Last, after selecting the core vocabulary, one of the teachers made a poster with some interesting thematic pictures to stimulate discussion. This was the chart the class would "visit" (see Figure 1). Visuals must stimulate sensory response and lead to discussion of key concepts and vocabulary. Other materials needed are sticky notes, a large marker, and a piece of chart

Figure 1
Vocabulary Visits Chart–Skeletons

The Vocabulary Visit

Jump-Start and First Write

Once the materials are prepared, the teacher gives the class a Jump-Start to help them activate their prior knowledge. He or she introduces the topic and asks students to talk, briefly, about some things they know about it. Then each student takes a piece of paper and does a First Write, which is a simple list of words they can think of that connects to the topic (see Figure 2). These are archived in a folder and serve as a preassessment. First Write is also a good diagnostic tool for teachers and can provide surprising insights. Speaking about a very shy and quiet little first

paper or poster board to make a poster. This chart forms a dynamic record of the visit.

grader, one teacher remarked, "I didn't know Keisha [pseudonym] knew so much about animals. It turns out she goes to the zoo almost every other week with her Daddy. I'll really have to draw on that in the discussions."

Group Talk

The next step is Group Talk. Students meet on the rug in the classroom, and the teacher brings out the poster and starts with the first question, "What do you see?" just as a teacher would on a regular field trip. As students contribute words related to what they see, the teacher records their contributions on sticky notes and puts them on the poster. For example, on the skeleton chart shown in Figure 1, the first word that came from the students was *skull*. The teacher recorded it on a sticky note and placed the word in a relevant

**Figure 2
First Write**

Name: _____

Here are some words I know about skeletons.

Ckincis | skins
Pitilas | patellas
hard
el bow
ribs

place on the chart. The second word to come up was *cranium*, which amazed the teacher. The children then informed her that Cranium was a game advertised for the holidays and was in the school game collection. This led to *head* and then *crown* followed by a chorus of the nursery rhyme "Jack and Jill."

As students make new suggestions, teachers must mediate as needed. They must make sure that supporting the students' learning with questions, explanations, and suggestions generates the targeted vocabulary. "Touch your skull. What is a skull for?" A student answered, "To protect your brain." The teacher added *brain* and *protect* to the chart and then asked, "How does it protect it?" This new question led to the word *hollow* for skull and then led to the teacher asking for an example of the word, which was supplied by a student who was surprised to find that his chocolate Easter bunny wasn't all chocolate. "Yeah, I hate that," agreed some of his classmates.

The words come fast, and it is the teacher's job to focus on the important ones, to ask for

clarification and an example ("Where is your wrist?"), and to group them in some relational way. Other senses besides sight are used. For example, in the visit about weather, the teacher asked, "What do you hear in a storm? What are some words for how you feel in rain?" After 5–10 minutes, there are usually quite a number of words on the chart, which the students have now heard, seen, discussed, and sometimes acted out.

Reading and Thumbs Up

The next step is the reading of the first book. Reading aloud to students has been found to be a significant way to increase vocabulary. However, research suggests that this reading should have some mediation involved for new words and should not be a dramatic performance (Dickinson & Smith, 1994). It should be like the kind of reading a parent does with a child, sometimes stopping to clarify or ask about something, much as the highly popular Richard Scarry books call for labeling and finding. We use the Thumbs Up procedure to help students become active listeners. Students put their thumbs up when they hear one of the new words. Sometimes the teacher stops or rereads a sentence when no thumbs go up for a critical term, but the goal is to have a fairly normal reading experience.

After the reading, the students discuss what they learned and add a few new words to the chart. If time permits, the teacher sometimes does semantic sorting activities with the words and tries to involve more of the students' senses. For example, for a unit on weather, the teacher asked, after reading the first book, if there were sound words that they associated with thunderstorms. The students came up with *crash*, *boom*, *thunder*, *thunderclap*, and other words; some of them were from the book and some were from personal knowledge.

Finally, a short writing activity occurs in which the students write about something learned or something that particularly interested them. The books are also put in a central location for reading during independent reading time, and students are asked to read at least one of the books each week and record it in their reading logs. One teacher noted,

> These books circulate four or five times more than they did last year. The read-alouds help my kids get interested in the topic and also make the other books accessible to them because they know some of the ideas and the vocabulary. It really works!

Follow-Up

The visit poster is kept on the classroom wall, and the activities are repeated for each book in the set. The students also start adding new words to the chart on their own and sometimes regroup the words. Over the course of the unit, students apply their new word knowledge through extension activities that include semantic sorting, word games, writing, reading new books on the same topic, and rereading the books the teacher has read. One participating teacher said,

> My students began making up some of their own activities. They would take the sticky notes and put them in new sets or make sentences with them. They got interested in the new words and were proud that they knew such grown-up ones.

Final Write

At the end of the entire five-book sequence, the students do two writing activities. One is a longer piece about their learning. In some classes, for example, students made their own books about the skeletal system, either to take home or to put in their classroom libraries. In others, students did a report on their favorite book. In first grade, this is often in the form of "The three most interesting things..." or "What the author could do to make this book better" (D. Gurvitz, personal communication, February 7, 2000) rather than a contrived book report form.

Students also do a Final Write, a list-writing activity of all the words they now can write that are associated with a certain topic. Their lists increased dramatically from First Write ($t = -8.453$, significance level $= .0001$). Those students who listed the fewest words at the beginning of the visit usually made the greatest gains, but even those starting with richer initial

	Record of Word Growth	
Student	Words before Vocabulary Visit cycle	Words added after Vocabulary Visit
1	8	20
2	7	23
3	4	6
4	6	23
5	7	27
6	4	32
7	4	13
8	7	8
9	5	10
10	7	26
11	3	10
12	4	18
13	5	11
14	5	11
15	0	6
16	0	6
17	0	14
18	0	19

vocabularies made significant gains. Teachers can also evaluate word learning by students' uses of the words in all of these final activities. Another anecdotal bit of evaluation was provided by reports from parents of new word use and sharing and requests to get books on class topics from the library and bookstores.

A Last Word

We learned so many things from our first trial of this process that we are now trying to add a randomized sample study of Vocabulary Visits. We need to extend our list of topics to provide more text sets, and some students are still not active enough in the Thumbs Up part of the process. We are searching for other methods to help students focus on the words without losing the thread of the read-aloud. We also want to find more sensible, uncontrived, and motivating ways to revisit the newly learned words.

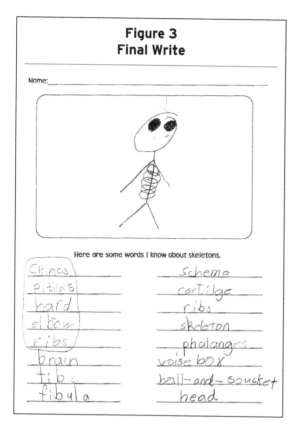

**Figure 3
Final Write**

Name:

Here are some words I know about skeletons.

Ckincs
pitilas
hard
elbow
ribs
brain
tibo
fibula

Schema
cartilge
ribs
skeleton
phalanges
voise box
ball-and-soucket
head

Vocabulary Visits has proved to be an exciting and effective research-based strategy for teachers to add attention to vocabulary in thematic units. The pre- and postwriting activities provide evaluation information in a way that is positive for students and teachers alike; it is motivating to see how many topical words are added in the Final Write (see Figure 3). As students work their way through the books in the thematic text set, they become more knowledgeable and confident as they encounter repeated and related vocabulary. They are proud of learning big and technical words, and the spread of words can be infectious, especially with those that are long, funny, or interesting sounding. After playground duty on a day that was growing stormy, an incredulous fifth-grade science teacher popped into one classroom to ask, "How in the heck did all you kids get to know *cumulonimbus*?" They had been using the word in the playground. In explanation, the students pulled him over to the classroom wall and treated him to a tour of their word chart—a Vocabulary Visit all of his own!

References

Anderson, R.C., & Nagy, W.E. (1991). Word meanings. In R. Barr, M.L. Kamil, P.B. Mosenthal, & P.D. Pearson (Eds.), *Handbook of reading research* (Vol. 2, pp. 690–724). New York: Longman.

Beck, I.L., McKeown, M.G., & Kucan, L. (2002). *Bringing words to life: Robust vocabulary instruction.* New York: Guilford.

Biemiller, A. (2001). Teaching vocabulary: Early, direct, and sequential. *American Educator, 25*(1), 24–28, 47.

Blachowicz, C., & Fisher, P. (2005). *Teaching vocabulary in all classrooms* (3rd ed.). Columbus, OH: Merrill-Prentice Hall.

Brett, A., Rothlein, L., & Hurley, M. (1996). Vocabulary acquisition from listening to stories and explanations of target words. *The Elementary School Journal, 96,* 415–422.

Cunningham, A.E., & Stanovich, K.E. (1998, Spring/Summer). What reading does for the mind. *American Educator,* 8–17.

Dickinson, D.K., & Smith, M.W. (1994). Long-term effects of preschool teachers' book readings on low-income children's vocabulary and story comprehension. *Reading Research Quarterly, 29,* 104–122.

Duke, N.K., Bennett-Armistead, V.S., & Roberts, E.M. (2003). Bridging the gap between learning to read and reading to learn. In D.M. Barone & L.M. Morrow (Eds.), *Literacy and young children: Research-based practices* (pp. 226–242). New York: Guilford.

Eller, G., Pappas, C.C., & Brown, E. (1988). The lexical development of kindergartners: Learning from written context. *Journal of Reading Behavior, 20,* 5–24.

Elley, W.B. (1988). Vocabulary acquisition from listening to stories. *Reading Research Quarterly, 24 ,* 174–187.

Farris, P.J., & Downey, P. (2004). Concept muraling: Dropping visual crumbs along the instructional trail. *The Reading Teacher, 58,* 376–380.

Hargrave, A.C., & Sénéchal, M. (2000). A book reading intervention with pre-school children who have limited vocabularies: The benefits of regular reading and dialogic reading. *Early Childhood Research Quarterly, 15,* 75–95.

Hart, B., & Risley, T.R. (1995). *Meaningful differences in the everyday experience of young American children.* Baltimore: Paul H. Brookes.

Johnson, D.D., Pittelman, S.D., Toms-Bronowski, S., & Levin, K.M. (1984). *An investigation of the effects of prior knowledge and vocabulary acquisition on passage comprehension* (Program Rep. No. 84-5). Madison: Wisconsin Center for Education Research, University of Wisconsin.

Paivio, A. (1971). *Imagery and verbal processes.* New York: Holt, Rinehart & Winston.

Penno, J.F., Wilkinson, I.A.G, & Moore, D.W. (2002). Vocabulary acquisition from teacher explanation and repeated listening to stories: Do they overcome the Matthew effect? *Journal of Educational Psychology, 94*, 23–33.

Robbins, C., & Ehri, L.C. (1994). Reading storybooks to kindergarteners helps them learn new vocabulary words. *Journal of Educational Psychology, 86*, 54–64.

Sadoski, M., Goetz, E.T., Kealy, W.S., & Paivio, A. (1997). Concreteness and imagery effects in the written composition of definitions. *Journal of Educational Psychology, 89*, 518–526

Sénéchal, M., & Cornell, E.H. (1993). Vocabulary acquisition through shared reading experiences. *Reading Research Quarterly, 28*, 361–374.

Sénéchal, M., Thomas, E., & Monker, J. (1995). Individual differences in 5-year-olds acquisition of vocabulary during storybook reading. *Journal of Educational Psychology, 87*, 218–229.

Snow, C. (1991). The theoretical basis for relationships between language and literacy development. *Journal of Research in Childhood Education, 6*, 5–10.

Stahl, S., & Fairbanks, M. (1986). The effects of vocabulary instruction: A model-based meta-analysis. *Review of Educational Research, 56*, 72–110.

Stanovich, K.E. (1986). Matthew effects in reading: Some consequences of individual differences in the acquisition of literacy. *Reading Research Quarterly, 21*, 360–407.

Wasik, B.A., & Bond, M.A. (2001). Beyond the pages of a book: Interactive book reading and language development in preschool classrooms. *Journal of Experimental Psychology, 93*, 243–250.

Whitehurst, G.J., Epstein, J.N., Angell, A.L., Payne, A.C., Crone, D.A., & Fischel, J.E. (1994). Outcomes of an emergent literacy intervention in Head Start. *Journal of Educational Psychology, 86*, 542–555.

Whitehurst, G.J., Zevenberg, A.A., Crone, D.A., Schultz, M.D., Velting, O.N., & Fischel, J.E. (1999). Outcomes of an emergent literacy intervention from Head Start through second grade. *Journal of Educational Psychology, 91*, 261–272.

Questions for Reflection

- Examples in this article are drawn from experiences in a first-grade classroom, using focal topics drawn from content area texts. How might you adapt this activity for use in other grades? What other sources are there for deciding on focal topics, and what texts might be used to support Vocabulary Visits centered on these topics?

- The authors note that the Thumbs Up portion of the activity is not always successful. What ideas do you have for helping students attend to vocabulary words during read-alouds, without interfering with their overall attention to the text they are listening to?

Sharing Alphabet Books in Early Childhood Classrooms

Barbara A. Bradley and Jennifer Jones

Young children need a strong foundation in literacy if they are to achieve academically. Although we believe that a variety of experiences are necessary to establish a firm foundation for literacy, knowledge of the alphabet is certainly one aspect (Snow, Burns, & Griffin, 1998). The purposes of this article are (a) to present the importance of alphabet knowledge and the components of that knowledge, (b) to describe an exploratory study about early childhood teachers' alphabet book read-alouds aimed at understanding what components of the alphabet teachers discuss, and (c) to describe how various genres of alphabet books may be used to introduce and to teach young children about literacy. We also describe other activities that teachers may use to teach young children about the alphabet.

Importance of Knowing the Alphabet and What It Takes to "Know" It

Knowledge of letter names prior to formal instruction is a strong predictor of later reading achievement (Snow et al., 1998). Although simply learning letter names has long been known to not necessarily produce significant improvement of reading ability (Gibson & Levin, 1975), letter-name knowledge may have indirect effects that facilitate the learning-to-read process. Specifically, letter-name knowledge may be necessary, though not sufficient, for children to develop phonological awareness (Stahl & Murray, 1994).

Alphabet knowledge is often measured by asking children to name letters or to make the sounds that letters represent. Full understanding of the alphabet, however, requires children to understand four separate yet interconnected components. According to Mason (1984), those components are (a) letter-shape knowledge or letter recognition, (b) letter-name knowledge, (c) letter-sound knowledge, and (d) letter writing ability.

Letter-Shape Knowledge

The ability to distinguish letters is a basic step in learning about the alphabet. To recognize letters, children must understand key visual features such as letter shape, orientation, and directionality. In addition to discerning key features, children must learn to recognize those features in letters presented in various sizes, fonts, cases, and handwriting styles (Adams, 1990). According to Gibson, Gibson, Pick, and Osser (1962), young children can begin to use key features (e.g., lines, curves, orientation, rotation, degree of closure) to identify letters and become more proficient over time and with experience.

Letter-Name Knowledge

A second component of alphabet knowledge is letter-name knowledge. To exhibit letter-name knowledge, children must learn that a letter is a symbol, that each letter has a given name, and that each letter name represents two symbols: an upper- and a lowercase letter. Further, children will discover that in many instances, letters are similar (e.g., *Cc, Ff, Kk*); however, some upper-

Reprinted from Bradley, B.A., & Jones, J. (2007). Sharing alphabet books in early childhood classrooms. *The Reading Teacher, 60*(5), 452-463.

and lowercase letters are not visually similar (e.g., *Aa, Dd, Gg*).

Treiman and Broderick (1998) found that children are able to learn all letter names equally well, although they tend to learn the first letter of their names more easily than the other letters of the alphabet. Children learn the first letter in their name and the names of important people in their lives more quickly because these names hold special significance and the capitalized first letter is visually more salient than the other letters in these names (Ferreiro, 1986; Share & Gur, 1999).

Letter-Sound Knowledge

A third component of alphabet knowledge is letter-sound knowledge. In written speech, letters—alone and in combination—represent sounds. As children learn letter sounds, they tacitly learn that a letter's name often provides a clue for the sound that the letter represents. Similar to learning that a letter name may represent two distinct symbols, children must learn that some letters represent more than one sound. For example, the letter *G* or *g* may represent a hard sound as in *goat* or a soft sound as in *George*. According to what Venezky (1975) referred to as the acrophonic principle, or that the most common sound that a letter represents is often the first sound of the letter name, letters can be grouped into five categories:

1. letter sound at the beginning of the letter name (*B, D, J, K, P, Q, T, V, Z*);

2. letter sound at the end of the letter name (*F, L, M, N, R, S, X*);

3. letter name represents a sound, but the letter also represents another sound (*A, E, I, O, U*);

4. letter sound at the beginning of the letter name, but the letter also represents another sound (*C, G*); and

5. letter names that do not contain the sound that the letter represents (*H, W, Y*).

Although letter-name knowledge is positively correlated to later reading achievement, evidence suggests that letter-sound knowledge accounts for more variance in early reading achievement

(McBride-Chang, 1999), and delays in early literacy skills may be linked to delays in letter-sound knowledge (Duncan & Seymour, 2000).

Letter Writing Ability

A fourth component of alphabet knowledge is the ability to write letters. Although young children's ability to write letters is rarely assessed (Dodd & Carr, 2003), it has been suggested that this ability should be included in assessments of their alphabet knowledge (Hiebert, 1981). Chomsky (1971) argued that children often begin to write before they learn to read and that children's early attempts at spelling demonstrate their awareness of letter–sound correspondences. Treiman and Broderick (1998) suggested that as children learn to write their own names they "search for links between the printed name and the oral name" (p. 114), helping them take an analytic stance toward identifying letter–sound associations. There is growing evidence to support this reciprocal relationship between children's name writing ability and other print-related concepts such as letter recognition and concept of word (Bloodgood, 1999; Welsch, Sullivan, & Justice, 2003).

As children have opportunities to learn and to develop fluent knowledge of the alphabet, their ability to read and to write will likely be facilitated. Accordingly, when teaching and when assessing children's alphabet knowledge, it is important to be aware of each of these four interconnected components.

Alphabet Book Sharing

Home-Experience Studies

Parents have opportunities to teach their children about the alphabet, and there are numerous studies describing how children from middle class homes learn about the alphabet (e.g., McGee & Richgels, 1989; Smolkin & Yaden, 1992; Yaden, Smolkin, & MacGillivray, 1993). Reading alphabet books is one means by which parents teach their children about the alphabet. Through alphabet book sharing, children learn letter features, letter names, letter sounds, and metalinguistic terms such as " __ is for __ " (Smolkin & Yaden; Yaden et al.). Although children often make inaccurate assumptions from the illustrations, and parents may not be aware of these misunderstandings (Smolkin & Yaden), reading alphabet books provides a medium in which print is discussed significantly more frequently when compared to storybook reading (Smolkin, Yaden, Brown, & Hofius, 1992).

School-Orientation Studies

Teachers, too, have many opportunities to introduce children to the alphabet. There are relatively few empirical studies, however, on how best to teach the alphabet, and we have found no peer-reviewed studies that examined reading alphabet books to children as a means of teaching alphabet knowledge. Murray, Stahl, and Ivey (1996) studied alphabet book read-alouds as a way to facilitate the phonemic awareness of young children. Although they found only limited support for their hypothesis that phonemic awareness develops at least in part through exposure to alphabet books, they speculated that alphabet book reading may still be beneficial to children.

To explore the potential of reading alphabet books to young children, we asked 13 early childhood teachers to read alphabet books aloud to their classes. Our purpose was to understand how teachers read alphabet books aloud to children and to explore how different genres of alphabet books might influence the read-aloud event.

Participants and Materials for the Current Study

Seven prekindergarten and six kindergarten teachers participated in the study. The seven prekindergarten teachers taught in a preschool facility in a rural community, and the six kindergarten teachers taught in an inner-city school district in the southeastern United States.

Numerous alphabet books in several genres are available. Two such genres, alphabet and letter-name (Murray, Stahl, & Ivey, 1996), were used in the present study. The first genre, alphabet books, focuses on alliteration. We chose

Dr. Seuss's ABC: An Amazing Alphabet Book! (Seuss, 1963) because it presents each letter of the alphabet with words or phrases that contain the initial sound of the letter. The second genre, a letter-name book, introduces the letters of the alphabet but does not contain examples of words or phrases that begin with each letter. For this genre, we chose Chicka *Chicka Boom Boom* (Martin & Archambault, 1989). Teacher participants also were asked to read *Toot & Puddle: Puddle's ABC* (Hobbie, 2000). This book is a story, like *Chicka Chicka Boom Boom*, but embedded within the story is a section devoted to the alphabet that contains alliteration, a characteristic of the genre alphabet books. In essence, *Puddle's ABC* is a combination of an alphabet book and a letter-name text.

Procedures and Results of the Current Study

Adhering to procedures employed by Smolkin and Donovan (2001), we gave each of the 13 teachers the three alphabet books along with instructions asking them to prepare for and to conduct the read-alouds as they normally would for the whole class. Further, teachers were asked to read only one alphabet book per day. Each read-aloud session was tape-recorded.

All audiotapes of teacher read-alouds were transcribed in full. We used a scheme adapted from Snow (1983) and Dickinson and Keebler (1989) to frame the coding and analysis of the transcripts. This scheme was used to determine if teachers focused children's attention on features of the alphabet (e.g., letter shape, name, sound) or features of the text (e.g., labeling or describing pictures), or encouraged children to engage in discussions about the text.

Analysis was conducted to investigate which aspect of the read-aloud events were emphasized by teachers within each genre of alphabet text (Donovan & Smolkin, 2002). Each read-aloud event was analyzed independently as a whole, and then each event was divided into three phrases: before, during, and after the read-aloud. Dividing the read-alouds into three phases allowed for detailed examination of when and how teachers emphasized the alphabet in relation to the read-aloud. In addition, detailed analyses explored the influence of genre on teacher talk.

Dimensions of Teacher Talk

Across all of the prekindergarten teachers, across all of the genres, and across all of the read-aloud events (before, during, and after), the greatest percentages of teacher talk were related to alphabet knowledge, text features, and involvement (see Table 1). With regard to alphabet knowledge, we found that prekindergarten teachers primarily made comments or asked questions related to letter-name knowledge; however, they also talked about letter sounds and letter shapes. Across all kindergarten teachers with all of the texts during the entirety of the read-aloud events, the greatest percentages of teacher talk were also related to alphabet knowledge, text features, and involvement (see Table 1). When we analyzed the talk related to alphabet knowledge, we found that kindergarten teachers primarily made comments or asked questions related to letter-name knowledge. Few teacher comments or questions were related to letter-sound or letter-shape knowledge. It is not surprising that early childhood teachers do discuss the alphabet when reading alphabet books to young children. However, the data also revealed a range of teacher comments and questions, or utterances, demonstrating that some teachers rarely interacted with the children during the read-aloud event, whereas other teachers did so constantly (see Table 1).

To obtain a detailed understanding of the read-aloud event we examined teacher talk during the three phases of the read-aloud event. Table 2 indicates that during each phase, the teachers' talk focused on involving children in the read-aloud event and on helping them make connections with the text. However, we also found differences between the three phases of reading aloud. Before reading, the teachers emphasized text-related talk on concepts such as the author and illustrator. During the read-aloud, teachers shifted their emphasis to alphabet knowledge. Kindergarten teachers also made attempts to involve the children and to help them make connections, and they encouraged children to notice features of the text and to recognize words. The

Table 1
Percentage of Teacher Talk per Category and Range of Number of Utterances per Teacher

	Prekindergarten teachers		Kindergarten teachers	
	Percentage of teacher talk	Range of utterances per teacher	Percentage of teacher talk	Range of utterances per teacher
Letter knowledge	28	1-89	26	16-126
Text	21	9-34	23	25-72
Involvement	22	3-105	17	12-71
Connections	14	1-39	16	12-67
Management	7	2-32	6	4-29
Words	4	0-10	8	5-36
Other	4	1-7	3	3-13
Phonological awareness	0	0-3	1	0-7

Table 2
Percentage of Teacher Talk Before, During, and After Read-Aloud for All Texts

	Prekindergarten teachers			Kindergarten teachers		
	Before reading	During reading	After reading	Before reading	During reading	After reading
Letter knowledge	3	45	7	11	27	24
Text	57	9	8	50	16	12
Involvement	15	17	48	11	21	18
Connections	11	13	18	13	14	29
Management	13	5	10	10	3	11
Words	>1	6	4	3	13	3
Other	>1	4	4	2	3	3
Phonological awareness		>1	1			2

prekindergarten teachers primarily attempted to involve children in the text after the read-aloud. The kindergarten teachers continued to emphasize alphabet knowledge after the read-aloud, and they encouraged children to make connections with the text and to participate in the discussions.

Effects of Genre

We compared the teacher talk among the three alphabet books and found some differences based on the genre. Table 3 shows the percentage of teacher talk during each read-aloud event by grade level and text type. With the letter-name book, *Chicka Chicka Boom Boom*, prekindergarten teachers placed less attention on letters when compared with the alphabet book, *Dr. Seuss's ABC*, or the combination book, *Puddle's ABC*. While reading *Chicka Chicka Boom Boom*, the prekindergarten teachers placed relatively greater emphasis on connections and involvement. Simply put, *Chicka*

Chicka Boom Boom is written like a story with letters of the alphabet for characters; so teachers asked questions or made comments to facilitate children's comprehension. With respect to *Dr. Seuss's ABC*, the prekindergarten teachers engaged the children in a relatively high proportion of involvement. Analysis of the transcripts indicates that the teachers used the clear pattern of introducing letters in *Dr. Seuss's ABC* to encourage participation.

The kindergarten teachers in our study also placed relatively less attention on the alphabet when reading *Chicka Chicka Boom Boom* as compared to readings of *Dr. Seuss's ABC* and *Puddle's ABC*. Further, for *Chicka Chicka Boom Boom*, the kindergarten teachers placed greater emphasis on involvement and words, as compared to the other two texts. This may be explained, in part, by teachers' utterances that encouraged children to recite or to read repetitive phrases that are part of the *Chicka Chicka Boom Boom* text.

Table 3
Percentage of Teacher Talk During Read-Aloud Based on Grade Level and Text Type

	Prekindergarten			Kindergarten		
	Chicka Chicka Boom Boom	*Dr. Seuss's ABC: An Amazing Alphabet Book!*	*Puddle's ABC*	*Chicka Chicka Boom Boom*	*Dr. Seuss's ABC: An Amazing Alphabet Book!*	*Puddle's ABC*
Letter knowledge	19	43	53	26	37	34
Texts	9	9	12	16	11	16
Involvement	22	18	11	25	16	15
Connections	25	7	11	14	13	16
Words	19	5	3	15	10	10

Discussion

It is not surprising that the present study demonstrates prekindergarten and kindergarten teachers do talk about and emphasize alphabet knowledge while reading alphabet books to children. Further, this study shows that most teachers ask questions or make comments that encourage children to become involved in the reading and to make connections with the text. According to our findings, the alphabet book genre influences what teachers emphasize. For example, *Chicka Chicka Boom Boom* is a story that has letters of the alphabet as the characters. While reading this text, the teachers' talk placed more emphasis on story comprehension than on learning specific aspects of the alphabet. *Puddle's ABC* also follows a story structure; however, embedded in the story is a section that introduces the letters of the alphabet with alliterative phrases (e.g., "Ballerina blowing bubbles"). This section facilitated greater emphasis on the alphabet, particularly letter names, formation, and sounds. Finally, because *Dr. Seuss's ABC* presents letters in both upper- and lowercase and uses alliteration to describe an odd collection of characters, rather than presenting a coherent story, this text allowed the teachers to emphasize various aspects of alphabet knowledge rather than comprehension.

This study supports and mirrors storybook research by demonstrating that teachers have different styles of reading alphabet books and that teachers tend to use the same reading styles consistently (Dickinson & Keebler, 1989; Martinez & Teale, 1993). That is, some teachers made comments and asked questions throughout the reading, whereas other teachers read straight through each text and rarely commented or questioned. Presumably, thoughtful questions and comments may help children to focus on ideas and concepts such as the alphabet. Therefore, it is reasonable to suggest that some children may benefit more from alphabet book read-alouds because their teachers emphasize the content.

Implications for Practitioners

Reading alphabet books is one means of introducing children to the alphabet. However, we believe that there are several issues that teachers should consider when reading alphabet books. First, teachers have individual book sharing styles that influence the read-aloud event, and, second, genre influences what teachers emphasize in read-alouds. Further, we believe that children need opportunities to learn about the alphabet in other meaningful contexts. Extrapolating from our data, we will address each of these issues in turn.

Book Sharing Styles Vary

First, teachers should be aware that they each have their own book sharing style. Thus, simply reading an alphabet book does not guarantee that a teacher will emphasize components of the alphabet, such as letter names or letter sounds. In the present study, teachers emphasized various aspects of each text, and some teachers provided numerous comments and questions, while other teachers did not. Although children may glean information about letters by participating in alphabet book read-alouds, it is plausible that, like research on storybook read-alouds and vocabulary development has shown, children benefit most from explicit talk surrounding the text (De Temple & Snow, 2003).

Genre Influences Focus

Teachers should be aware that the text structures of alphabet books influence how the text is read and what aspects of the text are emphasized (see Table 4 for a summary of some alphabet books). Thus, teachers should consider carefully the alphabet books they choose to read aloud and whether or not these texts lend themselves to teaching the alphabet, if that is the objective. For example, texts that portray the letters of the alphabet as characters, such as *Chicka Chicka Boom Boom*, likely will not facilitate talk about letter names and sounds. *Curious George Learns the Alphabet* (Rey, 1963), another popular book, presents the alphabet in the context of a story. Such a text is more likely to facilitate teacher talk about the story content and comprehension, rather than letters and sounds.

Texts using alliteration, such as *Dr. Seuss's ABC* and *Puddle's ABC*, encourage talk about letters and sounds. In another such text, *Bruno Munari's ABC* (1960), conversations about letters and sounds are facilitated by illustrations. For example, the illustrations for the letter *B* contain a blue butterfly, a banana, and a book.

Letter–picture correspondence is another feature to consider when choosing alphabet books. That is, the beginning sound of the picture should clearly represent the letter on the page. Pictures that provide teachers with the opportunity to discuss the multiple sounds of letters can be particularly helpful in teaching children to think flexibly about the alphabet. For example, in *ABC Discovery!* (Cohen, 1997), the letter *E* includes the illustrations of an eagle, an eel, an egg, and an elephant, among other things beginning with *E*. Opportunities to discuss multiple letter sounds also can be found in texts that use words from languages other than English, such as *Pedro, His Perro, and the Alphabet Sombrero* (Reed, 1995).

There are some cautions to consider related to letter–picture correspondence. For example, a letter, picture, and text stating "*A* is for Arcade" suggests that the letter *A* sounds like /r/. Silent letters, as in "*K* is for Knight," also may be confusing. Further, children may substitute a synonym for a picture or word on a page. For example, a prereader might read "*J* is for jacket" as "*J* is for coat." Although these types of letter, picture, and word correspondences are found in many alphabet books, these potentially confusing situations can be opportunities to teach children to think flexibly about the alphabet.

Alphabet books with clearly visible letters that have not been graphically altered lend themselves well to talk about letter-shape knowledge. For example, in *Flora McDonnell's ABC* (1997), letters in words are presented in either all upper- or all lowercase (e.g., *ALLIGATOR, ants*). However, some alphabet books, though visually intriguing, may be confusing for young children. For example, in *The Graphic Alphabet* (Pelletier, 1996), the letter *G* is portrayed in the illustration as a gear. Although the letter is creatively embedded within the illustration, it is difficult to distinguish and examine the configuration of the letter.

Finally, some alphabet books focus primarily on a theme by presenting specific concepts or words in alphabetical order. For example,

Table 4
Alphabet Books

Title and author	Salient feature of the text
	Alliteration
Base, G. (1986). *Animalia*.	Alliterative phrase for each target letter. Elaborate fonts and beautiful illustrations.
MacDonald, R. (2003). *Achoo! Bang! Crash! The noisy alphabet*.	Clever alliterative onomatopoeia and amusing illustrations.
Seeley, L.L. (1994). *The book of shadow boxes: A story of the ABCs*.	Alliteration and rhyming phrases in which the target letter, regardless of location in the word, is in bold. Illustrations representing the target letter.
	Letter, pictures, and words
Ehlert, L. (1989). *Eating the alphabet: Fruits & vegetables from A to Z*.	Illustrations of fruits and vegetables represent a target letter. Labels are written twice, once in all uppercase letters and again in all lowercase letters.
McDonnell, F. (1997). *Flora McDonnell's ABC*.	Illustration and words represent a target letter. The name of the larger object is written with uppercase letters, and the smaller object is written with lowercase letters.
Munari, B. (1960). *Bruno Munari's ABC*.	Bold illustrations and words represent a target uppercase letter.
	Concept focus
Floca, B. (2003). *The racecar alphabet*.	Phrases begin with a word containing the focus letter; uppercase only.
Musgrove, M. (1976). *Ashanti to Zulu: African traditions*.	Each uppercase letter introduces an aspect of Africa and its traditions.
Pallotta, J. (1994). *The desert alphabet book*.	Each upper- and lowercase letter introduces an object from the desert.
	Story
Lionni, L. (1968). *The alphabet tree*.	Story about letters on a tree that fall off when the wind blows. A bug teaches the letters how to make words, and later a caterpillar teaches them that their words should make meaningful sentences. Political message at the end. Rich vocabulary.
Reed, L.R. (1995). *Pedro, his perro, and the alphabet sombrero*.	A short story about Pedro and his perro who add objects to Pedro's new sombrero. Each object represents a target letter; object names are in Spanish.
Rey, H.A. (1963). *Curious George learns the alphabet*.	The man in the yellow hat teaches Curious George the alphabet. Upper- and lowercase letters are introduced, and the target letters are highlighted in words.
	Think, search, and find
Cohen, I. (1997). *ABC discovery!*	The upper- and lowercase letters are presented along with a long list of words beginning with the target letter. By searching an illustration, objects may be found that represent each word.

(continued)

Table 4	
Alphabet Books (*continued*)	
Title and author	**Salient feature of the text**
	Think, search, and find (continued)
McPhail, D. (1989). *David McPhail's animals A to Z.*	The uppercase letter is presented along with the name of an animal(s) that begins with a target letter. In addition to an illustration of the animal(s), other objects that begin with the target letter are represented.
	Visual/graphic
Fleming, D. (2002). *Alphabet under construction.*	A mouse constructs uppercase letters. Short phrase in which the verb begins with target letter.

The Racecar Alphabet (Floca, 2003) provides information about racecars. Talk about books in this genre, though valuable, is likely to center on concept development, rather than the alphabet.

Multiple Opportunities and Meaningful Contexts Matter

Teachers should also be aware that, in addition to reading alphabet books, they should provide children with further opportunities to learn about the alphabet and to use it in meaningful contexts. That is, reading alphabet books allows teachers to introduce and to discuss various components of the alphabet, but in the present study rarely did it encourage teachers to discuss the importance of alphabet knowledge within the meaningful contexts of reading and writing. Therefore, teachers should provide children with as many opportunities as possible to read and write.

One strategy for teaching children about the alphabet is to encourage them to recognize their name and the names of their peers. When children are first learning to recognize names in print, they often focus on the first letter because the first letter, an uppercase letter, is the most salient feature. By modifying a common classroom routine, teachers can encourage children to think critically about all the letters in names. For example, if a teacher holds up two or more names that begin with different letters (e.g., *E*dgar, *L*aShawn, *T*errel), this encourages children to learn to differentiate between the first letters. Holding up two or more names that begin with the same letter (e.g., *D*avid, *D*aniel, *D*aniesha) encourages children to look beyond the first letters in the names.

Dramatic play creates numerous opportunities to teach children about the alphabet. For example, in a dramatic play center of a grocery store, children can be encouraged to notice or read signs, labels, and coupons, as well as numbers on a scale. Children can be encouraged to write grocery lists and check off the items as they locate and purchase them. Texts such as cookbooks and magazines, grocery store flyers and coupons, and Ehlert's book *Eating the Alphabet* (1989) also may help to encourage children's play around literacy. Such activities encourage children to read and to write in meaningful contexts and provide opportunities for teachers to talk about various aspects of literacy, including the alphabet.

Creating a writing center allows children additional opportunities to explore the alphabet. Providing thematically related picture/word cards or a word wall encourages children to explore writing at their own pace. For example, picture/word cards or a word wall related to a grocery store or a unit on the food pyramid may contain pictures of food along with the item's written name (e.g., *B* is for *butter, beef, beans, blueberries, bread*). Pictures of other foods can be made available for children to glue into their journals, and some children may be encouraged to write words for the items using invented spelling. Children can then refer to the word wall or their journals to write grocery lists, create menus, or to invent recipes for the dramatic play center. Such opportunities not only promote knowledge of letter names and the sounds they represent but also facilitate concept development.

Writing class books is another strategy for teaching children about the alphabet. For example, to create a class phonebook, white pages could be made by printing or gluing a picture of each child onto a page and then asking the children to write their names and phone numbers onto the page with the first letter of their individual names. To create the yellow pages, children and their families could be encouraged to notice and suggest the names of local businesses that could be added in the class phonebook.

Creating alphabet books is another way to facilitate children's alphabet knowledge in meaningful contexts. Personalized alphabet books may be particularly motivating for children as they develop letter-sound knowledge. Such books, like the one in Figure 1 created by Hillary Meyer,

---

Figure 1
A Personalized Page of an Alphabet Book

Helga and Hillary hike happily.

Jake is a jolly jumper!

Ivana Iguana insists on imported indulgences.

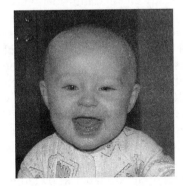

Kisses, kisses for Katy, Katy!

Note. Figure created by Hillary Meyer and used with permission.

could contain authentic photographs of the child's family and include direct letter–picture correspondences with alliteration on each page. Children also could create alphabet books that focus on a theme or concept. Although the primary purpose of such books is to teach content knowledge, it is done within the framework of the alphabet. Using a letter, children may dictate or write a sentence about a target word or concept. For example, after completing a unit on community helpers, a child who chooses the letter *D* might illustrate a picture of a doctor, and dictate or write a sentence. Laura Smolkin's Webbing Into Literacy website, http://curry.edschool.virginia.edu/go/wil/home.html, provides downloadable examples of concept-oriented alphabet books for each month of the year.

Finally, alphabet books may be constructed to maximize children's interactions with the text. For example, alphabet books may have removable pictures or letters attached with hook and loop tape. This type of interactive text allows children to sort pictures by sound and sort letters by font or configuration (Bear, Invernizzi, Templeton, & Johnston, 2004). For example, children sorting pictures by sound might place pictures of a snake, soap, and sun on the *S* page, or if sorting by letters children could place the *A*, *a*, *a*, and *A* together on a single page of the interactive text.

Alphabet Knowledge Is Part of the Foundation of Literacy

The present study gleaned information regarding teachers' alphabet book read-alouds with emergent readers. We learned that teachers have various book-reading styles when reading alphabet books, as they do when reading storybooks. We also highlighted the differences in teacher emphases during alphabet read-aloud events based on the genre of alphabet books and provided suggestions for using such books in early childhood classrooms. The results of the study merge with our experience in thinking about ways to incorporate alphabet knowledge and the foundations of literacy instruction. Future investigations might explore teachers' repeated readings of alphabet texts and their use of other meaningful contexts to teach children about the alphabet. Such data can extend teachers' awareness and suggest avenues for incorporating alphabet knowledge and their teaching. Further, such investigations will add to our knowledge of early literacy and to efforts that maximize meaningful alphabet learning opportunities for our emergent readers.

References

Adams, M.J. (1990). *Beginning to read: Thinking and learning about print.* Cambridge, MA: MIT Press.

Bear, D.R., Invernizzi, M., Templeton, S., & Johnston, F. (2004). *Words their way: Word study for phonics, vocabulary and spelling instruction* (3rd ed.). Upper Saddle River, NJ: Prentice Hall.

Bloodgood, J.W. (1999). What's in a name? Children's name writing and literacy acquisition. *Reading Research Quarterly, 34*, 342–367.

Chomsky, C. (1971). Write first, read later. *Childhood Education, 47*, 296–299.

De Temple, J., & Snow, C.E. (2003). Learning words from books. In A. van Kleeck, S.A. Stahl, & E.B. Bauer (Eds.), *On reading books to children: Parents and teachers* (pp. 16–36). Mahwah, NJ: Erlbaum.

Dickinson, D.K., & Keebler, R. (1989). Variation in preschool teachers' styles of reading books. *Discourse Processes, 12*, 353–375.

Dodd, B., & Carr, A. (2003). Young children's letter-sound knowledge. *Language, Speech, and Hearing Services in Schools, 34*, 128–137.

Donovan, C.A., & Smolkin, L.B. (2002). Children's genre knowledge: An examination of K–5 students' performance on multiple tasks providing differing levels of scaffolding. *Reading Research Quarterly, 37*, 428–465.

Duncan, L.G., & Seymour, P.H.K. (2000). Socio-economic differences in foundation level literacy. *British Journal of Psychology, 91*, 145–166.

Ferreiro, E. (1986). The interplay between information and assimilation in beginning literacy. In W.H. Teale & E. Sulzby (Eds.), *Emergent literacy: Writing and reading* (pp. 15–49). Norwood, NJ: Ablex.

Gibson, E.J., Gibson, J.J., Pick, A.D., & Osser, H.A. (1962). A developmental study of the discrimination of letter-like forms. *Journal of Comparative and Physiological Psychology, 55*, 897–906.

Gibson, E.J., & Levin, H. (1975). *The psychology of reading.* Cambridge, MA: MIT Press.

Hiebert, E. (1981). Developmental patterns and interrelationships of preschool children's print awareness. *Reading Research Quarterly, 16*, 236–260.

Martinez, M.G., & Teale, W.H. (1993). Teacher storybook reading style: A comparison of six teachers. *Research in the Teaching of English, 27*, 175–199.

Mason, J.M. (1984). Early reading from a developmental perspective. In P.D. Pearson, R. Barr, M.L. Kamil, & P. Mosenthal (Eds.), *Handbook of reading research* (pp. 505–543). New York: Longman.

McBride-Chang, C. (1999). The ABCs of the ABCs: The development of letter-name and letter-sound knowledge. *Merrill-Palmer Quarterly, 45*, 285–308.

McGee, L.M., & Richgels, D.J. (1989). "K is Kristen's": Learning the alphabet from a child's perspective. *The Reading Teacher, 43*, 216–225.

Murray, B.A., Stahl, S.A., & Ivey, M.G. (1996). Developing phoneme awareness through alphabet books. *Reading and Writing: An Interdisciplinary Journal, 8*, 307–322.

Share, D.L., & Gur, T. (1999). How reading begins: A study of preschoolers' print identification strategies. *Cognition and Instruction, 17*, 177–213.

Smolkin, L.B., & Donovan, C.A. (2001, November). *Science concepts and comprehension during science trade book read alouds.* Paper presented at the annual meeting of the National Reading Conference, San Antonio, TX.

Smolkin, L.B., & Yaden, D.B., Jr. (1992). "O" is for "mouse": First encounters with the alphabet book. *Language Arts, 69*, 432–441.

Smolkin, L.B., Yaden, D.B., Jr., Brown, L., & Hofius, B. (1992). The effects of genre, visual design choices, and discourse structure on preschoolers' responses to picture books during parent-child read-alouds. In C.K. Kinzer & D.J. Leu (Eds.), *Literacy research, theory, and practice: Views from many perspectives* (41st yearbook of the National Reading Conference, pp. 291–301). Chicago: National Reading Conference.

Snow, C.E. (1983). Literacy and language: Relationships during the preschool years. *Harvard Educational Review, 53*, 165–189.

Snow, C.E., Burns, M.S., & Griffin, P. (Eds.). (1998). *Preventing reading difficulties in young children.* Washington, DC: National Academy Press.

Stahl, S.A., & Murray, B.A. (1994). Defining phonological awareness and its relationship to early reading. *Journal of Educational Psychology, 86*, 221–234.

Treiman, R., & Broderick, V. (1998). What's in a name: Children's knowledge about letters in their own names. *Journal of Experimental Child Psychology, 70*, 97–116.

Venezky, R.L. (1975). The curious role of letter names in reading instruction. *Visible Language, 9*(1), 7–23.

Welsch, J.G., Sullivan, A., & Justice, L.M. (2003). That's my letter! What preschoolers' name writing representations tell us about emergent literacy knowledge. *Journal of Literacy Research, 35*, 757–776.

Yaden, D.B., Jr., Smolkin, L.B., & MacGillivray, L. (1993). A psychogenetic perspective on children's understanding about letter associations during alphabet book readings. *Journal of Reading Behavior, 25*, 43–68.

Children's Books Cited

Base, G. (1986). *Animalia.* New York: Penguin.

Cohen, I. (1997). ABC discovery! New York: Dial Books for Young Readers.

Ehlert, L. (1989). *Eating the alphabet: Fruits and vegetables from A to Z.* New York: Harcourt Brace.

Elting, M., & Folsom, M. (1980). *Q is for duck: An alphabet guessing game.* Ill. J. Kent. New York: Clarion.

Fleming, D. (2002). *Alphabet under construction.* New York: Holt.

Floca, B. (2003). *The racecar alphabet.* New York: Simon & Schuster.

Hobbie, H. (2000). *Toot & Puddle: Puddle's ABC.* Boston: Little, Brown.

Lester, M. (2000). *A is for salad.* New York: Grosset & Dunlap.

Lionni, L. (1968). *The alphabet tree.* New York: Dragonfly.

MacDonald, R. (2003). *Achoo! Bang! Crash! The noisy alphabet.* Brookfield, CT: Roaring Brook.

MacDonald, S. (1986). *Alphabatics.* New York: Simon & Schuster.

Martin, B., Jr., & Archambault, J. (1989). *Chicka chicka boom boom.* Ill. L. Ehlert. New York: Simon & Schuster.

McDonnell, F. (1997). *Flora McDonnell's ABC.* Cambridge, MA: Candlewick.

McPhail, D. (1989). *David McPhail's animals A to Z.* New York: Scholastic.

Munari, B. (1960). *Bruno Munari's ABC.* San Francisco: Chronicle.

Musgrove, M. (1976). *Ashanti to Zulu: African traditions.* Ill. L. Dillon & D. Dillon. New York: Dial.

Pallotta, J. (1994). *The desert alphabet book.* Ill. M. Astrella. Watertown, MA: Charlesbridge.

Pelletier, D. (1996). *The graphic alphabet.* New York: Scholastic.

Reed, L.R. (1995). *Pedro, his perro, and the alphabet sombrero.* New York: Hyperion.

Rey, H.A. (1963). *Curious George learns the alphabet.* New York: Houghton Mifflin.

Seeley, L.L. (1994). *The book of shadow boxes: A story of the ABCs.* Atlanta, GA: Peachtree.

Seuss, Dr. (1963). *Dr. Seuss's ABC: An amazing alphabet book!* New York: Random House.

Shannon, G. (1996). *Tomorrow's alphabet.* Ill. D. Crews. New York: Greenwillow.

Tryon, L. (1991). *Albert's alphabet.* New York: Atheneum.

Questions for Reflection

• In many school districts, kindergarten is now a full day. Further, in many neighborhoods, the majority of children attend preschool for at least a year prior to kindergarten entrance. Have you noticed any changes in the alphabet knowledge of the young children you work with based on changes in preschool experiences or in duration of the kindergarten day? At what age are children ready to work on alphabet knowledge? How significant of an emphasis should the alphabet receive in early literacy instruction in preschool versus kindergarten or first grade?

• Consider the alphabet books in your school or classroom library. Is a variety of genres represented? Which books do the children most like looking at on their own? Which ones are most appealing to them when they are read or shared aloud? Do you have books that are appropriate for English-language learners and for children from diverse racial, ethnic, and socioeconomic backgrounds and circumstances?

An Effective Framework for Primary-Grade Guided Writing Instruction

Sharan A. Gibson

Young writers need *instruction*. They do not improve their writing skills simply because teachers require them to write (Englert, 1992). Children need explicit scaffolding, constructed within expertly delivered instructional conversations that address the language, knowledge, and strategies required for problem solving in writing. Effective writing instruction provides "richly textured opportunities for students' conceptual and linguistic development" (Goldenberg, 1992, p. 317).

This article describes the theory and procedures for guided writing lessons, which are a specific format for primary-grade, small-group writing instruction based on (a) a sociocultural perspective (e.g., Vygotsky, 1978; Wertsch, 1991), (b) Clay's theories of literacy learning (2001), and (c) the author's study of second-grade guided writing instruction (Gibson, 2008). Guided writing is defined here as a small-group instructional framework presented to students who share similar needs at a particular point in time (Fountas & Pinnell, 2001). Guided writing provides an important context for teachers' in-the-moment assessment and immediate instructional scaffolding of students' construction of their own, individual texts. As students completed their hands-on examination of a celery stalk, for example, the following discussion supported their construction of an informative title for their own text.

Teacher: Okay, now that you've taken a good look at that celery stalk, I want you to think about one interesting idea about celery that you want to write about today. Sean, are you going to write about the strings that you found in the celery?

Sean: I'm going to say, *How do you get strings out of celery?* Hey, here's what I'm going to do. *First, snap it in two.*

Teacher: Good! *How to get the strings out of celery*. And you've thought of a good way to start your story as well.

Cari: That's his title. I don't want the strings.

Teacher: Are you thinking of your own title?

Cari: *Let me tell you how celery looks.*

Teacher: Great! You've all thought of one interesting idea to write about and are using a title to help your readers understand. I'll help you while you write your own text.

All writing is collaborative. Effective writing teachers collaborate with students, creating apprenticeships for them through guided practice (Englert, Mariage, & Dunsmore, 2006). Thus, writing instruction should include explicit teaching in which teachers step in to model and prompt and then step back to encourage students to make decisions and solve problems while writing (Englert & Dunsmore, 2002). Effective writing instruction should make the elements of good writing and the strategies of good writers visible and accessible to naïve writers (Vaughn, Gersten, & Chard, 2000). The *guided* in guided writing lessons, then, refers to the essential nature of the support provided by expert teachers while students write. This article connects guided reading to guided writing instruction with emphasis on children's internalization of the

Reprinted from Gibson, S.A. (2008). An effective framework for primary-grade guided writing instruction. *The Reading Teacher*, 62(4), 324-334.

thinking and self-scaffolding needed for effective writing.

The characteristics of effective reading instruction overlap with those of effective writing instruction. Reading and writing share rhetorical and communicative functions, knowledge, and cognitive processes (Nelson & Calfee, 1998). Critical shared knowledge between reading and writing includes metaknowledge, that is, knowing the functions and purposes of reading and writing; phonological and graphemic awareness; and procedural knowledge of the use of strategies (Fitzgerald & Shanahan, 2000). Clay (1998) emphasized the reciprocal relationship between learning to read and learning to write as well as the crucial role of strategic activity for both reading and writing acquisition. Both learning to read and to write requires the expansion of children's oral language resources and the application of these competencies to understanding and constructing texts within a variety of genres.

Poor writers' systems of learning and development (McNaughton, 1995) are both "limited and limiting" (Glasswell, 2001, p. 349). Young writers typically lack the control structures that allow them to use existing or developing skills to expand their knowledge base. However, these writers *do* learn strategic behavior for writing when such behavior is taught in supportive ways (Boocock, McNaughton, & Parr 1998; Bradley, 2001; Sipe, 1998). The study from which this article is derived (Gibson, 2008) analyzed the results of daily guided writing instruction presented by the author to five average-progress second-grade writers, referred to as Cari, Kim, Rachel, Sam, and Sean. This study addressed each child's internalization of strategic behaviors for problem solving during writing through analysis of videotaped weekly individual writing events as well as assessment of writing products. Each student demonstrated a strong, clear shift to a more active and strategic stance for writing, thus supporting expanded knowledge of language use for composing, for text and sentence structure, for phonemic awareness, and for orthography.

This article describes instructional steps and teaching behaviors for explicit primary-grade, small-group writing instruction in a supportive, guided context. Each section includes examples of teacher–student interaction during guided writing lessons. The article also describes two specific assessment procedures that support guided writing instruction.

A Framework for Guided Writing Instruction

Guided writing instruction in a small-group context allows teachers to provide high levels of immediate, targeted support while each student writes his or her own short but complete text. A typical format for a 20-minute guided writing lesson might include the following four steps:

1. Engagement in a brief, shared experience that is of interest to students, including both a linguistically and informationally rich activity and accompanying conversation, and expansion of students' ability to talk about content of interest

2. Discussion of strategic behavior for writing, including a presentation of a think-aloud or a cue for strategic activity along with active discussion of ways in which students can integrate this strategy into their own writing

3. Students' time to write individually with immediate guidance from the teacher, who "leans in" to interact with individual students about immediate decisions and strategies and uses prompts to guide students' thinking for problem solving while writing

4. A brief sharing activity in which the writer's immediate work is shared with an audience, and writers experience their newly written texts as a whole

Grouping practices are too often the missing link in effective writing instruction (Flood & Lapp, 2000). It is not necessary, however, for every student to participate in a guided writing lesson every day. Instead, teachers should make intentional, thoughtful decisions about which students are in need of a "shot in the arm" regarding writing at any point in time. A series of guided writing lessons might be presented to students who are not producing much text during classroom writing time, for example, or to students who write a sufficient quantity of text but lack a sense of ownership for their writing. Alternatively, the teacher may work with students who are not appropriating the elements of good writing described in whole-class lessons. Guided writing groups should be flexible in nature and based on observations of students' current needs. These lessons are most successful when presented on a daily basis to the same group of students, perhaps for several consecutive weeks.

The writing produced during guided writing will typically be the result of about 10 minutes of concentrated individual writing time and may or may not be extended, revised, or edited outside of the guided writing context. Guided writing lessons do not take the place of such frameworks as a writing workshop model (Graves, 1983) or interactive writing (McCarrier, Pinnell, & Fountas, 2000). A guided writing lesson might occur after a whole-class writing lesson has been completed and students are writing independently. Teachers typically spend the first weeks of each school year establishing expectations for independent work time prior to beginning guided writing lessons. Guided writing thus provides a strong context for teachers' support of students as they put whole-class instruction into practice. The instructional procedures for guided writing lessons are now described, divided into four steps.

Step 1: Brief, Shared Experience
The orientation provided for students when reading a new book insures that the meaning and language of this particular text are accessible to readers (Clay, 1991). The teacher

> creates a scaffold within which children can complete a first reading of a whole story. The teacher and children have rehearsed some responses; others are recent and familiar because the teacher modeled them. The children's own background knowledge has been called to mind, and some new knowledge has been introduced in a measured way. (p. 265)

As described in the next sections, Step 1 of guided writing lessons captures students' interests for writing and allows them to rehearse their use of important conceptual and linguistic resources.

Provide a Strong, Supportive Introduction.
The introductory section of guided writing lessons should (1) expand students' interest and orient them to the writing task, and (2) provide opportunities for students to hear and use the language structures needed for their writing. Possible activities include study of an interesting topic, a short read-aloud from one section of an informational text, and a brief experiment.

Teacher: Today we're going to try an experiment to see how many paperclips will stick to one magnet. I want you to think about the writing that you will do next, though, before you get your magnets. What would be a good first sentence for your own story?

Kim: I, I, I don't know.

Teacher: How could you tell your readers about the magnets and the paperclips?

Kim: *I test my magnets.*

Teacher: Yes. Do you think you want to write anything about the paperclips too? *First I tested...*

Rachel: Magnets and paperclips.

Sean: What did it stick on?

Teacher: Yes. You have to put some details in too, don't you? So your text might be about the magnet and the paperclips. You could start your own sentence with something like, *This experiment....*

Sean: *First, I did the experiment. I took my magnet and put the paperclips on it.*

Teacher: Good! Listen: *First, I did the experiment*, period. *I took my magnet and put the paperclips on it*, period. Say his sentences again: *First, I did the experiment. I took my magnet and put the paperclips on it.* You are thinking about great ways to start writing. Let's try our experiment, and then you can write your own story.

Engage Writers in Conversation and Rehearsal. In guided writing lessons, students rehearse new ways of talking about topics of interest using literate and increasingly complex forms of language. Discussion immediately prior to and during individual writing expands students' language base and prepares them to write well. Rehearsal of language structures should be explicit and well connected to the type of text and topic about which students are currently writing.

It is important to recognize the challenges faced by young writers as they work to appropriate the more complex structures of written language. Composing is a skill that has to be learned, just like spelling or the correct use of punctuation. It requires expertise with both overall organization and sentence structure. With strong and consistent input through discussion and teacher explanation, students' written texts can move from simple to complex uses of language. Sean's story about bats, for example (see Figure 1), was written during a guided writing session and supported by a discussion of a section of the book *Bat Loves the Night* by Nicola Davies. In contrast to his earlier writing, Sean began this text with a topic sentence and used a variety of sentence structures. He composed his text with relatively sophisticated details about bats, using specific vocabulary. Sean also wrote with an appropriate voice and stance for informational text, including a pronunciation guide for *echolocation* and a picture to illustrate this important concept. He completed this text in approximately seven minutes of sustained writing, supported by immediate discussion of the language, content, and writing strategies needed for his work.

Figure 1
Sean's Writing

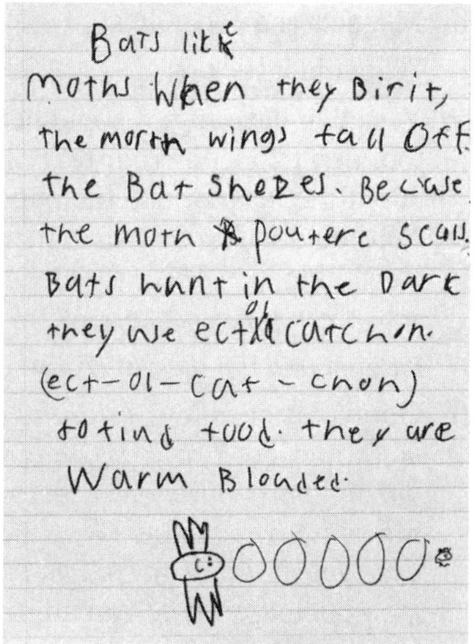
Bats like
moths When they Birit,
the morth wings fall Off
the Bat shozes. Because
the moth pouterc scall.
Bats hunt in the Dark
they we ectolacatchin
(ect-ol-cat-chon)
to find food. they are
Warm Blooded.

Step 2: Discussion of Strategic Behavior for Writing

Guided writing lessons provide maximum opportunities for active student engagement in their own writing, supported by the teacher's immediate guidance and explicit teaching of the strategic behaviors used by good writers. In Step 2, teachers work to expand their students' awareness of specific cognitive strategies for writing.

Describe Writing Strategies to Students. Following a brief shared activity, teachers can present a short think-aloud or introduce a cue card (Scardamalia & Bereiter, 1986) for a specific strategic activity to students (see Figure 2). Teachers and students should then discuss ways in which students can integrate this strategy into their own writing. In the following example, the teacher extends her think-aloud, demonstrating the construction of a strong opening sentence to students' own thinking.

Teacher: I want to be sure to write something about Velcro that people will think is interesting. This cue card can help me to remember what to think about as I start writing: *Think of a good first sentence.* That's what I'm going to do right now. I'm going to tell how Velcro works. The two sides, the hooks and the strings, are how it works. And I think most people don't know that. So this is my sentence: *Let me tell you how the strings and the hooks in Velcro work.* Put your cue card in front of you. What are you thinking about?

Sean: I really don't know what to write.

Teacher: You've got to make a choice, don't you?

Sean: I don't really know how Velcro works. I mean, I know the two different textures of the sides.

Teacher: And you know how the two sides work.

Sean: Yeah.

Kim: What does this side do to that side?

Cari: It kind of catches it, the hook.

Teacher: Yes, those are good details. How are you going to start writing?

Sean: *I think Velcro's so complicated! It's driving me nuts!*

Teach Students How to Write Well. Teachers need to do more than just tell young writers that they must include appropriate ending punctuation for all sentences or enough detail for clarity. If teachers present an immediately useful and well-contextualized way of thinking about writing, the stage is set for students' success. Writing is a cognitive process (Flower & Hayes, 1981), requiring instruction in how to think and act (Higgins, Miller, & Wegmann, 2006). When teachers provide mental, linguistic, and physical tools, such as cue cards, diagrams, graphic organizers, and clear examples of sentence and text structures, they are directly supporting students' use of procedural steps and higher order strategies for effective writing (Englert, Mariage, & Dunsmore, 2006).

Step 3: Students' Time to Write Individually With Immediate Guidance From the Teacher

The intent of guided writing lessons is not simply to provide more time to write. Instead, lessons are structured so that students are actively engaged in their own sustained, successful writing. Given well-supported, guided concentration on the immediate completion of a short but complete writing product, young writers are able to practice and internalize what they have been taught.

Provide Immediate Guidance for What Students Are Writing Next. After getting set up for success with a language- and content-stimulating activity combined with teacher think-alouds or cue cards for strategy use, students then write as independently as possible. Teachers should lean in and assist with what each student is *currently* constructing in his or her writing, providing strong "feed forward" for the individual writer. Feedback evaluates what the writer has already written. In contrast, feed forward focuses the writer's attention on what strategies to use next. In the following example, the teacher provided feed forward to Rachel as she became stuck while writing.

Teacher: Rachel, what do you need to say next in your writing?

Rachel: They're made of metal.

Teacher: So you're going to tell your readers about metal, different kinds of metal?

Rachel: Yeah. And this is different than the others.

Teacher: Think about what your readers would want to know. What could your sentence be?

Rachel: *They're made of different kinds of metal.*

Teacher: Great sentence. *Paperclips are made of different kinds of metal*, period. You're ready to keep writing now.

Scaffold Students' Writing Through Prompting.

Teachers should provide immediate guidance that will improve the writer's expertise, not just the written product itself (Gibson, 2007). Prompting during students' writing takes a proactive stance, guiding a young writer's ability to focus attention on composing and in-the-moment revising. Clay (2001) defines reading work as a strategic activity "when the reader directs attention, picks up and uses information, monitors the 'reading,' makes decisions, and activates self-correcting to revise a prior decision" (p. 128). Writing work, then, might be defined as an activity whereby the writer (1) directs his or her attention to key aspects of composing and transcribing tasks, (2) picks up and uses information from interests and resources, (3) monitors the writing piece as it is constructed, (4) makes decisions about the next steps, and (5) self-corrects to improve a text. Teachers should prompt for the in-the-moment writing work in which a student needs to engage.

Table 1 provides a list of prompts, organized by category, that may be useful for teachers during guided writing lessons. When leaning in to guide an individual writer, teachers must decide whether they are calling the student's attention to composing or transcribing processes or perhaps prompting the student to use a strategy to maintain fluency.

It is important to remember that any list of prompts serves only as shorthand for the conversational interaction between teacher and students. For example, as Kim finished writing about veins in an early guided writing lesson (see Figure 3), she lost momentum and asked for assistance.

Kim: I said about the veins.

Teacher: Do you know what to write next? What else do you think would be important to add?

Kim: I already put about to tear a leaf.

Teacher: Yes! Your idea is to write about discovering a leaf, and you added information about tearing and listening and then about seeing the veins in the leaf. Have

Table 1
Teacher Prompting During Guided Writing Lessons

Category	Teacher prompting
Directing students' attention to key aspects of composing tasks	• Pick one small but interesting idea to write about. • Think of a title that tells what you are writing about. • What would be an interesting first sentence for your story? • How will you introduce your readers to the next part of your story? • What word(s) would make your readers know what you really mean? • Could you start the next sentence like this...?
Directing students' attention to key aspects of transcribing tasks	• Say your sentences. Can you hear where the period/question mark/exclamation point might go? • Say that word slowly to yourself. What sounds do you hear? • Clap that word to help you know what parts to write.
Prompting students to use information from interests and resources	• Think about everything you know about this topic. • Did you read or write something like this that you could look at to help yourself?
Prompting students to monitor their writing as it is being constructed	• Say it to yourself before you write it. How should your sentence sound? • Have you included enough details so that your readers will understand and be interested?
Supporting students' decisions about the next steps to take for writing	• What could you do now to help yourself keep writing? • What information are you thinking about next? • When you get stuck, rereading will help you to start writing again. • When you get stuck, talking to yourself or to a friend about your ideas will help you to start writing again.

you included enough details so that readers will understand?

Kim: I could say about oxygen.

Teacher: Good! What do people want to know about leaves and oxygen? Go ahead and write!

The teacher structured her talk to improve Kim's ability to integrate an awareness of information already included in her writing with the need for further details, using prompts like, Have you included enough details so that readers will understand?

Provide Lots of "Just Right" Help as Soon as Students Struggle. Writing teachers need to provide high levels of instructional scaffolding. Teachers should provide more and appropriate kinds of help as soon as a student is struggling and then either fade the kind and amount of further support or raise the level of challenge (Wood, 1998). Teacher prompting guides students' immediate thinking by directing their attention to both the visible (e.g., use of space on the page, letter formation) and invisible (e.g., phonemes, language choices) aspects of writing. Teachers can provide instructional scaffolding

Figure 3
Kim's Writing

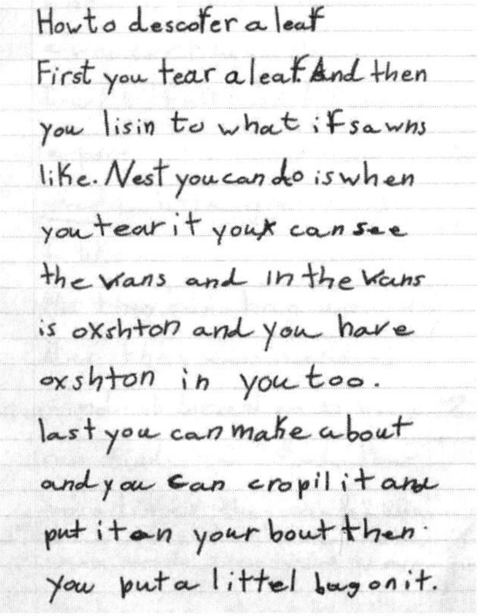

How to descofer a leaf
First you tear a leaf And then
you lisin to what if sawns
like. Nest you can do is when
you tear it yous can see
the vrans and in the vrans
is oxshton and you have
oxshton in you too.
last you can mabe about
and you can cropil it are
put it an your bout then.
You put a littel bag on it.

on a continuum from full modeling and explana-tion to independent task completion (Gaskins et al., 1997). Prompting during writing (see Table 2) requires teachers to decide whether full mod-eling of a task is necessary (e.g., *"When bats are asleep,* comma, *you shouldn't wake them up.* Listen to where I put the comma.") or whether simple cueing of aspects of the task (e.g., "How can you help yourself get started writing?") is the right amount of support.

Step 4: Connecting Students' Immediate Writing to an Audience

Writers need an audience. Young writers typical-ly dedicate significant attention to transcription and need to experience their own newly writ-ten texts as a whole. Dedicate a few minutes for sharing that same day's texts at the end of each guided writing lesson; this provides an immedi-ate audience and context within which the text is revisited. This sharing also supports the develop-ment of students' active attempts to convey infor-mation to readers clearly and focuses instruction on writers' decision making.

Teachers may want to highlight a differ-ent student's writing each day, reading it aloud to the group and asking the writer to comment on decisions made while writing. As his teacher read his story to the group, for example, Sean explained his decision to include parenthetical information.

Teacher: Oh, parentheses!

Sean: Yeah, I put *echolocation.* So when peo-ple read it and say, *What's that?* then they'll find out.

Students in the group may read their com-pleted text to a partner or switch papers and read a piece of writing independently. It may also be feasible to extend the audience beyond the small-group context. Each author may choose a friend in the classroom and invite him or her to the guided writing table to share a text.

It is also useful to maintain individual port-folios of the texts constructed during guided writ-ing lessons. A three-ring binder or blank journal can be used for all writing accomplished during a series of lessons. These portfolios become a strong resource for students' extended writing and for the teacher's ongoing assessment and sharing of student progress.

Assessment for Guided Writing Instruction

Effective instruction cannot occur in the absence of ongoing and insightful assessment practices. During guided writing instruction, teachers develop a strong knowledge of individual stu-dents' writing expertise in a detailed manner, allowing for accurate on-the-spot decisions regarding task difficulty. This section describes an instructional level for writing tasks as well as two specific assessment procedures for guided writing instruction.

Tasks presented to students through teacher prompting should be at an instructional level so that students will encounter some challenges requiring strategy use but will also be able to complete much of the task accurately and flu-ently. Therefore, one of the primary goals of the

Table 2
Instructional Scaffolding During Guided Writing Instruction

Instructional scaffolding stages	Scaffolding during writing instruction
Full modeling and explanation	T: *When bats are asleep,* comma, *you shouldn't wake them up.* Did you hear where I put the comma?
Element identification through assisted modeling and generic questions	T: Here's my sentence about straw. *I think the reason the water stays in the straw is because of the air pressure.* What sentence about the way a straw works are you thinking about?
Cueing aspects of tasks, naming and reinforcing strategies	T: We're going to do an experiment today so that you'll have something very interesting to write about. But first of all, I want you to think about your writing. How can you help yourself know how to get started? S1: First, think of things. T: Like one little thing that's interesting? S3: Why not make it easy? You could have an object to look at and write about it. T: So then you have it in front of you to help you choose ideas.
Strategy naming and prompting	T: I heard you clapping. Did the clapping help you? You put *under.* What part of the word do you need to write next? S: *Under stand.*

Note. Framework adapted from Gaskins et al. (1997).

teacher's instructional scaffolding during writing is to ensure a high level of student success with a few opportunities for problem solving. As teachers observe students' success with these challenges, they are then able to introduce new strategic processes that raise the difficulty level appropriately.

Anecdotal Observation of Student Writing Behavior

Learners are always appropriating, learning, and adapting a series of strategies from which they choose for the particular task at hand (Siegler, 2005). Assessment procedures, then, need to identify those strategies that are well within a student's independent control, those that the student can use but only with the teacher's input (as well as some effort and a few errors), and those that are presently beyond the student's reach.

Although it is not practical to attempt something as systematic and comprehensive as a running record (Clay, 2002) for writing behavior, anecdotal notes made both during and immediately after each lesson will help teachers know what aspects of instruction have or haven't been appropriated by students. Table 3, for example, shows anecdotal notes made as Kim wrote her text describing her examination of a leaf. [A blank form is available with the online version of this article as originally published in *The Reading Teacher*, at dx.doi.org/10.1598/RT.62.4.5.] The teacher identified four specific points during the writing for which Kim demonstrated interesting writing behavior. During the lesson, the teacher took brief notes, indicating the text being written at each point in time as well as Kim's writing behavior and any support provided to her. After the lesson, the teacher analyzed these notes and made tentative plans for the next steps in

Table 3
Analysis and Anecdotal Observation of Kim's Writing Behavior

Text written	Description of observed writing behavior	Assistance provided	Analysis	Comments
"descofer" (discover)				
"lisin" (listen)	Kim tapped on table and articulated slowly	None	Listens for syllables and phonemes	• Hears most phonemes well
• f/v confusion				
• Needs stronger focus on orthographic patterns				
"and"/"And,"	Kim self-corrected; during rereading, heard need for new sentence; smiled at teacher to celebrate a success	None	Monitors the sound of sentences for ending punctuation	• Needs to become more automated and fluent at sentence structures
"Next you can do is when you tear it you can see the veins."	Kim repeated first, next to self	Peer assisted with idea for veins; Kim consulted her own texts	Uses resources well	• Attempts complex sentences with difficulty
	Kim stuck; requested assistance	Teacher prompted: What else is important?	May have had limited interest in this topic	• Needs more attention to planning and elaboration of ideas

Note. Framework adapted from Gaskins et al. (1997).

instruction. In this instance, Kim's teacher noted aspects of Kim's spelling, sentence structure, and composing processes. The teacher found that Kim needed to move beyond an alphabetic stage (Bear, Invernizzi, Templeton, & Johnston, 2004) for spelling while writing and expand her language base for informational text.

Teachers may want to focus anecdotal notes on a different student during each lesson or keep a clipboard at hand to take notes for any student as time allows. These observations should not interrupt instruction but should be made as time allows.

Analytic Assessment of Written Products

Periodic analytic assessment (Fearn & Farnan, 2001) of the writing products arising from guided writing lessons—focused specifically on those strategies that have been taught to students—will help teachers fine-tune their short- and long-term teaching decisions.

Analytic assessment (Fearn & Farnan, 2001) does not rely on any checklist or rubric, but it is closely matched to instruction. The teacher determines a short list of those skills and strategies that he or she has already taught to a guided writing group and examines a set of recently written texts for those specific factors. The teacher should always be teaching to and assessing both composing and transcribing behavior, from generating ideas to sentence structure and mechanics. Analytic assessment provides a format within which a teacher investigates the degree to which each student has appropriated this instruction. It is important to ask: Are my students actually using the strategies I have taught?

For example, during one point in time, specific strategies for writing clear, understandable texts, with lead sentences, details, and signal words as well as the spelling of high-frequency words, had been taught to Cari, Kim, Rachel, Sam, and Sean. Each student's current text was examined for these specific factors (see Table 4). Based on this analysis, their teacher determined that (a) Rachel was in need of higher levels of support for the planning and structure of ideas within her writing, (b) all students in the group needed to become comfortable writing with more complex sentence structures, and (c) fur-

ther instruction on spelling strategies would be helpful to all students. This analysis provided specific instructional targets for language development, composing, and spelling. To address spelling, the teacher introduced a more sophisticated spelling strategy to students in the next lesson.

Teacher: You know how to say a word slowly and listen for sounds. Another way to spell a word is to clap it so that you can hear the parts. Then think of another word that's like it. Let's try it. Clap the word *magnet*. What's the first part you hear?

Cari: *Mag.*

Teacher: That's the first part of the word. Does *mag* sound like the word *bag*? *Bag* is spelled B-A-G. So how would you spell the first part of the word *magnet*?

Rachel: M-A-G.

Teacher: So when you need to spell a word today while you write, you can clap and hear its parts and maybe think of another word like it. Will that work?

Table 4
Analytic Assessment

	Writing clear/ informative	Lead sentence	Details	Signal words	Correctly punctuated sentences	Correctly capitalized sentences	Sight word spelling errors
Sean	+	+	+	First second	4/4	0/4	to/two
Kim	+	+	+	(none)	1/11	5/11	thar/they're cinds/kinds
Rachel	–	✓	–	And	2/3	3/3	do'not/don't
Cari	+	+	+	(none)	4/5	5/5	meny/many
Sam	✓	+	✓	and then, next	2/2	1/2	wite/white

Note. Analytic Assessment described in Fearn & Farnan (2001).
+ = strong, ✓ = adequate, – = weak

Rachel:　Like when it has two syllables?

Teacher:　Yes. If you hear two syllables, then you can think about how each syllable should look.

Summary

Young writers need instruction. The missing link in effective writing instruction may not only be grouping practices (Flood & Lapp, 2000) but also teaching to each student's ability to write better *drafts* over time. Drafting is absolutely central to the planning, revision, editing, and publishing processes. Conversely, each student's ability to produce text is dependent on his or her ability to engage in *immediate* planning, revision, editing, and consideration of readers' viewpoints.

Guided writing lessons provide opportunities to observe and teach intensively, using an instructional framework that includes (1) engagement in a linguistically and informationally rich activity, (2) discussion of strategic behavior, (3) immediate teacher guidance while each student writes his or her own short but complete text, and (4) sharing of texts. Thus, guided writing lessons will help students to bridge the gap between whole-class writing instruction and their own active engagement in successful, independent writing.

References

Bear, D.R., Invernizzi, M., Templeton, S., & Johnston, F. (2004). *Words their way: Word study for phonics, vocabulary, and spelling instruction* (3rd ed.). Upper Saddle River, NJ: Merrill.

Boocock, C., McNaughton, S., & Parr, J.M. (1998). The early development of a self-extending system in writing. *Literacy Teaching and Learning, 3*(2), 41–58.

Bradley, D.H. (2001). How beginning writers articulate and demonstrate their understanding of the act of writing. *Reading Research and Instruction, 40*(4), 273–296.

Clay, M.M. (1991). Distinguished educator series: Introducing a new storybook to young readers. *The Reading Teacher, 45*(4), 264–273. doi:10.1598/RT.45.4.2

Clay, M.M. (1998). *By different paths to common outcomes.* York, ME: Stenhouse.

Clay, M.M. (2001). *Change over time in children's literacy development.* Portsmouth, NH: Heinemann.

Clay, M.M. (2002). *An observation survey of early literacy achievement* (2nd ed.). Portsmouth, NH: Heinemann.

Englert, C.S. (1992). Writing instruction from a sociocultural perspective: The holistic, dialogic, and social enterprise of writing. *Journal of Learning Disabilities, 25*(3), 153–172.

Englert, C.S., & Dunsmore, K. (2002). A diversity of teaching and learning paths: Teaching writing in situated activity. In J. Brophy (Ed.), *Social constructivist teaching: Affordances and constraints* (pp. 81–130). Amsterdam: JAI Press.

Englert, C.S., Mariage, T.V., & Dunsmore, K. (2006). Tenets of sociocultural theory in writing instruction research. In C.A. MacArthur, S. Graham, & J. Fitzgerald (Eds.), *Handbook of writing research* (pp. 208–221). New York: Guilford.

Fearn, L., & Farnan, N. (2001). *Interactions: Teaching writing and the language arts.* Boston: Houghton Mifflin.

Fitzgerald, J., & Shanahan, T. (2000). Reading and writing relations and their development. *Educational Psychologist, 35*(1), 39–50. doi:10.1207/S15326985EP3501_5

Flood, J., & Lapp, D. (2000). Teaching writing in urban schools: Cognitive processes, curriculum resources, and the missing links—management and grouping. In R. Indrisano & J.R. Squire (Eds.), *Perspectives on writing: Research, theory, and practice* (pp. 233–250). Newark, DE: International Reading Association.

Flower, L., & Hayes, J.R. (1981). A cognitive process theory of writing. *College Composition and Communication, 32*(4), 365–387. doi:10.2307/356600

Fountas, I.C., & Pinnell, G.S. (2001). *Guiding readers and writers grades 3–6: Teaching comprehension, genre, and content literacy.* Portsmouth, NH: Heinemann.

Gaskins, I.W., Rauch, S., Gensemer, E., Cunicelli, E., O'Hara, C., Six, L., et al. (1997). Scaffolding the development of intelligence among children who are delayed in learning to read. In K. Hogan & M. Pressley (Eds.), *Scaffolding student learning: Instructional approaches and issues* (pp. 43–73). Cambridge, MA: Brookline.

Gibson, S.A. (2007). Preservice teachers' knowledge of instructional scaffolding for writing instruction. *Mid-Western Educational Researcher, 20*(2), 9-15.

Gibson, S.A. (2008). Guiding writing lessons: Second-grade students' development of strategic behavior. *Reading Horizons, 48*(2), 111–132.

Glasswell, K. (2001). Matthew effects in writing: The patterning of difference in writing classrooms K–7. *Reading Research Quarterly, 36*(4), 348–349.

Goldenberg, C. (1992). Instructional conversations: Promoting comprehension through discussion. *The Reading Teacher, 46*(4), 316–326.

Graves, D.H. (1983). *Writing: Teachers and children at work.* Portsmouth, NH: Heinemann.

Higgins, B., Miller, M., & Wegmann, S. (2006). Teaching to the test...not! Balancing best practice and testing requirements in writing. *The Reading Teacher, 60*(4), 310–319. doi:10.1598/RT.60.4.1

McCarrier, A., Pinnell, G.S., & Fountas, I.C. (2000). *Interactive writing: How language & literacy come together, K–2*. Portsmouth, NH: Heinemann.

McNaughton, S. (1995). *Patterns of emergent literacy: Processes of development and transition*. New York: Oxford University Press.

Nelson, N., & Calfee, R.C. (1998). The reading–writing connection. In N. Nelson & R.C. Calfee (Eds.), *The reading–writing connection* (97th yearbook of the National Society for the Study of Education, Part II, pp. 1–52). Chicago: University of Chicago Press.

Scardamalia, M., & Bereiter, C. (1986). Research on written composition. In M.C. Wittrock (Ed.), *Handbook of research on teaching* (3rd ed., pp. 778–803). New York: Macmillan.

Siegler, R.S. (2005). Children's learning. *American Psychologist*, 60(8), 769–778. doi:10.1037/0003-066X.60.8.769

Sipe, L.R. (1998). Transitions to the conventional: An examination of a first grader's composing process. *Journal of Literacy Research*, 30(3), 357–388.

Vaughn, S., Gersten, R., & Chard, D.J. (2000). The underlying message in LD intervention research: Findings from research syntheses. *Exceptional Children*, 67(1), 99–114.

Vygotsky, L.S. (1978). *Mind in society: The development of higher psychological processes* (M. Cole, V. John-Steiner, S. Scribner, & E. Souberman, Eds. & Trans.). Cambridge, MA: Harvard University Press.

Wertsch, J.V. (1991). *Voices of the mind: A sociocultural approach to mediated action*. Cambridge, MA: Harvard University Press.

Wood, D. (1998). *How children think and learn: The social contexts of cognitive development*. Malden, MA: Blackwell.

Questions for Reflection

- Young writers often need help with the mechanics of writing along with guidance in the processes of organization, composition, and effective expression. How do you achieve the right balance in your classroom? How can you teach the importance of spelling, punctuation, and grammar without de-emphasizing students' creative expression?

- Research has shown that writing for authentic audiences can be a strong motivator for young writers. How might you extend small-group guided writing to provide a broader audience and enhance engagement without losing the immediacy of the guided writing experience?

Strategy Instruction During Word Study and Interactive Writing Activities

Cheri Williams and Ruth P. Lundstrom

Strategy instruction has received consider-able attention recently in the professional literature. A host of textbooks written especially for classroom teachers (e.g., Almasi, 2003; Fountas & Pinnell, 2006; Harvey & Goudvis, 2000; McEwan, 2004; Miller, 2002) as well as a number of research articles (e.g., De la Paz & Graham, 2002; James, Abbott, & Greenwood, 2001; Schorzman & Cheek, 2004; Smith, 2006) call for explicit strategy instruc-tion throughout the literacy program. Teachers are encouraged to arm students with a variety of strategic tools that support fluent reading and writing. This is especially important for children who experience difficulty in learning to read and write. Providing effective instruction early on will go a long way in ameliorating their literacy problems (see Graham & Harris, 2002).

As experienced teachers of young children, we know the importance of teaching every stu-dent to read and write strategically. We also know that explicitly teaching a series of strat-egies may not be enough to enable students to use those tools independently and productively. We found this to be the case when we examined primary-grade students' independent use of spe-cific spelling strategies we had taught. The chil-dren easily used the strategies to spell unfamiliar words during teacher-directed games and activi-ties, but they rarely did so when writing indepen-dently (Williams & Phillips-Birdsong, 2006). We realized that in addition to explicit instruc-tion, the students also needed guided practice in applying those strategies to extended writing. So, we designed a follow-up study that investigated explicit strategy instruction paired with guided practice in using those strategies during authen-tic writing activities. In this article, we report the results of that second project and discuss the implications of our findings for primary-grade literacy instruction.

Background of the Study

Ruth is an experienced first-grade teacher with a master's degree in literacy education and Reading Recovery training. She teaches Reading Recovery and Title I (a federally funded program for at-risk students) reading in a U.S. school dis-trict near the large urban university where Cheri teaches. This study began as a teacher researcher assignment but eventually grew into a collabora-tive research project.

We conducted our investigation with one of Ruth's Title I reading groups—six first graders who were struggling with learning to read and write. Ruth met with the children every day for 30 minutes. On Monday, she devoted the entire time to explicit word study instruction. On Tuesday through Friday, she spent the first 10 minutes focused on word study and the remaining 20 minutes on guided reading instruction. Twice a month, Ruth used the 30-minute time slot for an interactive writing lesson. This arrangement provided an authentic context for our investiga-tion; it allowed us to examine explicit strategy instruction during word study as well as the ways in which Ruth scaffolded the children's use of those strategies during the interactive writing lessons. We also examined whether the students

Reprinted from Williams, C., & Lundstrom, R.P. (2007). Strategy instruction during word study and interactive writing activities. *The Reading Teacher, 61*(3), 204-212.

subsequently used the strategies to spell unfamiliar words while writing in their journals. We asked three specific questions:

1. Which spelling strategies were taught during the daily word study lessons?

2. How did the teacher researcher scaffold the children's use of those strategies during interactive writing events?

3. Which spelling strategies did the children use to spell unfamiliar words while writing in their journals in the regular first-grade classroom?

Theoretical Framework

We grounded our work in Wertsch's (1998) concept of mediated action and Rogoff's (1990) theory of cognitive development as an apprenticeship. Mediated action focuses on the ways in which learners interact with specific cultural tools. Cultural tools can be physical objects (e.g., pens, rulers, computers) as well as cognitive processes. Wertsch suggested that as students interact with cultural tools they learn to use them with facility and may eventually appropriate these tools for their own purposes. This framework was helpful to us because we view word study as a set of cultural tools that students can use to mediate spelling, both during spelling activities and extended writing events.

Rogoff (1990) suggested that learners appropriate the use of specific cultural tools through apprenticeship—by participating in activities with adults and more experienced peers who scaffold the learner's understanding of and skill in using particular cultural tools. We believed that interactive writing could provide an authentic and meaningful apprenticeship in the use of word study as a cultural tool, and we designed our project to examine this assumption.

Relevant Research Literature

We also grounded our investigation in the available research on word study instruction and interactive writing. Word study is a relatively new approach to spelling instruction that focuses on active exploration of the principles of English orthography (Bear, Invernizzi, Templeton, & Johnston, 2004). Teachers engage students in a variety of hands-on activities that help them to discover the regularities, patterns, and derivations in English words. The approach was important to this project because it also involves explicit strategy instruction; teachers purposefully teach a variety of strategies that students can use to spell (or read) unfamiliar words.

Word study is described in detail in a number of professional textbooks (e.g., Bear et al., 2004; Cunningham & Hall, 1994; Pinnell & Fountas, 1998) and myriad articles describe word study games and activities (e.g., Aiken & Bayer, 2002; Barnes, 1989; Fresch, 2000; Invernizzi, Abouzeid, & Bloodgood, 1997; Johnston, 1999; Zutell, 1998). But surprisingly little research is available that examines the impact of word study on students' writing. When we searched the research literature, we located several projects that investigated word study and children's spelling achievement (Abbott, 2001; Brandt & Gielbelhaus, 2000; Joseph, 2000; Sabey, 1999) as well as their word-level reading development (Carlisle, 2000; Joseph & McCachran, 2003; Lovett, 1999; Rasinski & Oswald, 2005; White, 2005). But, to date, we have identified only one investigation that specifically addressed word study and young children's writing (Dahl et al., 2004). The study was particularly relevant because the researchers examined children's use of the spelling strategies that had been taught during word study instruction.

Dahl and colleagues (2004) asked students to circle in their writing the words "they really had to think about" (p. 311) and then to describe, retrospectively, the strategies they had used to spell those words. Students' strategy use was also examined in process, with researchers interviewing children as they were writing. Results of the project indicated that children self-reported using multiple strategies to spell single words and that students' strategy use differed across developmental stages. The researchers argued for explicit strategy instruction during word study lessons as well as teacher demonstrations of strategy use during daily writing activities. They also recommended that teachers hold conferences with students who do not appear to connect word study concepts to their own writing.

Interactive writing is an approach to beginning writing instruction in which a teacher and group of children coconstruct an oral message and then "share the pen" to get that message into print (Pinnell & McCarrier, 1994, p. 159). The teacher scaffolds the children's participation in the writing event, helping students to use the conventions of print—space, direction, capitalization, punctuation—to make the text readable. Throughout the activity, students have opportunities to write words they do not know how to spell, and the teacher scaffolds their use of specific spelling strategies and orthographic patterns they have learned (Lyons & Pinnell, 2003). The goal of the activity is to teach students the letter–sound relationships, concepts about print, writing conventions, and spelling strategies they need to become competent, independent writers (McCarrier, Pinnell, & Fountas, 2000).

Button, Johnson, and Furgerson (1996) conducted one of two published studies that examined the efficacy of interactive writing as an instructional approach. At the beginning of their kindergarten year, Furgerson assessed her students' literacy knowledge and behaviors using Clay's (1993) Observation Survey. Students' scores served as a pretest measure and provided important information for literacy instruction. Initially, Furgerson directed most aspects of the interactive writing lesson, but as the year progressed she gradually released responsibility while scaffolding the children's participation in the writing event. The researchers observed growth in the children's phonemic awareness, use of letter–sound correspondences, and print conventions. Students' posttest results on the Observation Survey also indicated considerable progress, particularly on the Hearing Sounds in Words test.

In a more recent study, Craig (2003) compared the effects of "interactive writing-plus" to "metalinguistic games-plus" on kindergarten children's phonological awareness, alphabet knowledge, and early reading development. The "plus" component of each approach was supplemental letter–sound instruction. The 87 children who participated in the study were randomly assigned to small intervention groups and received instruction from literacy teachers outside their regular classroom for 20 minutes 4 times each week for 16 weeks. While no differences were found between groups for phonological awareness or spelling, results of the project indicated that children in the interactive writing-plus group outperformed children in the metalinguistic games-plus group on word identification, passage comprehension, and word reading development.

Both of these studies demonstrated the efficacy of interactive writing as an instructional approach, but neither study addressed students' extended writing. That is not altogether surprising, as both projects were conducted in kindergarten classrooms. Our investigation goes one step further by examining the efficacy of interactive writing for supporting young children's writing development.

Methods

To achieve our research purposes, we used a qualitative approach to data collection and analysis (Bogdan & Biklen, 1982; Miles & Huberman, 1984). In her role as teacher researcher, Ruth collected all of the data for our study from October 15 through May 10. She gathered five kinds of evidence: (1) daily lesson plans, (2) reflective notes following the daily lessons, (3) in-process and postlesson field notes on bimonthly interactive writing activities, (4) field notes on weekly observations of the children during journal writing in their regular first-grade classroom, and (5) photocopies of the children's journal entries for each observation. Ruth photocopied the entire data corpus and sent a copy to Cheri, who, in her role as university collaborator, assisted with data analysis.

Patton (2002) suggested that important insights can surface when two researchers examine the same set of data, so we analyzed the data separately. We followed specific steps we had outlined in advance, using techniques borrowed from content analysis (Krippendorff, 1980;

Weber, 1990). First, we systemically reviewed Ruth's lesson plans and postlesson reflective notes and teased out the specific spelling strategies she had taught. We listed each strategy on a Spelling Strategies Chart and noted the date of instruction as well as any review lessons. Our second step was to analyze the data collected during interactive writing. We reviewed Ruth's field notes and identified her prompting and scaffolding of each student. We created six coding sheets—one for each student—and listed each prompt or scaffold on the left side of the student coding sheet by date. We then teased out the students' overt responses and recorded those on the right side of the student coding sheet. For example, on April 19, when Brad (all children's names are pseudonyms) was struggling to write the word *bad*, Ruth prompted him to "Say the word slowly and listen for the sounds" he could hear. We recorded her prompt on the left side of Brad's coding sheet next to the date. Then, on the right side, we coded Brad's response, noting that he said, "/b/.../æ/.../d/" and wrote *BAD* on the interactive writing chart. The third step in our analysis was to systemically examine Ruth's field notes on journal writing to document students' overt use of the spelling strategies that were taught. Again, we created six coding sheets. Each time Ruth's field notes indicated that a student had used a spelling strategy we coded this behavior on his or her sheet. On February 27, for example, when Andrew was trying to write the word *last*, Ruth heard him say, "/l/.../æ/.../s/.../t/, like *fast*." We coded this overt behavior as his use of two strategies, "Say the word slowly and listen for the sounds you hear," and "Think of a word you know that rhymes with the word you're trying to spell."

When our individual analyses of the data were complete, we compared them and found that our coding was strikingly similar. From our coding scheme we moved to major categories (see Strauss & Corbin, 1990). We determined that the spelling strategies Ruth taught and subsequently scaffolded fell into two broad categories. We named these Tools of the Trade and Tools of the Mind to reflect the nature of the strategic behavior involved. Establishing these two categories provided a framework within which we determined the final outcomes of our project. In the sections that follow, we describe those outcomes. We begin with a brief description of Ruth's word study lessons, and then we turn to the strategic behaviors that were taught, prompted, and learned.

Lesson Format

Ruth's daily word study instruction reflected the general format, procedures, and activities recommended in Pinnell and Fountas's (1998) *Word Matters*, but the scope and sequence of her instruction were constrained by the need to follow her district's required spelling list. While the district's goal was memorization of specific words, Ruth's objective was for students to learn *about* words; that is, to understand how English words work. Each week, as she taught the required spelling words, she made explicit the ways in which specific orthographic features of those words could be used to read and spell other words. On November 5, for example, when Ruth introduced the required spelling word *away*, she highlighted the *ay* spelling pattern and connected it to the word *play*, which she had introduced and displayed on the word wall on October 15. She reminded the children of a relevant spelling strategy she had previously taught: "Remember that when you're trying to spell a new word, you can look for a word on the word wall that will help you." Then, she gave the children dry erase boards and they used the *ay* pattern to generate a number of rhyming words (e.g., *day, may, say, way, stay, clay, tray*). Ruth then explicitly taught another relevant strategy, "When you're trying to spell a new word, think of a word you know that rhymes with the word you're trying to spell," and she related this new strategy to the day's activities.

Each word study lesson followed this general format, and, across the academic year, Ruth covered the district's mandated spelling curriculum (144 Dolch words), focused the children's attention on many orthographic patterns that could be generalized widely to their reading and writing, and explicitly taught a number of strategies the children could use to "solve the spelling" of unfamiliar words.

Tools of the Trade and Tools of the Mind

Our analysis revealed that Ruth explicitly taught 10 spelling strategies during word study instruction. While each strategy involved cognitive processing, four strategies required the use of a physical cultural tool to mediate the strategic behavior. We categorized these as Tools of the Trade:

1. Look for the word on the word wall.
2. Find a word on the word wall that will help you (*could* → *should*).
3. Look for the word in your dictionary.
4. Look for the word in print around the classroom.

We categorized the remaining strategies as Tools of the Mind:

5. Say the word slowly and listen for the sounds you hear.
6. Think about different spelling patterns that can spell the sound you hear (*ou*t vs. d*ow*n).
7. Say the word slowly and listen for any parts you know how to spell (*and* in *candy*).
8. Think about the word in your head. Can you "see" the word?
9. Think of a word you already know how to spell that will help you spell this word.
10. Think of a word you know that rhymes with the word you're trying to spell.

Ruth reviewed these strategies regularly across the academic year. In each word study lesson, she engaged the children in games and activities that required them to apply particular strategies to "solve the spelling" of sample words that reflected specific orthographic principles.

Prompting With a Purpose

One of the primary functions of an interactive writing lesson is to provide meaningful opportunities for students to figure out or solve the spelling of the words to be written. Word solving engages students in strategic behavior as they consider and apply specific orthographic principles and spelling strategies they have learned (Lyons & Pinnell, 2003; Pinnell & Fountas, 1998). Our analysis of the data for interactive writing revealed a myriad of opportunities for students to solve words and highlighted the ways in which Ruth scaffolded their ability to do so.

During the 15 interactive writing lessons, Ruth prompted strategic behavior 61 times. Slightly more than half of her prompts (38) encouraged students to use Tools of the Mind, particularly "Listen for the sounds you hear" (prompted most often in the beginning of the year) and "Listen for a part you know" (prompted most often later in the year). The following excerpts from our data analysis are illustrative:

November 16
Ben is trying to write the word *dog*.
Ruth draws Elkonin boxes on a practice sheet and prompts him: "Say the word slowly and listen for the sounds you hear."
He does so and writes the letters in the boxes. Then, he spells the word correctly in the story.

March 1
Hannah is trying to write the word *didn't*.
Ruth prompts, "Say it slowly and listen for a part you know."
Hannah says the word slowly and then writes *DID* on the paper.

It is interesting that Ruth's third most frequent prompt encouraged students to use their knowledge of word wall words (that is, their spelling words) in conjunction with another strategy. Students either knew how to spell these words or could easily find them on the word wall, as the following examples demonstrate:

February 15
Matt is trying to spell the word *let*.
Ruth prompts, "That word rhymes with the word wall word *get*."

Matt looks for *get* on the word wall and uses it to spell *let*.

March 22
Andrew is trying to spell the word *under*.
Ruth prompts, "Can you think of any other words that are like this word? Like the word wall word *her*?"
Andrew knows the word *her* and so he spells *under* correctly.

May 10
Brad is trying to write the word *frightened*.
Ruth prompts, "Listen for the first part. It begins like a word wall word."
Brad finds *from* on the word wall and uses it to write *fr* on the paper.

The students' responses to Ruth's prompts demonstrated their understanding and their ability to act on her scaffolding. Our data indicated that for every teacher prompt, the student successfully spelled the word or word part in question. On at least one occasion, a student's oral response made her cognitive processing transparent to Ruth and to her peers:

May 3
Caroline is trying to write the word *diver*.
Ruth prompts, "Say it slowly and listen for a part you know."
Caroline says the word slowly and then says, "The end is like the word wall word *under*," and she spells *diver* correctly.

As an experienced teacher, Ruth was careful to provide sufficient wait time for students to enact strategic behavior on their own. Her instructional decision making proved fruitful because on 23 occasions students used the spelling strategies independently—without teacher prompting—as they "shared the pen." The most common strategy observed was checking the word wall (11 times), but students also said words slowly to listen for sounds (5 times) or for parts they knew (5 times). The following excerpts illustrate the children's independent, strategic behavior during the interactive writing lessons:

February 8
Caroline is trying to spell the word *helps*.

She looks over at the word wall and searches under the *H* column until she finds the word. She writes it correctly and adds the final *s*.

April 26
Andrew is trying to write the word *street*.
He says the word slowly and writes *stret* on the paper.
Ruth praises him for using a spelling strategy and then adds, "The /ē/ in *street* is spelled like the word wall word *see*."
They use correction tape, and Andrew spells the word with *ee*.

April 26
Brad is spelling the word *car*.
He says, "*Car* starts like the word *can* but ends with *ar*."
He writes the word correctly.

May 3
Hannah is writing the word *thing*.
She says, "I know two parts to that word, *th* and *ing*."
She spells the word correctly.

These overt, independent uses of the spelling strategies Ruth had taught demonstrated the children's appropriation of particular cultural tools—both Tools of the Mind and Tools of Trade. Moreover, as the children used the strategies independently, they were, in essence, modeling strategic behavior for their peers.

A third finding surfaced as we analyzed the data for interactive writing: The children were learning their spelling words. As they took their turns at the chart, the students independently spelled correctly 36 of the spelling words Ruth had taught during the daily word study lessons (e.g., *my, like, is, and, she, was, we, too, of, for, with, got, want*). The students may have used specific strategies covertly to spell these words, but we suspect mastery came through repeated word study and guided reading instruction. An added benefit, then, of interactive writing was the opportunity it afforded the students to use the spelling words they were learning.

Taking Tools to Task

A primary goal of early writing instruction is to arm students with the tools they need to become independent, fluent, and confident writers. Our analysis of the data for journal writing suggests that these six struggling learners appropriated a number of the tools that were taught. The most frequently observed strategy was "Look on the word wall" (34 times). This did not surprise us, as Tools of the Trade are far more observable than Tools of the Mind. Nor were we surprised to learn that students used the word wall in conjunction with other strategies. On November 26, for example, when Ben was trying to spell the word *because*, he said the word slowly and isolated the parts *be* and *cause*, and then he looked on the word wall for *be*. On April 24, when Hannah wanted to write the word *fun*, she said the word slowly and isolated all three sounds, and then she checked the word wall, presumably to confirm the spelling of the vowel.

Ruth also observed the children using Tools of the Mind to mediate their spelling. She heard students listening for sounds (2 times), listening for parts they knew (3 times), using a known word (4 times), and saying words that rhymed with the words they wanted to spell (8 times). Ruth often heard the children combining strategies as they wrote in their journals. The following examples are illustrative:

> *February 27*
> Matt is trying to spell the word *something*. He breaks it into the syllables *some* and *thing* and then says, "I know how to spell *some* and *ing*."

> *March 22*
> Hannah wants to write the word *sister*. She says, "*Sister* ends like the words *her* and *under.*"

> *March 22*
> Caroline is trying to spell the word *boring*. She says the word slowly and isolates the parts *bor* and *ing*," and then says, "Like the word *for* with *ing*.

> *March 25*
> Brad is trying to spell the word *fun*. He says it slowly, articulating each sound, and then says, "That's part of *funny*."

Unlike the researchers in the Dahl et al. (2004) study, Ruth was not at liberty to talk with the children as they worked; as a consequence, we could not investigate their covert strategy use. Moreover, she was able to observe the children only once each week. We suspect our findings may not reflect the degree to which the students appropriated the spelling strategies that were taught.

Our analysis of the students' journal entries, however, provided convincing evidence that many of the spelling words had become a part of the children's writing vocabularies. Word learning was not a focus of this investigation, but when our data for interactive writing suggested that the children were learning the spelling words, we decided to examine the photocopies of their journal entries. We recorded 53 different correctly spelled spelling words—with multiple repetitions of each. It was clear that the children had learned many of the spelling words that were taught.

Embrace Word Study and Interactive Writing Instruction

Young children's early writing development is strongly related to their later literacy success (Juel, 1988). It is crucial that we identify instructional approaches and techniques that are effective with beginning writers. The design of our study cannot presume cause and effect, but our results clearly point to the efficacy of both word study and interactive writing instruction for *supporting* young children's spelling growth and, ultimately, their early writing development. We believe both of these instructional activities should be key components of a comprehensive literacy program for beginning learners, and especially for those who find literacy learning difficult.

Word study in this project went well beyond typical spelling instruction. The daily word study lessons not only provided opportunities for Ruth to teach the required spelling words, but also she was able to make explicit the ways in which specific orthographic features of those words generalized to other words. And she taught a variety of fundamental spelling strategies. We know that explicit and systematic strategy instruction can improve young children's writing performance (Beal, Garrod, & Bonitatibus, 1990; Harris, Graham, & Mason, 2006), and, while we did not examine the children's use of specific orthographic features, our findings clearly demonstrate that the students learned and used a number of the spelling words and spelling strategies that were taught. We recommend that primary-grade teachers embrace a word study approach to spelling instruction (even if they are required to teach a prescribed list of words) because it supports word solving in addition to word learning (Pinnell & Fountas, 1998).

Word solving strategies took two forms, Tools of the Mind and Tools of Trade, and our findings support the teaching of both. Ruth's students used physical cultural tools as well as mental cultural tools to mediate their spelling (Wertsch, 1998). Tools of the Trade can be made readily available to students in school settings, and these tools—especially the word wall—provide strong support for early word learning. Tools of the Mind are not dependent on the physical artifacts of schooling and thus lead to greater independence. Teachers may want to emphasize these strategies once students have developed some competence with Tools of the Trade. Our study certainly provides support for a combined approach, teaching, for example, the ways in which a child can listen for sounds in the word he or she is trying to write and then confirm the spelling in a dictionary.

Interactive writing proved effectual in at least three ways. We mentioned earlier that students had many opportunities to use their spelling words during interactive writing activities. This additional practice helped the students to learn the required words. What was more important was that interactive writing provided guided practice in strategic word solving behavior. Each interactive writing lesson called upon the students to apply the spelling strategies they had learned. If they needed assistance, Ruth provided it. As the students worked at the chart to solve the spelling of specific words, they engaged in a cognitive task that was considerably more demanding than that of the word study games and activities. They were solving the spelling of words as they were writing continuous text, which is exactly what students must do during independent writing activities. This guided practice paid off: Students gradually appropriated a number of strategic tools and used them independently both during group writing events as well as while writing in their journals (Rogoff, 1990; Vygotsky, 1934/1978; Wertsch, 1985, 1991). Finally, and equally important, interactive writing made transparent the link between word study and writing. As the students participated in the interactive writing lessons, specific features common to word study and to writing became clear and made the children's knowledge and strategies relevant (Rogoff, Radziszewska, & Masiello, 1995). When students recognize the relationship between instructional activities, they are more likely to apply the knowledge and skills they learned in one context to the other (Vygotsky, 1934/1978).

We recommend that primary-grade teachers embrace interactive writing as a powerful context for guided practice with strategic cultural tools and also as an instructional activity that will build a bridge between word study lessons and students' independent writing endeavors. Word study provides opportunities for children to apply spelling strategies to isolated words, but interactive writing engages students in word solving behaviors in the midst of authentic composition, which better prepares them for independent writing. The children who participated in our project were struggling writers. Pairing word study lessons with interactive writing activities successfully supported their appropriation of specific cultural tools that they eventually used to accomplish their own purposes during journal writing in their regular classroom. We believe this kind of success at school writing tasks builds confidence as well as motivation (Gaskill & Murphy, 2004; Graham, Harris, & Mason, 2005; Morrow & Sharkey, 1993)—key factors in learning, especially for children who find literacy learning difficult.

References

Abbott, M. (2001). Effects of traditional versus extended word-study spelling instruction on students' orthographic knowledge. *Reading Online, 5*(3). Retrieved May 21, 2002, from www.readingonline.org/articles/art_index.asp?HREF=abbott/ index.html

Aiken A., & Bayer, L. (2002). They love words. *The Reading Teacher, 56*, 68–74.

Almasi, J. (2003). *Teaching strategic processes in reading.* New York: Guilford.

Barnes, W. (1989). Word sorting: The cultivation of rules for spelling in English. *Reading Psychology, 10*, 293–307.

Beal, C., Garrod, A., & Bonitatibus, G. (1990). Fostering children's revision skills through training in comprehension monitoring. *Journal of Educational Psychology, 82*, 275–280.

Bear, D., Invernizzi, M., Templeton, S., & Johnston, F. (2004). *Words their way: Word study for phonics, vocabulary, and spelling instruction* (3rd ed.). Upper Saddle River, NJ: Prentice-Hall.

Bogdan, R.C., & Biklen, S.K. (1982). *Qualitative research for education: An introduction to theory and methods.* Boston: Allyn & Bacon.

Brandt, T., & Gielbelhaus, C. (2000, October). *Word study and spelling achievement.* Paper presented at the annual meeting of the Mid-Western Educational Research Association, Chicago, IL.

Button, K., Johnson, M., & Furgerson, P. (1996). Interactive writing in a primary classroom. *The Reading Teacher, 49*, 446–454.

Carlisle, J.F. (2000). Awareness of the structure and meaning of morphologically complex words: Impact on reading. *Reading and Writing: An Interdisciplinary Journal, 12*, 169–190.

Clay, M.M. (1993). *An observation survey of early literacy achievement.* Portsmouth, NH: Heinemann.

Craig, S.A. (2003). The effects of an adapted interactive writing intervention on kindergarten children's phonological awareness, spelling, and early reading development. *Reading Research Quarterly, 38*, 438–440.

Cunningham, P., & Hall, D. (1994). *Making words: Multilevel, hands on, developmentally appropriate spelling and phonics activities.* Parsippany, NJ: Good Apple.

Dahl, K., Barto, A., Bonfils, A., Carasello, M., Christopher, J., Davis, R., et al. (2004). Connecting developmental word study with classroom writing: Children's descriptions of spelling strategies. *The Reading Teacher, 57*, 310–319.

De la Paz, S., & Graham, S. (2002). Explicitly teaching strategies, skills, and knowledge: Writing instruction in middle school classrooms. *Journal of Educational Psychology, 94*, 687–698.

Fountas, I., & Pinnell, G.S. (2006). *Teaching for comprehending and fluency: Thinking, talking, and writing about reading, K–8.* Portsmouth, NH: Heinemann.

Fresch, M.J. (2000). What we learned from Josh: Sorting out word sorting. *Language Arts, 77*, 232–240.

Gaskill, P., & Murphy, K. (2004). Effects of a memory strategy on second-graders' performance and self-efficacy. *Contemporary Educational Psychology, 29*, 27–49.

Graham, S., & Harris, K.R. (2002). Prevention and intervention for struggling writers. In M. Shinn, H. Walker, & G. Stone (Eds.), *Interventions for academic and behavior problems II: Preventive and remedial approaches* (pp. 589–610). Bethesda, MD: National Association of School Psychologists.

Graham, S., Harris, K., & Mason, L. (2005). Improving the writing performance, knowledge, and motivation of struggling young writers: The effects of self-regulated strategy development. *Contemporary Educational Psychology, 30*, 207–241.

Harris, K., Graham, S., & Mason, L. (2006). Improving the writing, knowledge, and motivation of struggling young writers: Effects of self-regulated strategy development with and without peer support. *American Educational Research Journal, 43*, 295–337.

Harvey, S., & Goudvis, A. (2000). *Strategies that work: Teaching comprehension to enhance understanding.* Portland, ME: Stenhouse.

Invernizzi, M., Abouzeid, M., & Bloodgood, J. (1997). Integrated word study: Spelling, grammar, and meaning in the language arts classroom. *Language Arts, 74*, 185–192.

James, L.A., Abbott, M., & Greenwood, C. (2001). How Adam became a writer: Winning writing strategies for low-achieving students. *Teaching Exceptional Children, 33*(3), 30–37.

Johnston, F. (1999). The timing and teaching of word families. *The Reading Teacher, 53*, 64–75.

Joseph, L.M. (2000). Developing first graders' phonemic awareness, word identification and spelling: A comparison of two contemporary phonic instructional approaches. *Reading Research and Instruction, 39*, 160–169.

Joseph, L.M., & McCachran, M. (2003). Comparison of a work study phonics technique between students with moderate to mild mental retardation and struggling readers without disabilities. *Education and Training in Developmental Disabilities, 38*, 192–199.

Juel, C. (1988). Learning to read and write: A longitudinal study of 54 children from first through fourth grades. *Journal of Educational Psychology, 80*, 437–447.

Krippendorff, K. (1980). *Content analysis: An introduction to its methodology.* Thousand Oaks, CA: Sage.

Lovett, M.W. (1999). Defining and remediating the core deficits of developmental dyslexia: Lessons from remedial outcome research with reading disabled children. In R.M. Klein & P. McMullen (Eds.), *Converging methods for understanding reading dyslexia* (pp. 111–132). Cambridge, MA: MIT Press.

Lyons, C., & Pinnell, G.S. (2003). Reading and writing and reassessment. *Journal of Staff Development, 24*(2), 23–31.

McCarrier, A., Pinnell, G.S., & Fountas, I.C. (2000). *Interactive writing: How language and literacy come together, K–2*. Portsmouth, NH: Heinemann.

McEwan, E.K. (2004). *Seven strategies of highly effective readers: Using cognitive research to boost K–8 achievement*. Thousand Oaks, CA: Corwin Press.

Miles, M., & Huberman, A.M. (1984). *Qualitative data analysis: A sourcebook of new methods*. Thousand Oaks, CA: Sage.

Miller, D. (2002). *Reading with meaning: Teaching comprehension in the primary grades*. Portland, ME: Stenhouse.

Morrow, L.M., & Sharkey, E.A. (1993). Motivating independent reading and writing in the primary grades through social cooperative literacy experiences. *The Reading Teacher, 47*, 162–165.

Patton, M.Q. (2002). *Qualitative evaluation and research methods* (3rd ed.). Thousand Oaks, CA: Sage.

Pinnell, G.S., & Fountas, I.C. (1998). *Word matters: Teaching phonics and spelling in the reading/writing classroom*. Portsmouth, NH: Heinemann.

Pinnell, G.S., & McCarrier, A. (1994). Interactive writing: A transition tool for assisting children in learning to read and write. In E. Hiebert & B. Taylor (Eds.), *Getting reading right from the start: Effective early literacy interventions* (pp. 149–170). Boston: Allyn & Bacon.

Rasinski, T., & Oswald, R. (2005). Making and writing words: Constructivist word learning in a second-grade classroom. *Reading and Writing Quarterly, 21*, 151–163.

Rogoff, B. (1990). *Apprenticeship in thinking: Cognitive development in social context*. New York: Oxford University Press.

Rogoff, B., Radziszewska, B., & Masiello, T. (1995). Analysis of developmental processes in sociocultural activity. In L. Martin, K. Nelson, & E. Tobach (Eds.), *Sociocultural psychology: Theory and practice of doing and knowing* (pp. 125–149). New York: Cambridge University Press.

Sabey, B. (1999). Metacognitive responses of an intermediate speller while performing three literacy tasks. *Journal of Literacy Research, 31*, 415–455.

Schorzman, E., & Cheek, E. (2004). Structured strategy instruction: Investigating an intervention for improving sixth-graders' reading comprehension. *Reading Psychology, 25*, 37–60.

Smith, L.A. (2006). Think-aloud mysteries: Using structured, sentence-by-sentence text passages to teach comprehension strategies. *The Reading Teacher, 59*, 764–773.

Strauss, A., & Corbin, J. (1990). *Basics of qualitative research: Grounded theory procedures and techniques*. Thousand Oaks, CA: Sage.

Vygotsky, L.S. (1978). *Mind in society: The development of higher psychological processes* (M. Cole, V. John-Steiner, S. Scribner, & E. Souberman, Eds. & Trans.). Cambridge, MA: Harvard University Press. (Original work published 1934)

Weber, R.P. (1990). *Basic content analysis* (2nd ed.). Newbury Park, CA: Sage.

Wertsch, J.V. (1985). *Vygotsky and the social formation of mind*. Cambridge, MA: Harvard University Press.

Wertsch, J.V. (1991). *Voices of the mind: A sociocultural approach to mediated action*. Cambridge, MA: Harvard University Press.

Wertsch, J.V. (1998). *Mind as action*. New York: Oxford University Press.

White, T. (2005). Effects of systematic and strategic analogy-based phonics on grade 2 students' word reading and reading comprehension. *Reading Research Quarterly, 40*, 234–255.

Williams, C., & Phillips-Birdsong, C. (2006). Word study instruction and second-grade children's independent writing. *Journal of Literacy Research, 38*, 427–465.

Zutell, J. (1998). Word sorting: A developmental spelling approach to word study for delayed readers. *Reading and Writing Quarterly: Overcoming Learning Difficulties, 14*, 219–238.

Questions for Reflection

• This study involved struggling learners, but many of the instructional techniques it describes could be used with other groups of children. What might Tools of the Trade and Tools of the Mind look like for English-language learners? For gifted students? For the full range of young writers you have in your classroom?

• Scaffolding is an important part of the instructional approach described in this article. How aware are you of your own use of scaffolding? How do your students respond to your scaffolding? Are they successfully internalizing the strategies you teach? Consider asking a colleague to observe your teaching over the course of a few days, and then trade places so you can observe your colleague's teaching for a similar period. Then, meet to discuss what you noticed and how your teaching practice might change as a result.

What's Your News? Portraits of a Rich Language and Literacy Activity for English-Language Learners

Patrick C. Manyak

David stretches his hand high above his head, anxious to ask Jesus a question. (All teacher and student names are pseudonyms.) Ms. Page's combination first- and second-grade class has just read the "news" that Jesus narrated earlier to a pair of peer "reporters." The story dealt with a particularly gory eye gouging: Jesus's father, a landscaper, had been hit in the eye by a stick while trimming some trees. David, motioning as if pulling out his eyeballs, asks enthusiastically, "*¿Tu papá, se le salían así los ojos?*" (Your dad, did his eyes pop out like this?) Jesus, pointing to his right eye, responds with equal enthusiasm, "*No. ¡No más este!*" (No, only this one!)

During two years of research in two U.S. primary-grade English immersion classes of Spanish-dominant Latino students, I frequently observed this type of fervent engagement in the classroom activity known as daily news. During each day's production and sharing of the news, the students eagerly related, scribed, edited, read, and, as in the case above, negotiated understandings of the events that filled their lives outside of school. Furthermore, the activity created an ideal context for the teachers, Ms. Page and Mr. Grant, to foster the students' language development, provide explicit instruction and meaningful practice in various writing skills, and produce supplemental reading texts that captured the children's interest. Given the fact that literacy instruction for English-language learners (ELLs) tends to focus on drill and practice of decontextualized skills (Fitzgerald, 1995; Gutiérrez, 2001; Neufeld & Fitzgerald, 2001), daily news stood out as a meaning-centered instructional activity that drew on students' diverse language resources and created space in the classroom for their unique out-of-school experiences. Consequently, I consider daily news, as I observed it in Ms. Page and Mr. Grant's classrooms, a valuable example of rich language and literacy instruction for ELL students. In this article I use transcripts of actual classroom interactions to create detailed portraits of key aspects of daily news. These portraits provide concrete examples of the type of principles for teaching ELL students that are often presented in abstract, summary, or hypothetical fashion (Fitzgerald, 1993; Lenters, 2004; Mohr, 2004).

In the following section, I provide a backdrop for understanding the dynamics of daily news by discussing important insights from previous research focusing on language and literacy instruction for linguistically diverse students. Next, I briefly describe the classes in which I conducted my studies. I then offer a series of glimpses into the nature of daily news in the two classrooms, calling attention to the ways that it facilitated the students' language and literacy learning. Finally, I conclude by highlighting the important lessons that this portrait of daily news offers with regard to constructing rich instruction for young ELLs.

Reprinted from Manyak, P.C. (2008). What's your news? Portraits of a rich language and literacy activity for English-language learners. *The Reading Teacher, 61*(6), 450-458.

Rich Instruction for Young English-Language Learners

Recent research has demonstrated that children can acquire initial literacy in a language they are just beginning to speak (Fitzgerald & Noblit, 1999; Geva & Zadeh, 2006; Lesaux & Siegel, 2003). Furthermore, several of these studies have shown that the basic processes of children learning to read in a second language parallel those of children learning to read in their first language, and that explicit instruction in phonemic awareness and word recognition is as crucial for ELLs as it is for young English-speaking children (Geva & Zadeh, 2006; Lesaux & Siegel, 2003). However, numerous scholars have stressed the importance of balancing such explicit, code-based instruction with rich instruction that fosters ELLs' oral language development, acknowledges their unique linguistic and cultural resources, and provides them with opportunities to interact with print in meaningful ways (Fitzgerald, 1993; Gutiérrez, 2001; Lenters, 2004; Lesaux & Siegel, 2003; Moll & González, 1994). Like these scholars, I believe that this type of rich language and literacy instruction is critical to ELLs' long-term reading achievement, to their development of a positive view toward their primary language and bilingualism, and to their appreciation of the value of literacy within their own social and cultural worlds. In the remainder of this section, I discuss three key themes that I have distilled from previous research on ELL instruction that provide a framework for understanding the special power of daily news as a language and literacy activity.

First, longstanding principles of second-language acquisition stress the critical nature of providing learners with comprehensible input in the target language and of scaffolding their output by providing consistent routines, frequent modeling, familiar and enjoyable topics for discussion, and feedback that causes learners to elaborate on their utterances (Ernst, 1994; Krashen, 1981; Wong-Fillmore, 1985). More recently, Toohey, Waterstone, and Jule-Lemke (2000) have employed the notion of carnival to depict another dimension of robust second-language learning environments. These authors used carnival to describe a classroom interaction that featured an informal tone, spontaneity and playfulness, and students' active participation. Although such a setting may not represent the full scope of instruction and practice necessary for effective second-language acquisition, robust environments do allow young ELLs to experiment in valuable ways with the forms and functions of and the speaking positions offered by the new language. Therefore, I suggest that powerful second-language instruction should provide ELL students with careful input, modeling, and feedback and foster carnivalesque interactions in which they can engage actively and playfully with the new language.

Second, a number of studies focused on classrooms with native Spanish-speaking students have documented the vibrant nature of instruction that recognizes bilingualism as an emblem of academic competence and fosters students' biliteracy development (Manyak, 2004; Moll & Dworin, 1996; Moll & Whitmore, 1993). For instance, in previous work, I described a primary-grade classroom in which young bilingual students frequently engaged in acts of translation during literacy activities (Manyak, 2004). By acting as translators, the students facilitated class literature discussions and demonstrated a special linguistic ability that captured the attention of their monolingual peers. Furthermore, many students composed bilingual books by translating stories written in one language into the other, a practice that led to simultaneous development of literacy in Spanish and English. These examples highlight the unique linguistic potential of ELL students and suggest the importance of using and extending this potential in the classroom.

Third, research has revealed that students from culturally and linguistically diverse families possess a wealth of cultural knowledge and experiences that can be used to enhance their literacy development (Moll & González, 1994). Instruction that brings together the official school curriculum and these students' out-of-school knowledge, activities, and purposes often generates deep engagement in significant meaning-making processes (Gutiérrez, Baquedano-López,

& Tejada, 1999). For instance, Moll and his colleagues (Moll, Amanti, Neff, & Gonzalez, 1992) documented the vast funds of knowledge, or "socially distributed cultural resources," possessed by Mexican immigrant families in Tucson, Arizona, and then worked together with teachers to create literacy instruction units that built on these funds of knowledge. These units produced dynamic contexts for students' literacy and content learning.

Taken together, these themes suggest the linguistic and literate potential of ELLs and underscore the multiple factors that teachers must consider when seeking to provide these students with rich instruction. I believe that daily news, as I documented it in Ms. Page and Mr. Grant's classrooms, represents an exemplary literacy activity that demonstrates how skillful teachers can simultaneously create the kind of interaction patterns important for second-language acquisition; acknowledge and use students' diverse linguistic and cultural resources; and provide meaningful, engaging, and instructive experiences with print.

The Research Settings and Method

My research in these two classrooms followed the passage of California's Proposition 227, the voter initiative that mandated English immersion schooling for the state's large number of ELL students. Early research revealed that this mandate was interpreted and implemented in widely divergent ways across and within districts and schools (García & Curry-Rodriguez, 2000). I specifically chose to study classes taught by former bilingual teachers who remained committed to valuing and using their students' knowledge of Spanish and to providing meaning-centered literacy activities. In particular, I sought to document literacy activities that allowed for students' full participation regardless of their level of English proficiency, created conditions for English language development, and effectively supported the students' initial steps toward literacy in two languages.

During the 1998–1999 school year I conducted research in Room 110, a first- and second-grade English immersion class at Adams School, and the following year I studied Room 12, a first-grade English immersion class at Foothill School. (All school names are pseudonyms.) The schools were both on the outskirts of Los Angeles and served large numbers of impoverished Latino students. Ms. Page, the teacher in Room 110, was a middle class white woman in her second year of teaching. She approached fluency in Spanish and had taught a bilingual K–1 class the previous year. Her class included 15 first-grade and 5 second-grade Latino students, all of whom spoke Spanish as their primary language and had little or no instruction in English literacy. Mr. Grant's first-grade English immersion class consisted of 20 Latino students whose home language was Spanish. Eighteen of the students had attended English immersion classes at Foothill School the previous year. Mr. Grant, a middle class white man, was fluent in Spanish and had taught in bilingual programs for five years prior to the advent of Proposition 227.

In order to richly describe the classroom communities, I used a qualitative approach to data collection and analysis. I made 165 research visits to the two classrooms. In both classes I acted as a participant-observer, typically sitting alongside the students, taking notes and asking simple questions while they worked on reading and writing activities. To supplement these observations, I also frequently audiotaped classroom literacy activities. My analysis of this data was ongoing during the collection phase in both studies. On a weekly basis I coded field notes and transcripts and used these codes to identify key themes that captured and explained the important storylines of the classroom instruction that I observed. In this article, I present findings detailing four such themes related to daily news.

An Overview of Daily News in Rooms 110 and 12

Although daily news occurred every morning in both classrooms, it is important to note that it was just one part of the teachers' comprehensive literacy instruction. Ms. Page and Mr. Grant each implemented versions of shared and guided reading, word study, interactive writing, writing workshop, and literature study units. Although there were a few subtle differences in the way that each class conducted daily news, the activity followed the same basic sequence in both classes. This was largely because I had recommended the activity as I had observed it in Ms. Page's room to Mr. Grant prior to my research in his classroom. During the first semester in each class, the teachers and the students met on the rug to write daily news together. The entire session typically lasted about 15 minutes. During the activity a pair of students volunteered to share news about events from their home or school lives and the teachers, after prompting the students to clarify and add detail to their narratives, scribed the stories on a large sheet of lined paper. As the teachers wrote, they called attention to particular spelling patterns and punctuation and frequently asked the students to participate by stretching out words and offering spelling suggestions. The class then read the news chorally. Although some of the volunteers shared their stories in Spanish, Ms. Page wrote in English, asking the students for help in translating their peers' words. Both teachers saved each day's version of daily news and, at the end of the month, bound them into a book that was added to the class library. At the beginning of the second semester, both teachers turned the task of writing the news over to the students. This evolution resulted from the children's growing competence as writers and the teachers' desire to, in Ms. Page's words, "let them take responsibility and to feel what it is like to be a writer."

The second stage of daily news provided the students with new and more central roles and responsibilities. Every morning at the beginning of the literacy block, the class helper-of-the-day chose a partner to share the job of reporter and two peers who served as news givers. The two student reporters then called back each news giver and scribed their narratives without the teachers' supervision. This part of the activity typically took about 15 minutes, during which time the classes continued with their introductory routines and moved on to their writing time. When the class reconvened on the rug at the end of their literacy block, the teachers briefly engaged the class in editing that day's news, and then the authors recopied the revised version for inclusion in the monthly volume. In both classes, the reporters were free to work in English or Spanish.

This sketch provides a skeletal outline of daily news, but it only hints at the rich tapestry of explicit instruction, scaffolding, collaboration, and playfulness that the event produced. In the following sections I flesh out this outline, presenting detailed portraits of the teachers and students' words and actions.

Scaffolding Participation and English-Language Development

During the first months of school, the teachers established the ground rules for daily news, teaching the children how to share and elaborate on their news, coaxing them to participate in a variety of ways, and fostering an enthusiasm for the event. For instance, Mr. Grant explained to the students several times that "we tell things that we've done, important or exciting things." Additionally, he encouraged the children's participation in translating and dictating their peers' narratives, offering spelling suggestions, and reading the finished news. For example, he often stopped the choral reading to remind the students, "I want to hear everybody reading." Both teachers also taught the students how to elaborate the important details of their experiences, frequently prompting them with who, when, where, and what questions. Along with this explicit instruction, the teachers encouraged the students' coparticipation in various phases of activity. For instance, the teachers used oral cloze as a strategy to involve the students in dictating the words of the news givers' narratives as they wrote. The children responded eagerly to this strategy, filling in the appropriate words whenever the teachers hesitated. In addition, the teachers regularly prompted the students to question the news givers about their news, to offer spelling suggestions during the scribing process, and to join in each day's choral reading of the news.

By allowing the students to share their news in Spanish, the teachers enabled even the most limited English-speaking students to participate in daily news. This situation also created conditions that benefited the students' acquisition of English. The teachers often used English to question students who then shared news in Spanish. On one typical occasion, I observed as Roberto shared in Spanish that his parents were buying him a skateboard. Ms. Page, indicating that she had not heard well, questioned him:

Transcript 1 (Manyak, 2001, p. 448)

Ms. Page: They are buying you it?

Roberto: *Sí.*

Ms. Page: Hey Roberto, are you going to wear a helmet, *un casco*, when you ride it?

Roberto nods.

Ms. Page: That's good. You wouldn't want to fall down and hit your head.

Roberto smiles and nods.

Because Ms. Page's questions and comments centered on the topic of Roberto's own narrative, they were comprehensible to him and he responded appropriately through gesture and Spanish. This form of teacher response exemplifies the condition known as semantic contingency. Semantic contingency is a key strategy for making language comprehensible to a learner, because the learners themselves establish the topic of conversation and thus have a clear sense of the meaning of a contingent response. Although semantically contingent talk appears to be somewhat rare in classrooms (Wells, 1986), daily news provided Ms. Page and Mr. Grant with many opportunities to prompt their students to elaborate on their self-chosen topics.

By encouraging the students to translate their own and their peers' Spanish narratives, Ms. Page also challenged them to produce comprehensible output in English. The translations often developed into a collaborative production in which their voices overlapped and inter-twined. This collaboration pushed the limits of the students' English, allowing them to perform beyond their individual levels of competence. For example, after Ana had shared in Spanish that she was going to the movies, Ms. Page challenged the students to act as translators.

Transcript 2 (Manyak, 2001, p. 444)

Ms. Page: Let's try to do that in English. Ana, can you help me out and think how to say that in English?

Ana shakes head, "no."

Karen raises her hand.

Ms. Page: Are you sure? Sandra.

Sandra: Ana went to a movie.

Karen: Is going to a movie.

Student 1: A movie.

Student 2: The movies.

Ms. Page: The movies. Which day is she going to the movies?

Students: *El sábado.*

Ms. Page: On Saturday. Ana is going to the movies on Saturday. OK, all eyes up here on the board. Ana, help me out with the words. (Ms. Page begins to write.)

This transcript demonstrates how the children built on one another's efforts to produce a translation. It also highlights how Ms. Page worked to scaffold the students' efforts by providing key phrases and weaving together the various contributions into sound grammatical utterances.

These brief examples illustrate some of the many ways that daily news provided developing bilingual students with opportunities to extend their English and to engage in sophisticated language practices like translation. Perhaps more important, they also suggest how even those students who knew little English were able to participate fully in the event, sharing news in Spanish and experimenting with English by mouthing words silently, imitating a peer, or interjecting a word or phrase during the translation, dictation, or choral reading.

Building Bridges and Creating Carnival

Because daily news revolved around episodes from the students' lives outside of school, it served to bridge home and school worlds. Ms. Page identified this as one of her main objectives for the activity, noting that it made experiences that occurred outside the school into topics that can be talked about in school. As a consequence of the union between the formal school curriculum and familiar world of the children, the activity prompted the children to weave reading and writing into the fabric of their daily lives. The exchange about Jesus's father's eye injury that opens this article demonstrates how the familiar content of the news captivated the children and frequently led to an enthusiastic negotiation of meaning. By sanctioning such subject matter as appropriate for classroom literacy tasks, daily news repositioned the children's sociocultural experience as a legitimate source of knowledge and demonstrated to them that literacy was an effective tool for recording and reflecting on their lived experience.

Furthermore, the activity was characterized by a particularly comfortable and lively atmosphere. The teachers clearly enjoyed and contributed to this atmosphere. For his part, Mr. Grant established a familiar and playful tone by offering humorous responses to the children's stories. For example, when Marisol shared that her mother was going to take her to Disneyland, Mr. Grant asked if she was "going to take the whole class?" This sense of familiarity and playfulness quickly permeated the practice of the daily news and intensified when the children began to write the news independently. As children in both classes worked on the news, they engaged in lively discourse saturated with humor and local knowledge. Even the students' physical positioning during the activity—they often sprawled on the table to get a good look at the scribe's work—testified to its unceremonious nature and, equally, to the children's intense engagement in it.

Fostering Productive Collaboration

From the outset, daily news was a highly interactive and collaborative activity. When the students took over the task of writing the news independently, I regularly observed them, without the teachers' supervision, engage in a dense, web-like pattern of collaboration. Their shared history with the activity appeared to guide them as they worked. The student reporters knew to begin by writing the title and date at the top of the page, to question the news givers in order to elicit more detailed accounts, and to use environmental print as a resource for spelling. For their part, the news givers spoke in phrases or dictated word by word so that the reporters could more easily record their narratives. Thus, although the students worked relatively independently, they evidenced a sense of commitment to producing the public document expected of them. This is not to say that disputes, teasing, and critiques of others' efforts did not occur. Still, the students' clear sense of their task and of the multiple ways to contribute to it tended to prompt quick and relatively equitable resolutions of conflict.

Every day, students helped their peers by guiding a hand to form letters correctly, stretching out syllables for the writer to hear the sounds, spelling out a word, pointing to necessary letters or words in environmental print, or taking the pen to write a difficult part of a word. Although struggling writers received a great deal of support from their partners, just as frequently the shifting patterns of collaboration placed such students in a position to provide expert help. The following excerpt from my field notes captures a typical moment in which assistance flowed in all directions during the composing of the news.

Field notes: Room 12

Edgar says, "I want to write, 'On the last day of this week, it's going to be my happy birthday.'" Yesenia shouts, "The date!" and puts the date on the top of the page. Sergio dictates the words for Marisol, stretching them out, "O-o-o-n. *La o*." Marisol writes, "On the *L*" and Edgar tells her to make "*la chiquita*" [the lower case *l*].... Marisol now writes Edgar's name. Yesenia runs to the name cards on the wall and shouts out the letters to Marisol, "*La g, la a, la r.*" [The *g*, the *a*, the *r*.] Edgar is also telling her the letters. Marisol writes *is* and then begins *going*. Edgar tells her, "That's the word!" after *go*. She says, "Going?" and completes the word. Yesenia writes her name at the bottom of the page. Marisol continues to write as the other two stretch out the words and suggest letters. Edgar then adds, "They are going to take me to Mountain Water." Marisol says, "*They*, I don't know how to write *they*." Edgar begins to spell it for her, "*T....*" A moment later Edgar turns to me and asks, "Mr. Manyak, how do you write Mountain Water?" I write out the words on a piece of paper, and Edgar spells it out for Marisol.

In this brief exchange Edgar shared news, corrected Marisol when she made an uppercase letter, and offered spelling support; Yesenia added the date, dictated a spelling using environmental print, and later scribed for the next news giver; and Marisol served as the scribe, disregarded Edgar's incorrect advice on *going*, and asked for his help on *they*. I was even called upon to contribute a difficult spelling to the group. The episode demonstrates the distributed nature of expertise that epitomized the writing of the daily news. During such interactions, no one student laid exclusive claim to a high ground of competence vis-à-vis his or her peers. As a result, the students appeared intensely engaged in the collaborative work, each waiting for opportunities to momentarily display their expertise.

Focusing on Writing

During the first stage of daily news, the event functioned as a shared writing experience. At this point, the teachers' objectives were, in Ms. Page's words, "to model the thought processes that occur while writing: the editing decisions, the connection between speech and the written word" and "to teach the school register, the formal speech that occurs at school: speaking loudly, clearly, giving details." As they scribed the students' news, the teachers modeled and commented upon numerous aspects of the composing process. This instruction was highly contingent on the text that they were writing and on the stu-

dents' comments and questions. For instance, on one occasion Marisol informed Mr. Grant that he had forgotten "the little mark" at the end of a sentence. Because the sentence was a question, Mr. Grant had used a question mark and he then discussed this usage.

When they took over the responsibility for writing the news, the students benefited from the focused writing practice and the satisfying experience of creating a document that had an ongoing and highly visible presence in the life of the class. In fact, the students reveled in fulfilling the reporter job. In a particularly poignant case, I observed Daniel, one of Mr. Grant's most reluctant writers, enthusiastically embrace the role of reporter. After successfully completing the news and boasting about how long it was, he raised his hand to be a reporter again the following day. When Edgar remarked, "You already went," Daniel responded, "I wanna go again."

The daily editing sessions were another powerful dimension of the activity. Each day the teachers and students corrected various errors in spelling and punctuation from that day's news. Although the teachers provided specific instruction during this time, students also offered solutions to spelling and grammar problems. Late in the year the reporters, anticipating this editing conference, often reread their work and made their own corrections. For instance, in the editing session in mid-March, Mr. Grant emphasized replacing *and* with a period to break up run-on sentences. The next week I observed Edgar, David, and Jessica apply this lesson as they wrote the news in Spanish.

Transcript 3

Edgar (rereading what he has written): *En la casa David estaba haciendo un libro de perros.* [David is making a book about dogs at home.]

David (continuing to dictate): *Y todavia no lo acabo.* [and I still haven't finished it.]

Edgar & David (as Edgar writes): *Y-y-y.* [And.]

Jessica: *No, es—* [No, it's]

David: *¡Un punto!* [A period!]

Jessica: *¡Un punto!* [A period!]

David: *¿Te acuerdas? Un punto.* [Do you remember? A period.]

Jessica: *Y despues de hacer un punto, verdad que empiezas con una letra mas grande.* [And after making a period, you start with a bigger letter.]

David: *Mas grande.* [Bigger.]

This transcript demonstrates the students' developing ability to edit their own writing as they applied the lessons that they learned during the class's editing sessions.

Overall, with regard to writing instruction, daily news represented an exceptional example of the principle of the gradual release of responsibility (Pearson & Gallagher, 1983). Throughout the first semester, the teachers provided clear models of and contextualized instruction in spelling and composing. As the students' knowledge of reading and writing increased, they assumed the roles and responsibilities previously performed by the teachers. However, even during this period of independent writing, the teachers continued to share their special knowledge of writing conventions through the class editing session.

Rich Instruction for ELLs: Lessons From Daily News

Although previous scholars have outlined a number of excellent teaching and learning principles to guide teachers in their work with ELL students (Fitzgerald, 1993; Lenters, 2004; Mohr, 2004), I have taken a different and complementary tack in this article. I have tried to portray, in rich detail, an activity that incorporated many of these principles and that created deep engagement and learning in two classes of young Spanish-dominant students. I hope that this portrait has captured the imagination of my readers and that they will embrace the challenge of developing similarly robust instruction for their ELL students. To conclude, I would like to highlight several key lessons from daily news that might guide teachers in this task.

First, given the fact that teachers have at times relied on simple, repetitive instruction with young ELLs (Fitzgerald, 1995; Neufeld &

Fitzgerald, 2001), I hope that my portraits of the students at work during daily news demonstrate that ELLs can engage in and learn from sophisticated, meaning-centered language and literacy activities. Although I would again stress that recent research clearly indicates the value of solid phonemic awareness and phonics instruction for young ELLs (Lesaux & Siegel, 2003), I believe that these children's participation in rich activities such as daily news is equally crucial to their long-term language and literacy development.

Second, I believe that daily news provides an important example of a robust context for second-language acquisition that simultaneously provides ELL students a comfortable, familiar environment to try out English and allows them to work carefully with the teacher to elaborate on their utterances and see their words set down in print.

Third, I believe that the process of peer translation that occurred during daily news represents an intriguing instructional tool. Although this process may not be possible in every classroom or appropriate for every activity, in specific settings such as daily news it has the potential to bolster the participation of students with limited English skills, validate students' competence in their primary languages, and create a rich occasion for language acquisition. My own research occurred in classrooms where the teachers were bilingual, but I suggest that even a monolingual teacher, after getting the gist of a peer translation, could then help the students refine it much the same way that Ms. Page did in Transcript 2.

Fourth, Ms. Page and Mr. Grant's bilingualism contributed in important ways to their students' participation in daily news, underscoring the value of teachers who speak the language of their ELL students. However, clearly, there are numerous cases in which teachers have little or no knowledge of their ELL students' primary languages and there is no possibility for peer translation. Although this situation requires somewhat different interaction patterns than those that I documented, I believe that there are still several reasons to consider daily news as a valuable tool for supporting ELLs' language and literacy development in such settings. The familiar content typically produced during daily news (i.e., birthdays, trips to favorite spots) and the comfortable atmosphere are important elements of positive second-language learning environments. The process of scribing the words typically results in careful and deliberate rehearsal of the narratives, further enhancing their comprehensibility for English learners. The scribing of the news makes visual the act of translating speech into print, thus making more comprehensible the teacher's real-time commentary on his or her writing processes. Also, daily news provides ELLs very low-risk forms of participation—chorally dictating words as they are scribed and joining the choral reading of the news—that pave the way to more central participation as their English competency grows.

Fifth, the students in these classrooms negotiated the challenges of peer collaboration created by daily news in a largely positive way and often contributed to one another's language and literacy development. I concluded that this productive collaboration was strongly influenced by the shared history of practice resulting from the long period during which the classes produced the news together and by the fact that the activity provided for various forms of participation. Thus, I suggest that a shared history of practice, which makes clear to all participants the nature of the task and the various ways to contribute to it, serves as an important resource for students in overcoming the social and technical challenges of student-directed literacy tasks.

Finally, although research has documented the rich resources for learning that linguistically diverse students acquire in their homes and communities (Moll & Gonzalez, 1994), visions for using these resources have often been large-scale projects involving researchers (Gutiérrez et al., 1999; Moll et al., 1992). I believe that daily news presents a valuable model of how teachers might incorporate diverse students' out-of-school experiences with classroom instruction in a more practical way.

In conclusion, my experiences as a teacher and later as a researcher in multilingual classrooms have acquainted me with the challenges of providing rich language and literacy instruction for young ELLs. It is a weighty task to enable students who may understand and speak little English to participate fully in classroom activities, create the conditions that facilitate language acquisition, appreciate and use the students' unique cultural and linguistic resources, and provide excellent beginning literacy instruction. By taking readers inside the classrooms of two skillful teachers and offering glimpses of young ELLs at work in an engaging, language-rich literacy activity, I hope that this article both encourages and informs educators committed to undertaking this urgent task.

References

Ernst, G. (1994). "Talking Circle": Conversation and negotiation in the ESL classroom. *TESOL Quarterly, 28,* 293–322. doi:10.2307/3587435

Fitzgerald, J. (1993). Literacy and students who are learning English as a second language. *The Reading Teacher, 46,* 638–647.

Fitzgerald, J. (1995). English-as-a-second-language reading instruction in the United States: A research review. *Journal of Reading Behavior, 27,* 115–152.

Fitzgerald, J., & Noblit, G. (1999). About hopes, aspirations, and uncertainty: First-grade English-language learners' emergent reading. *Journal of Literacy Research, 31,* 133–182.

García, E., & Curry-Rodriguez, J. (2000). The education of limited English proficient students in California schools: An assessment of the influence of Proposition 227 in selected districts and schools. *Bilingual Research Journal, 24*(1–2), 15–35.

Geva, E., & Zadeh, Z. (2006). Reading efficiency in native English-speaking and English-as-a-second-language children: The role of oral proficiency and underlying cognitive-linguistic processes. *Scientific Studies of Reading, 10,* 31–57. doi:10.1207/s1532799xssr1001_3

Gutiérrez, K. (2001). What's new in the English language arts: Challenging policies and practices, ¿y qué? *Language Arts, 78,* 564–569.

Gutiérrez, K., Baquedano-López, P., & Tejeda, C. (1999). Rethinking diversity: Hybridity and hybrid language practices in the third space. *Mind, Culture, and Activity, 6,* 286–303.

Krashen, S. (1981). *Second language acquisition and second language learning.* Oxford, England: Pergamon.

Lenters, K. (2004). No half measures: Reading instruction for young second-language learners. *The Reading Teacher, 58,* 328–336. doi:10.1598/RT.58.4.2

Lesaux, N., & Siegel, L. (2003). The development of reading in children who speak English as a second language (ESL). *Developmental Psychology, 39,* 1005–1019. doi:10.1037/0012-1649.39.6.1005

Manyak, P. (2001). Participation, hybridity, and carnival: A situated analysis of a dynamic literacy practice in a primary-grade English immersion class. *Journal of Literacy Research, 33*, 423–465.

Manyak, P. (2004). "What did she say?": Translation in a primary-grade English immersion class. *Multicultural Perspectives, 6*, 12–18. doi:10.1207/S15327892mcp0601_3

Mohr, K. (2004). English as an accelerated language: A call to action for reading teachers. *The Reading Teacher, 58*, 18–26. doi:10.1598/RT.58.1.2

Moll, L., Amanti, C., Neff, D. & Gonzalez, N. (1992). Funds of knowledge for teaching: Using a qualitative approach to connect homes and classrooms. *Theory Into Practice, 31*, 132–140.

Moll, L., & Dworin, J. (1996). Biliteracy development in classrooms: Social dynamics and cultural possibilities. In D. Hicks (Ed.), *Discourse, learning, and schooling* (pp. 221–246). New York: Cambridge University Press.

Moll, L., & González, N. (1994). Lessons from research with language-minority children. *Journal of Reading Behavior, 26*, 439–456.

Moll, L., & Whitmore, K. (1993). Vygotsky in classroom practice: Moving from individual transmission to social transaction. In E. Forman, N. Minick, & C. Stone (Eds.), *Contexts for learning: Sociocultural dynamics in children's development* (pp. 230–253). New York: Oxford University Press.

Neufeld, P., & Fitzgerald, J. (2001). Early English reading development: Latino English learners in the "low" reading group. *Research in the Teaching of English, 36*, 64–105.

Pearson, P.D., & Gallagher, M. (1983). The instruction of reading comprehension. *Contemporary Educational Psychology, 8*, 317–344. doi:10.1016/0361-476X(83)90019-X

Toohey, K., Waterstone, B., & Jule-Lemke, A. (2000). Community of learners, carnival, and participation in a Punjabi Sikh classroom. *Canadian Modern Language Review, 56*, 421–436.

Wells, G. (1986). *The meaning makers: Children learning language and using language to learn*. Portsmouth, NH: Heinemann.

Wong-Fillmore, L. (1985). When does teacher talk work as input? In S. Gass & C. Madden (Eds.), *Input in second language acquisition* (pp. 17–50). Rowley, MA: Newbury.

Questions for Reflection

• The classrooms in this article included only children who were English-language learners. If you have a mixture of native English speakers and ELLs in your classroom, how could you adjust the daily news activity to involve all learners? What sort of peer mentoring or coaching might work among your students? What grouping arrangements would be most effective in maximizing learning for all?

• Although the author acknowledges that it is not possible to have bilingual teachers available for all English learners, his comments about the support Ms. Page and Mr. Grant were able to provide highlight the importance of knowing at least something about the language backgrounds of English learners. What do you know about the home languages of your English learners? How can you find out more? How might you adapt your instructional approach for learners as a result?

Beginning Reading Instruction in Urban Schools: The Curriculum Gap Ensures a Continuing Achievement Gap

William H. Teale, Kathleen A. Paciga, and Jessica L. Hoffman

The literacy achievement gap refers to the disparity in academic performance between different groups—different, for example, in income, cultural background, or gender. In the United States, the literacy achievement gap means that, as a group, children from poverty backgrounds score significantly lower in reading and writing than children from middle and high income backgrounds and that a similar gap exists between African American and Latino students and their higher scoring Caucasian peers (e.g., see results from the National Assessment of Educational Progress [NAEP] at nces.ed.gov/nationsreportcard/pdf/main2005/2006451.pdf).

Because disproportionately high percentages of low-income, African American and Latino children are found in most urban environments, the achievement gap is a particularly acute issue for urban schools. In fact, NAEP studies of 4th and 8th grade reading achievement in 11 urban districts conducted in 2005 and 2003 show that most of the existing gaps are significantly larger for urban students than for the overall student population (see Table 1).

Addressing the Literacy Achievement Gap

In an ambitious attempt to address the achievement gap, the federal government of the United States has taken on early reading achievement. Guided by the findings of the National Reading Panel (National Institute of Child Health and Human Development, 2000) and implemented under the auspices of the No Child Left Behind (NCLB) legislation of 2001, the move to enhance beginning reading instruction, raise reading achievement for all students, and provide targeted support for the teaching of reading to the most economically challenged schools has been underwritten with more federal funding than many of us ever imagined. Since 2002, through Reading First (RF), more than US$4 billion (yes, that's a *b*) was spent to improve reading instruction in the primary grades (K–3, students from 5 to 9 years old). The monies have primarily gone for teacher professional development, instructional materials, and literacy assessment programs. Reading First focuses on "putting proven methods of early reading instruction in classrooms...to ensure that all children learn to read well by the end of third grade" (from www.ed.gov/programs/readingfirst/index.html). RF funds are aimed at helping schools with high percentages of children from families with incomes below the poverty line (www.ed.gov/programs/readingfirst/index.html).

Reading First has experienced some recent problems (Dillon, 2006), but there are also arguments that it is having positive effects on early literacy achievement (Spellings, 2007). We are pleased as can be about the investment of almost US$1 billion per year in improving early literacy instruction, and we firmly believe that the "big five" foundational pillars upon which Reading

Reprinted from Teale, W.H., Paciga, K.A., & Hoffman, J.L. (2007). Beginning reading instruction in urban schools: The curriculum gap ensures a continuing achievement gap (Issues in Urban Literacy department). *The Reading Teacher, 61*(4), 344-348.

Table 1
Magnitude of the Achievement Gap, Reported in Differences of NAEP Scale Scores

	African American/ Caucasian gap		Latino/Caucasian gap		Poverty/nonpoverty gap	
	National	Urban	National	Urban	National	Urban
Grade 4						
2005	29	32*	27	29*	27	32*
2003	30	34*	28	30*	28	26
2002	29	35*	28	30*	23	n/a
Grade 8						
2005	28	30*	25	27*	23	27*
2003	26	29*	26	29*	25	22
2002	27	31*	26	29*	22	n/a

Note. *Significantly higher gap. Sources for the data were nces.ed.gov/nationsreportcard/pdf/main2005/2006451.pdf and nces.ed.gov/nationsreportcard/pdf/dst2003/2004459.pdf.

First is based—phonological awareness, phonics, vocabulary, fluency, and comprehension—are indispensable components of a quality beginning reading program.

The Curriculum Gap—What Is It, Why Is It, and Why Does It Matter?

We have noted, however, a disturbing trend in the current reforms related to early literacy instruction, as legislation becomes classroom practice. We refer to this trend as the curriculum gap. In recent years the implementation of NCLB and Reading First has, in many K–3 classrooms, resulted in the absence of or insufficient attention to curriculum elements critical for success in reading and writing. Our visits to urban primary-grade classrooms and our conversations with curriculum directors, reading specialists, and literacy coaches indicate that there are three significant dimensions to the curriculum gap, as follows:

- Comprehension instruction
- Instruction focused on developing children's knowledge of the world in general

and of core concepts in content domains like science and social studies

- Writing instruction

The professional development teachers receive and the student assessment instruments typically used as part of RF are based on the five pillars mentioned previously. But, the message that large numbers of K–3 teachers in urban schools have taken from their participation in RF and from the tests that measure adequate yearly progress under NCLB is that reading instruction in the early grades is exclusively about children learning phonological awareness, how to decode, and how to read words accurately and fluently.

Other writers have commented at length on the limiting influence of NCLB high-stakes assessment on curriculum, instruction, and school experience (e.g., Meier & Wood, 2004), and we shall not reiterate the details of those arguments here. But, it is important to point out that state achievement tests (typically administered at grade 3) and the screening and progress monitoring assessments deemed appropriate for RF classrooms have, in many teachers' minds, reinforced instructional practices focused on a limited set of foundational literacy skills. In that sense, such assessment processes contribute directly to the curriculum gap addressed here.

Comprehension Instruction Gap

Sustained and strategic attention to comprehension is absent in far too many primary-grade urban classrooms. We suspect this is so largely because the litany many primary teachers have taken to heart goes something like the following:

- Reading words accurately and fluently is the key to comprehension.
- Lots of practice with grade-level text is the key to developing fluent word recognition.
- The conceptual load in K–3 grade-level texts is simple.
- Therefore, as long as one teaches word recognition skills, comprehension will pretty much take care of itself.

There is quite a bit of truth in the first three points. But the final point is problematic, and using all four as the guiding principles for a beginning reading program means that teachers get the message that comprehension instruction is something that can (or even should) be put off until later grades. For two main reasons we believe such a perspective is, in the long term, a recipe for reading problems—especially for urban children.

First, the fact of the matter is that an unacceptably large number of primary-grade children in urban schools historically have failed to master two of the foundational skills of reading— phonics and fluency. But these skills are not all that is necessary to help children become successful readers. During the primary grades it is also essential to teach children appropriate comprehension strategies and skills that enable them to understand texts that are more complex than those made of everyday words they already know and conversations they routinely hear.

Second, focusing merely on accurate and fluent word recognition makes the content and quality of what children read less important for teachers to consider. Teachers and children in the United States are fortunate to have a rich body of children's literature available, but that literature gets little more than lip service because of the prevailing RF emphasis on short-term reading achievement goals coupled with the relative lack of attention to long-term goals. When we think long term, one of the most important questions to be asked is, What is going to make young children be readers, now and when they are teenagers and adults? The answer to that question lies solidly in the realm of ideas—the stories and information in the pages of books and magazines and on the screens of computers. Successful readers are not developed merely by having young children practice reading texts that have transparent, innocuous, or sometimes rather inane ideas. Good books are a key to creating good readers. And for the many urban children who do not find much support in their home or community environments for interacting with extended written texts, the school is an especially important source of their developing comprehension abilities.

Background/Domain Knowledge Gap

All states in the United States have learning standards for social studies and science in each of the primary grades. Also, almost every teacher we work with is well aware of the connection between background knowledge and reading comprehension. Yet, when we examine what is currently happening in primary-grade classroom instruction, we come to the conclusion that in many instances the connection between background knowledge and early literacy achievement is not viewed as a priority.

A recent study completed by the Center on Education Policy (CEP, 2007) is very telling on this point. The CEP surveyed 349 school districts and conducted additional in-depth district- and school-level interviews in 13 school districts. Results showed that about 62% of districts overall and 77% of urban districts had increased time for English language arts instruction considerably since 2002; *and* that to enable this increase, 44% of districts substantially reduced instructional time in other subject areas. Moreover, the reduction in instruction in other content areas was even greater in districts that had at least one school identified as needing improvement under NCLB and in urban districts. For example, more than half of the districts with at least one identified school reduced instructional time in social studies, by an average of 90 minutes per week; and 43% of such districts cut science instruction by an average of 94 minutes per week (CEP, 2007, p. 7).

What this means is that many primary-grade children in urban schools are being short-changed on domain specific knowledge. "So what?" some would argue—those children are getting a better foundation in literacy. It could appear that way, and it may even show up that way in mandated K–3 assessments: Scores on tests of phonics skills, word recognition, and word reading speed and accuracy may well rise a bit in the short run. But what happens in fourth or seventh or tenth grade when what it takes to be a good reader depends on vocabulary knowledge, domain knowledge, and the ability to comprehend a variety of genres of text at a deep level? Our prediction is that the initial "bump" will at best fade away by fifth or sixth grade and at worst translate into an even larger achievement gap. Why? Because what are being treated *in practice* as the foundational skills of reading represent only a part of what children need to learn during the primary grades to be good readers in upper elementary school, middle school, and high school. In other words, we may well be losing more than we are gaining by increasing attention to reading instruction, if it is being done at the expense of instruction in content areas such as science and social studies.

Writing Instruction Gap

Indicators suggest that Reading First has resulted in many urban primary-grade classrooms becoming focused on just that—*reading* first. Chicago Public Schools (CPS), for example, has—since 2000—implemented a Reading Framework that equally emphasizes instruction in word knowledge, fluency, comprehension, and writing at all grade levels. There are more than 100 RF classrooms in CPS, and Jodie Dodds Kinner, Director

of Elementary Literacy for the district, pointed out that the 2006–2007 school year's program evaluation data from primary-grade classrooms indicated such a lack of instructional attention to writing that CPS has focused its entire district-wide literacy professional development on writing for the 2007–2008 school year (Personal communication, July 2007).

The pattern observed in CPS recurs in other urban districts. Instead of capitalizing on the well-documented connections between reading and writing (Shanahan, 2005), many classrooms concentrate solely on the elements of Reading First in their "literacy block," which does not specifically include time for writing, thus symbolically and in practice cutting the ties between reading and writing. Writing is an excellent way to foster phonological awareness skills (Snow, Burns, & Griffin, 1998) and awareness of the functions and uses of literacy, as well as being important for its own sake as a significant part of early literacy learning.

The Curriculum Gap and Urban Schools—What Is to Be Done?

The first years of school are critical to children's development as capable and lifelong readers and writers. This period is the time for learning foundational literacy skills and dispositions. But it is essential—especially for children who depend heavily on the school as a place for their early literacy learning—that the curriculum encompasses all aspects of the foundation in order to promote long-term growth in literacy. A focus on phonological awareness/decoding, word recognition, and fluency instruction is central to early literacy development. However, as we have attempted to show, other foundational aspects of literacy are also essential but often missing from or only attended to in passing in daily instruction in urban K–3 classrooms, thus creating a severe curriculum gap. Lack of sustained instructional attention to comprehension, content knowledge, and writing in the early grades is rather like expecting children to grow up to be healthy teenagers with a childhood diet of meat and potatoes but no fruits or vegetables.

The curriculum gap must be bridged if we hope to ameliorate the achievement gap. This necessitates rethinking programs so that they systematically attend to helping children develop comprehension and writing skills as well as letter knowledge, letter–sound correspondence, and word-recognition skills. It also necessitates rethinking how much and in what way subjects like social studies and science are taught in the primary grades. Such instructional changes likewise imply reform of early literacy assessment programs, so that what is counted in terms of early literacy development is what really counts. In essence, we encourage primary-grade educators to think comprehensively about what constitutes a good beginning in reading and writing, because a good ending is far more likely when there is a good beginning.

Note

The authors thank Jennifer McMurrer at the Center on Education Policy for supplying additional statistics used in this column to disaggregate the achievement gap data.

References

Center for Education Policy. (2007). *Choices, changes, and challenges: Curriculum and Instruction in the NCLB era.* Washington, DC: Author.

Dillon, S. (2006, September 23). Report says education officials violated rules in awarding initiative grants. *The New York Times.* Retrieved September 25, 2007, from www.nytimes.com/2006/09/23/education/23education.html

Meier, D., & Wood, G. (2004). *Many children left behind: How the No Child Left Behind Act is damaging our children and our schools.* Boston: Beacon Press.

National Institute of Child Health and Human Development. (2000). Report of the National Reading Panel. *Teaching children to read: An evidence-based assessment of the scientific research literature on reading and its implications for reading instruction.* (NIH Publication No. 00-4769). Washington, DC: U.S. Government Printing Office.

Shanahan, T. (2005). Relations among oral language, reading, and writing development. In C. MacArthur, S. Graham, & J. Fitzgerald (Eds.), *Handbook of writing research* (pp. 171–185). New York: Guilford.

Snow, C.E., Burns, M.S., & Griffin, P. (Eds.). (1998). *Preventing reading difficulties in young children.* Washington, DC: National Academy Press.

Spellings, M. (2007, April). *Reading First: Student achievement, teacher empowerment, national success.* Retrieved July 30, 2007 from www.ed.gov/nclb/methods/reading/readingfirst.html

Questions for Reflection

• This article was published in 2007, during the George W. Bush administration in the United States. Do you see any changes in educational priorities emerging? If so, how do you think they will—or won't—address the curriculum gap the authors describe? What, particularly, are the implications for urban children or for children living in poverty in other settings? How can these implications be addressed?

Choice of Action: Using Data to Make Instructional Decisions in Kindergarten

Mary Ann Reilly

Query the phrase *data-driven decision making* on the Internet and you'll get more than 1 million hits represented by a range of text focusing on technology frameworks to support data decisions, software to manipulate data, and professional development "quicktips" to simplify the use of data. Lost against the certainty of such text is the uncertainty that always frames fine teaching and is equally inherent in the collection, selection, interpretation, and use of data. Yet, negotiating uncertainty is a requisite stance for informed teaching (Edwards, Gilroy, & Hartley, 2002; Reilly, 1998; Vinz, 1996). Being data rich does not necessarily translate into being data smart. Teachers form and reform themselves by the decisions they make. As Dewey (1916) noted, "The self is not something ready-made, but something in continuous formation through choice of action" (p. 351). It is the decision making that precipitates choice of action that most interests me when I think of kindergarten teacher Margo Calderon, a 15-year veteran from a northern New Jersey school district, who uses data to guide her instructional decisions in an effort to prevent reading difficulties.

Teachers like Calderon can provide essential early intervention instruction within their classrooms and prevent reading difficulties from occurring (Snow, Burns, & Griffin, 1998). Without effective intervention, a reading performance gap develops early and widens as children progress across school years (Stanovich, 1986), and the majority of the less able readers remain so throughout elementary school (Juel, 1988). What types of data help Calderon to make instructional decisions that make children's reading success more likely?

Selecting Assessments: A Tiered Practice

During the last three years, the school district's data collection process has been streamlined in order to reduce the fragmentation educators experienced and to provide the district leadership with general screening and progress monitoring information. Previously, teachers spent an inordinate amount of time administering lengthy assessments to all students in response to district demands.

Calderon explained,

One of my weaknesses has always been documenting a student's progress, because I always found it such an overwhelming task. I would assess students, hand the scores to an administrator, and then file them away. I literally would assess here and there, never use the results, and concentrate on whole-group instruction. Individual needs based on assessment were never taken into consideration.

Like Calderon, many teachers, feeling overwhelmed, administered but did not analyze results, and they were often unable to use the data to guide instruction. Now primary-grade teachers have developed student goals related to screening and progress monitoring benchmarks that specify literacy outcomes for children and help teachers to prioritize and organize instruction (Little, 1987; McGonagill, 1992; Schmoker, 1999, 2003). Calderon and her colleagues use

Reprinted from Reilly, M.A. (2007). Choice of action: Using data to make instructional decisions in kindergarten. *The Reading Teacher,* 60(8), 770-776.

three types of assessment to guide their instructional decisions.

1. Dynamic Indicators of Basic Early Literacy Skills

In kindergarten, phonemic awareness (Torgesen, 1998) and letter-name knowledge are reliable predictors of later reading achievement, especially during the early stages of reading acquisition (Blachman, 1984; Ehri & Sweet, 1991; Rathvon, 2004; Scanlon & Vellutino, 1997). It was with this in mind that the school district where Calderon is employed established screening and progress monitoring measures that were used by all teachers at particular grade levels across each of the elementary schools.

At the kindergarten level, classroom teachers administer the Dynamic Indicators of Basic Early Literacy Skills (DIBELS; Good & Kaminski, 2002). DIBELS are brief, individually administered fluency-based measures designed to screen and monitor children's prereading and reading skill development from preschool through third-grade levels. At the beginning of kindergarten the Initial Sound Fluency (ISF) and Letter Naming Fluency (LNF) measures are administered. The ISF measures the number of initial sounds a kindergarten child can identify within a minute. In September, the benchmark is eight correct sounds per minute. By January, the benchmark progresses to 25 correct sounds per minute. The LNF measures the number of letters a child can correctly identify within a minute. In September the benchmark is 8 correct letters per minute. By January the benchmark progresses to 27 correct letters per minute. Although the ISF has less reliability than the other DIBELS measures (Rathvon, 2004), the district believed that ISF coupled with the LNF, which has a very high reliability (Kaminski & Good, 1996), would help teachers to identify potential students at risk for reading difficulties. Following the established benchmarks (Good, Simmons, Kame'enui, Kaminski, & Wallin, 2002), kindergarten students who scored less than 4 on the ISF *and* less than 2 on the LNF at the beginning of the school year were identified.

2. Discretionary Assessments Determined by Teachers

In addition to the DIBELS, kindergarten teachers also use, at their discretion, three portions of the Observation Survey (Clay, 1993): the Letter Identification (LI) task, the Hearing and Recording Sounds in Words (HRSIW) task, and the Writing Vocabulary (WV) spree. The Observation Survey has demonstrated a high correlation with other standardized, norm-referenced tests (Gómez-Bellengé & Thompson, 2005; Pinnell, Lyons, DeFord, Bryk, & Seltzer, 1991) and provides teachers with information about how each child works with print (Clay).

The LI task allows teachers to assess what letters a child can identify and the child's preferred mode of identification. Students are asked to identify uppercase and lowercase letters, naming the correct letter or substituting a correct representative sound or word for the given letter. A sentence dictation task, the HRSIW allows teachers to determine how well a child can represent sounds and sound clusters in written text. The WV task requires a child to correctly write as many words as he or she can in a 10-minute time frame. This assessment allows teachers to determine the extent of a child's personal resource of words. In addition, observation of the child while completing these tasks might also reveal information about the child's sense of directionality, sequencing letters in words, letter formation, placement of words, spacing between words, visual discrimination of print, and visual memory.

3. Computer-Assisted Assessment

A third program in use in all K–2 classrooms in the district is the Waterford Early Reading Program (WERP), a computer-based program that provides teachers with detailed information about each student's knowledge of print concepts, phonological awareness, and letter recognition (Waterford Institute, 2001/2002). Each classroom is outfitted with three to five computers, and kindergarten students spend 15 minutes each day using level 1 of the software. WERP courseware is personalized for each student's learning, and teachers retrieve information about students' progress on a weekly basis. WERP is used as a supplement to the district's primary reading program.

Analyzing Data and Planning Instruction

Calderon administers the ISF and LNF to her students in order to screen incoming students and measure their progress during kindergarten. In fall 2004, the majority of Calderon's students were considered to be at risk, with 11 out of 20 students unable to identify any initial sounds or correctly name more than two letters. By January, 6 of those 11 students met the ISF and LNF benchmarks and 5 students remained at risk for reading difficulties.

In addition to the ISF and LNF, Calderon also chooses to assess her students using the LI, HRSIW, and WV tasks (Clay, 1993). Her interpretation of these data is held alongside her formal and informal observations of students as they work. Literacy assessments are discursive practices (Egan-Robertson, 1998; Gee, 1996; Johnston & Rogers, 2002) that are informed by what Calderon knows, values, and believes. Calderon also uses the Concepts About Print (Clay, 1993) assessment with selected students as needed and reviews weekly data provided through WERP.

Using multiple assessments allows Calderon to build richer understandings of which concepts the children have learned, not learned, or find confusing while maintaining the flow of inquiry (Schön, 1983). For example, Calderon says that she now waits until the end of October to administer the ISF, because she has found that when her children first arrive in September they often do poorly on this task. "What I find is when they come in, so many of the kids will do poorly on the initial sounds that it is almost not an accurate reading for me. I prefer to look at the LI task," explained Calderon. Once students understand the ISF task, Calderon assesses and finds that the results are more reliable as children understand what she is asking them to do. By coupling results, a deeper understanding can be reached. Where a single set of data may suggest one interpretation, the coupling of data, including data sets that may offer contradictory information, helps Calderon to plan more effectively.

"ISF, letter ID, and my observations allow me to pinpoint specific weaknesses that I address with each child as opposed to using an assessment with one score for multiple literacy components," explained Calderon.

Benchmark assessments and progress monitoring allow Calderon to customize her instruction and employ flexible grouping. She explained,

> I just completed the final progress monitoring before the January assessments. I created a new, much smaller group of students who are still not performing as well as I would like to see and need intensive instruction. I will concentrate on teaching them how to isolate initial sounds using consonant sorting activities while building their oral language skills. Using data to inform my instruction has helped my children to achieve higher levels of success in literacy. I think years ago the students at risk of reading difficulties made progress at a much slower pace because the instruction wasn't geared toward their needs. Using data to drive my instruction, certainly to intensify it, seems to assist the children in meeting benchmarks sooner.

Students' literacy success in Calderon's class has been documented, with all of her students last year achieving the district's literacy benchmarks, and perhaps even more notably, maintaining those gains into first grade. Five years ago, only 18% of the district's fourth graders passed the state literacy assessment; last year, nearly 80% of the district's fourth graders passed the same assessment. Across the last five years, the systematic use of multiple sources of data by teachers like Calderon to inform instructional and programmatic decisions is arguably one reason for the increased student achievement (Schaffer, 1988).

Connecting Data Analysis With Instructional Planning: Shared Writing

Calderon plans for specific instruction by using her analysis of the formal data alongside her observation of children. What she does in order to ensure the development of her students' phonological awareness skills during the first half of the school year could be characterized as hybrid instruction. She has adapted several multisensory approaches and has embedded them within an interactive shared writing experience called Message Time Plus (Children's Literacy Initiative, 2004), which is designed to increase children's knowledge of print conventions. Message Time Plus is an instructional process in which a teacher plans a message and then writes it as the children watch, make predictions, and read along out loud. When the message has been written and reread, the children come to the board to identify any letters, numbers, words, or print elements they know. The teacher then extends each child's knowledge through scaffolded minilessons.

Using the beginning of the year data and progress monitoring results, Calderon keeps specific literacy benchmarks in mind when designing instruction and asks, What language or processes are children using and confusing? How might I use this lesson to help the students clarify what they are learning?

For example, during a lesson in late November, Calderon has written a brief mathematics message to the children based on a Rosemary Wells story. The children have been engaged in an author study and are familiar with the stories featuring Max and Ruby, the main characters in many Wells stories. This familiarity will help them when it comes time to read the message, and Calderon will congratulate them for using their story knowledge to help them read the message. In Calderon's class, students are immersed in rich oral language, while also writing and hearing and reading quality literature. Calderon has prepared a message in advance that will include the following sight words: *for*, *you*, *he*, and *went*. Because she is also interested in ensuring that the children are able to determine relevant from irrelevant information in a mathematics problem, she has written a mathematics problem.

On this early morning, Calderon gathers the children in front of a whiteboard and tells them,

"I need to think about what I will write." The children are quiet as Calderon thinks. Although only the 12th week of school, the children are aware that writers need to think in order to compose. Calderon will write, "Max went to the store to buy milk for Ruby. He paid 2¢ for the milk and 3¢ for Red-Hot Marshmallow Squirters. How much money did Max spend?" While writing the message, she will scaffold the children's learning by seeing what they attempt to use but confuse, and she will continually remind them that they are using known sounds and words in order to read. Against the discrete work of identifying sounds and letters, Calderon is well aware of the larger lesson at hand: that students connect their successful attempts at finding letters and sounds with the metaknowledge that effective readers use these tools to help to make meaning while they read.

For example, after writing the first word, *Max*, Calderon prompts the children to predict what she will next write, telling them, "word-wall word." This phrase is one she uses with the children to indicate a word they can find on the class word wall. As she begins to write the word *went*, a child says "we." Calderon finishes writing *went* and then says, "We is a great prediction, because I see we." She tells them this while pointing to the first two letters in the word, *went*. "But it is really," she says stopping and the children reread and then chorally say, "went." By rereading, the children rely on both syntactic and semantic knowledge to determine that *we* wouldn't make sense or fit. Calderon will complete writing the first sentence and then direct the children to reread the entire sentence as she points to each word.

"Guess what just happened? It's only day 53. We have only been in school 53 days. Did you hear me read that sentence? I didn't have to read that sentence. You were able to read that sentence without me. Are you readers?" The children respond, "yea," and Calderon affirms, "Yes, you're readers."

Calderon begins to write the next sentence, stops and tells the children that she does not have enough room to write the next word, and asks them what she should do. "Sweep left," they chorally respond. As she continues writing, she provides directions for children to tell what they know. For example, when she begins to write the word *paid*, she asks the children to give her the sound the initial letter in the word makes. The children say /p/ and Calderon follows by saying, "paid," stressing the initial sound. Again, knowing her learners, Calderon asks students to do what she thinks is important at this point in the school year.

After completing the message and rereading it, Calderon is now ready for individual children to find within the message any sounds, letters, words, numbers, and punctuation marks that they know. The teaching assistant in Calderon's classroom will keep track of three types of information: the message that Calderon wrote, what each child finds in the message, and the scaffolding that Calderon does to reinforce each child's learning or to extend the learning. This information is then used by Calderon to plan instruction (see Figure 1). Because Calderon is well aware of how each student is progressing, she can individ-ualize instruction. Her analysis of data informs the occasions she will develop to build students' reading schema.

"Find me a letter, a sound, or a word," Calderon prompts, as 5-year-old Tyronne (student names are pseudonyms) approaches the board. Using the pointer, he locates the letter *M* in the word *Max*, saying, "I found the letter *M*." There is great celebration in the classroom at Tyronne's discovery because he has only spoken about 20 words aloud during the school year. Tyronne was unable to name any initial sounds on the ISF or identify any letters on the LNF and LI tasks at the beginning of the school year. Calderon has routinely monitored his progress through assessments and her daily observations. Tyronne has made some progress by November and is able to name 8 initial sounds and identify 13 letters.

"I've seen you do this when we sit alone," Calderon says softly to Tyronne. She and Tyronne have worked one on one to develop his phonological awareness. "Tell me, what sound does *M* make?"

Figure 1
Data Collection for Message Time Plus

Date:
Teacher's message:

Child's name	What the child finds in the message	How the teacher reinforces or scaffolds the learning

---

Tyronne responds by making the sound of the letter *M*, and Calderon writes *M m* on the board and leads the children to say, "*M* says /m/ and *m* says /m/." As she speaks, she writes the uppercase and lowercase letter in the air. The children quickly mimic her because this routine is well known.

Calderon attempts to anchor Tyronne's new learning by having Tyronne say a word that begins with the /m/ sound. Again, Calderon is concerned that Tyronne continues to struggle identifying initial sounds and uses all opportunities to strengthen his phonological skills. "Tyronne, can you give me a word that starts with /m/?" Tyronne is unable to do so. "Do you want to use the chart? You can use the name chart or the picture (alphabet) chart. Whichever you want to use." Tyronne walks to the alphabet chart, surveys the letters and pictures and focuses his attention on the letter *M*.

"Tyronne, use my pointer and point to the picture you're looking at. Find the *M*." Tyronne uses the pointer to point to the letter *M*, but is unable to also say that the picture below the letter *M* is a mouse and that the word *mouse* begins with /m/.

Calderon redirects by prompting Tyronne to look at the name chart. Calderon's name chart contains the children's first names, alphabetized and grouped by initial letter. Next to the children's names are their photographs. Tyronne looks at the names and finally selects Kemberly, placing the pointer under the lowercase letter m. Realizing that Tyronne has selected Kemberly because the letter *m* appears in the name, Calderon, supports his learning by saying, "Tyronne, you want it to be the first letter."

She further prompts him by saying, "Look," and places the pointer that Tyronne is still holding on the letter *M*. "Do you see the *M*? Who is that?" she asks, directing Tyronne to look at the picture. "Mary," answers Tyronne. "Good. Mary starts with /m/. Now you say it," she directs, emphasizing the positional word *starts* and the letter sound. "Mary starts with /m/."

As Tyronne returns to his seat, Calderon extends her students' learning by having them offer other words that begin with /m/. *Mark*,

monkey, mouse, moth, and *mountain* are offered. After recording these words and having some of the children provide sentences for the words they have offered, Calderon has the children repeat the list. "I'll say it. You say it," she prompts as she puts the pointer on the first word, *Mary*, and says it. The children repeat each word in chorus.

During this half hour of instruction, the children will find additional letters, numbers, and word-wall words and will explain what is relevant and irrelevant in the message with respect to solving the word problem. Calderon will reinforce their learning by having children use words in a sentence. At other times she will direct a child to pound out the syllables in a word, as she does with Anthony when she asks him how many syllables he hears in *watermelon*, a word he has offered for the letter *W*. "Five," he says. "Do it with me," Calderon directs, and they pound out each syllable, hitting the closed fist of their right hand against the palm of their left hand. "Water- mel- on," says Calderon as Anthony mimics, pounding each syllable. "How many syllables?" "Four." "Right. Everyone, let's pound out all of the *W* words we've written."

Pockets of Learning

There are small moments in the classroom—pockets of learning—that appear insignificant at first glance but when coupled together with other learning experiences provide a rich nexus of support for learners like Tyronne and Anthony. Bernhardt (1996) explained that "data can help us replace hunches and hypotheses with facts concerning what changes are needed" (p. 1). I wonder about Bernhardt's certainty in light of the work that Calderon does as a teacher—for doesn't Calderon rely in part upon informed hunches and hypotheses? Perhaps interpretation rests in a dialogic (Bakhtin, 1981) that accounts for the contemporality among facts, hunches, and hypotheses.

As the intensive work with Tyronne and Anthony suggests, Calderon must be diligent in attending to what each child understands and misunderstands. She will continue to monitor children's understandings, make choices about what data to value, and then design occasions to deepen her students' learning. Throughout this process, Calderon is being shaped by what she learns, fails to learn, unlearns, and relearns. It is this dynamic flux that is at the center of data-driven decision making and that complicates the process and our ability to make sense of the data in ways that can directly assist children.

William Carlos Williams in *The Desert Music, and Other Poems* asked, "How shall we get said what must be said?" and responded, "the poem, only the made poem." Williams wrote of the struggle the poet has to create the made poem of an experience. He concluded, "And I could not help thinking/of the wonders of the brain that/hears the music and of our/skill sometimes to record it" (1962, p. 120). I think of Williams's keen observation concerning the tentativeness of one's ability to record experience in light of what Calderon must do to compose interpretations of data, read her students' intentions, and to then use each to fashion instruction for Tyronne, Anthony, and her other students. The teaching adjustments she needs to make require her to continually ask, What do I know about this child that can help me to understand why he or she said or did *x*? Against this question, Calderon's knowledge of the student via her analysis of data and observations acts as a bifurcating force, shaping her decisions and allowing her to work more closely within each child's zone of proximal development (Vygotsky, 1934/1986). This process ultimately allows her to be more effective as a teacher.

References

Bakhtin, M.M. (1981). *The dialogic imagination* (M. Holquist, Ed. & Trans., & C. Emerson, Trans.). Austin, TX: University of Texas Press.

Bernhardt, V.L. (1996). Data makes the difference with school reform. *Quality Digest*. Retrieved March 30, 2005, from http://www.qualitydigest.com/sep96/school.html

Blachman, B.A. (1984). Relationship of rapid naming ability and language analysis skills to kindergarten and first-grade reading achievement. *Journal of Educational Psychology, 76*, 610–622.

Children's Literacy Initiative. (2004). *Message time plus*. Philadelphia: Author.

Clay, M. (1993). *An observation survey of early literacy achievement*. Portsmouth, NH: Heinemann.

Dewey, J. (1916). *Democracy and education: An introduction to the philosophy of education*. New York: Macmillan.

Edwards, A., Gilroy, P., & Hartley, D. (2002). *Rethinking teacher education: Collaborative responses to uncertainty*. New York: Routledge/Falmer.

Egan-Robertson, A. (1998). Learning about culture, language and power: Understanding relationships among personhood, literacy practices, and intertextuality. *Journal of Literacy Practices, 30*, 449–487.

Ehri, L.C., & Sweet, J. (1991). Fingerpoint-reading of memorized text: What enables beginning readers to process the print? *Reading Research Quarterly, 26*, 442–462.

Gee, J. (1996). *Social linguistics and literacies: Ideology in discourses* (2nd ed.). London: Taylor & Francis.

Gómez-Bellengé, F.X., & Thompson, J.R. (2005). *U.S. norms for tasks of an observation survey of early literacy achievement* (NDEC Rep. No. 2005-02). Columbus: Ohio State University, National Data Evaluation Center.

Good, R., & Kaminski, R. (2002). *Dynamic indicators of basic early literacy skills*. University of Oregon. Retrieved October 25, 2005, from http://dibels.uoregon.edu

Good, R.H., Simmons, D., Kame'enui, E., Kaminski, R.A., & Wallin, J. (2002). *Summary of decision rules for intensive, strategic, and benchmark instructional recommendations in kindergarten through third grade* (Tech. Rep. No. 11). Eugene: University of Oregon.

Johnston, P.H., & Rogers, R. (2002). Early literacy development: The case for "informed assessment." In S. Neuman & D. Dickinson (Eds.), *Handbook of early literacy research* (pp. 377–389). New York: Guilford.

Juel, C. (1988). Learning to read and write: A longitudinal study of fifty-four children from first through fourth grade. *Journal of Educational Psychology, 80*, 437–447.

Kaminski, R.A., & Good, R.H. (1996). Toward a technology for assessing basic early literacy skills. *School Psychology Review, 25*, 215–227.

Little, J.W. (1987). Teachers as colleagues. In V. Richardson-Koehler (Ed.), *Educator's handbook* (pp. 491–518). White Plains, NY: Longman.

McGonagill, G. (1993). *Overcoming barriers to educational restructuring: A call for "system literacy."* Arlington, VA: American Association of School Administrators. (ERIC Document Reproduction Service No. ED357512)

Pinnell, G.S., Lyons, C.A., DeFord, D.E., Bryk, A.S., & Seltzer, M. (1991). *Studying the effectiveness of early intervention approaches for first grade children having difficulty in reading*. Columbus: Ohio State University, Martha L. King Language and Literacy Center.

Rathvon, N. (2004). *Early reading assessments: A practitioner's handbook*. New York: Guilford.

Reilly, M.A. (1998). Difficult flows and waves: Unfixing beliefs in a grade 8 language arts literacy class. *English Education, 31*, 26–41.

Scanlon, D.M., & Vellutino, F.R. (1997). A comparison of instructional backgrounds and cognitive profiles of poor, average, and good readers who were initially identified as a risk for reading failure. *Scientific Studies of Reading, 1*, 191–215.

Schaffer, R.H. (1988). *The breakthrough strategy: Using short-term successes to build the high-performing organization.* New York: Harper Business.

Schmoker, M. (1999). *Results: The key to continuous school improvement* (2nd ed.). Alexandria, VA: Association for Supervision and Curriculum Development.

Schmoker, M. (2003). First things first: Demystifying data analysis. *Educational Leadership, 60*(5), 22–24.

Schön, D. (1983). *The reflective practitioner: How professionals think in action.* New York: Basic Books.

Snow, C.E., Burns, M.S., & Griffin, P. (Eds.). (1998). *Preventing reading difficulties in young children.* Washington, DC: National Academy Press.

Stanovich, K.E. (1986). Matthew effects in reading: Some consequences of individual differences in the acquisition of literacy. *Reading Research Quarterly, 21*, 360–407.

Torgeson, J.K. (1998, Spring/Summer). Catch them before they fail: Identification and assessment to prevent reading failure in young children. *American Educator, 22*, 32–39.

Vinz, R. (1996). *Composing a teaching life.* Portsmouth, NH: Boynton/Cook.

Vygotsky, L.S. (1986). *Thought and language* (A. Kozalin, Trans.). Cambridge, MA: The MIT Press. (Original work published 1934)

Waterford Institute. (2001/2002). *Research compendium: The Waterford early reading program.* Sandy, UT: Waterford Research Institute.

Literature Cited

Williams, W.C. (1962). *Pictures from Brueghel and other poems: Collected poems 1950–1962.* New York: New Directions.

Questions for Reflection

- Consider all the data sources about your students that you have available to you, including results over time on formal and informal assessments, work samples, and observations. How do you use these data, in isolation or together, to guide your instruction? What types of data are missing from your collection, and how could you collect them?

- The teacher described in this article uses DIBELS along with several other assessments to monitor her students' progress during their kindergarten year. DIBELS is widely used, but it is not without its detractors. What do you know about the strengths and limitations of DIBELS? If this assessment is in use in your school, do you feel it is being applied appropriately? Why or why not?

Leyendo Juntos (Reading Together): New Directions for Latino Parents' Early Literacy Involvement

Robert W. Ortiz and Rosario Ordoñez-Jasis

I want my children to have a better life than me, to succeed in anything they choose to do. To be literate, to be well educated, opens worlds for them and is something no one can take away, no one.... I've had to work since I was 14 and I didn't have certain opportunities, but for my children things will be different. (36-year-old Mexican agricultural worker and parent of four elementary school-aged children, personal communication, July 15, 2002)

Teacher educators in the United States are often asked by their students how schools can develop better family literacy programs and initiatives aimed toward Latino families. For many teachers, it appears that parent involvement in Latino families may not have produced the same positive results in academic success as in some other families. In the courses we teach, teachers and preservice teachers are urged to take a nonprescriptive stance toward family literacy, one that promotes family strengths and reciprocity and works to establish a more balanced partnership between schools and families.

Auerbach (1995) contended that recent trends in family literacy programs mask underlying differences in values, goals, ideological orientations, and pedagogical approaches to literacy. These programs sometimes aim to change parents' abilities and beliefs about their role in literacy development, proposing only school-like literacy interactions with their children. As an alternative, new directions for Latino parents' involvement in early literacy point to a renewed understanding and validation of the depth and diversity of home-based knowledge as children begin to acquire formal literacy skills.

Indeed, the importance of traditional parent involvement in their children's education has been well documented in the literature (Cairney & Munsie, 1995; Epstein & Dauber, 1991; Morrow, 1997), and it is associated with higher test scores, better attendance, and stronger cognitive skills (Slavin, Madden, Karweit, Dolan, & Wasik, 1994). Further research on parent involvement in early literacy development, in particular, has shown how early reading experiences better prepare children for the benefits of formal literacy instruction and build a foundation for later reading success (Genishi, Stires, & Yung-Chan, 2001; Stewart, 1986; Wells, 1985). Yet other researchers (McCarty & Watahomigie, 1998; Moll, Amanti, Neff, & Gonzalez, 1992) agree that nonmainstream parents can and do assist their children with reading and writing development through sometimes overlooked life events and community interactions that families experience daily. These nontraditional interactions and events should be the basis for developing culturally enriched literacy programs, for they have the potential to enhance children's education (Darling, 1992; Nieto, 2002).

Latino Schooling: A Diverse Community, a Diverse Pedagogy

There is an abundance of existing literature from a diversity of conceptual frameworks that

Reprinted from Ortiz, R.W., & Ordoñez-Jasis, R. (2005). *Leyendo juntos* (reading together): New directions for Latino parents' early literacy involvement. *The Reading Teacher, 59*(2), 110–121.

has attempted to explain the historical, sociological, and ideological aspects of the "Latino educational experience" in the United States for the past 40 years. However, researchers and practitioners alike face a challenge while attempting to explore the voices of a complex, dynamic community that encompasses a multitude of realities as rich and as diverse as Mexican farm workers in New Mexico, urban Puerto Rican youth in New York, or Cuban refugees in Florida. This diversity is addressed by using the term *Latinos* or the phrase "people generally related to Latin American origin or ancestry" (Jasis, 2000, p. 22) to describe this vast population segment. But the overt intention is to avoid an over-generalization of the hopes, challenges, and aspirations of the various communities and individual families. Thus, the term *Latino* is incorporated more as a concept nurtured out of a shared bond of culture, history, and often social oppression and inequality (Acuña, 1988; Barrera, 1997; Garcia, 2002). The challenge implied in sharing these literacy development approaches among educators is to include in our practice a variety of pedagogical notions that are flexible and creative enough to address the many realities of Latino students and their families.

A review of the literature indicates that, despite its diverse social and cultural indicators, the Latino community shares substandard school experiences across the United States, as well as a historical involvement in collective efforts to improve schooling for its members (Donato, 1997; Hero, 1992; Soto, 1997). Current statistics reveal that, although the conditions of Latino schooling have improved in many ways, Latino students are still dropping out of high school in large numbers and tend to be disproportionately represented in special education programs for slow learners (Daugherty, 2001). In 2000, only 64.1% of all Latino 18- through 24-year-olds had completed high school. This compares with 91.8% of white, 83.7% of black, and 94.6% of Asian students (National Center for Education Statistics, 2002). In an attempt to explain these disparities, the majority of research on these students has focused primarily on deficiencies of the individual, home, and culture. The predominant deficit-based paradigms have been widely mentioned in the literature. They include genetic inferiority (Herrnstein & Murray, 1994; Jensen, 1973; culture of poverty (Lewis, 1966), and deprivational theories (Valdés, 1996). The deficit-based model is so persistent that it has "the longest history of any explanatory model for understanding the achievement of low-status students discussed in the educational literature and is deeply imprinted in our individual and collective psyches" (Baca & Almanza, 1991, p. 2).

Deficit-based theories also have shaped the interactions that schools have had with Latino families. Despite evidence to the contrary (Ada, Campoy, & Zubizarreta, 2001; Moll, 1992; Ordoñez-Jasis, 2002; Ortiz, 1998), Latino parents are often viewed as nonsupportive of their children's school success, and their involvement is either unrecognized or perceived as counterproductive by many school officials (CTB/McGraw-Hill, 1988; Garcia, 2001; Teale, 1986).

While it appears that academicians, administrators, and researchers continually offer families from diverse linguistic and ethnic backgrounds hope that parents' engagement in reading and writing activities with their children will lead to academic achievement, Auerbach (1995) has correctly argued that current approaches in family literacy programs, particularly those targeted toward low-income families, tend to take a neo-deficit approach. That is, despite the recent discourse on family strengths, schools have failed to fully recognize, incorporate, or tap into the wealth of information, skills, and knowledge parents may hold in the area of literacy. As a result, a narrow definition of literacy, coupled with a one-dimensional view of parent involvement, may lead to misconceptions of families' strengths and abilities in these areas (Allen et al., 2002; Lareau, 1994; Moll, 1999; Ordoñez-Jasis, 2003).

Power Structures and Familial Literacy Models

Defining Literacy

Definitions of literacy can vary from the simple to the complex. At a basic level, literacy is generally associated with the ability to read and write. For example, Kaestle (1988) defined *literacy* as, "the ability to decode and comprehend written language at a rudimentary level, that is, the ability to look at written words corresponding to ordinary oral discourse, to say them and to understand them" (p. 96). But literacy can be viewed in a broader sense, that is, as the ability to think and reason within a particular society (Green & Dixon, 1996). Being literate was described as "mastery over the processes by means of which culturally significant information is coded" by de Castell and Luke (1988, p. 159). According to theorists, literacy cannot be content or context free, for it is always used as a mechanism of or is filtered through one's culture (Gee, 1992; Snow, 1983; Vygotsky, 1978). Because of the predilection toward social interaction in the construction of meaning and knowledge in one's world, a "sociocultural" perspective was selected as the paradigmatic construct when defining literacy for this article. (Additional information on the sociocultural concept and its relationship to familial literacy practices is offered in a following section.)

Because of the difference in perceptions of what constitutes "appropriate" literature and literacy activity between mainstream society and families from diverse ethnic backgrounds, we believe that reliable data on parental involvement practices become hard to find (Applebee, 1991). Devine (1994) highlighted the significance of how literacy is defined and understood differently among dominant and subordinate cultures in her interpretation of the "Muted Group Theory" (see Ardener, 1975, for the original formulation of the theory). Devine attributed the perceived literacy failure on the part of minority families within U.S. society as a mismatch between divergent sets of literacy attitudes and practices—those of the socially powerful mainstream culture and those of diverse ethnic and cultural groups.

Similarly, Valdés's (1996) research emphasized how Latino families have historically attended schools that have "failed to legitimize the forms of knowledge brought to school by [these] groups," validating only the literacy behaviors, activities, and events of the dominant group (p. 19). Furthermore, Miramontes (1991) suggested that many teachers regard the language environments of English-language learners as a limiting factor to literacy acquisition and academic success. At best, her research showed teachers feel that very little literacy learning is occurring in the home. At worst, very little occurs that is of value in school. Miramontes has found that teachers' assessments of students' abilities are often based on parents' willingness to become traditionally involved in their children's schooling, particularly with reading and writing tasks. Thus, it becomes difficult for non–English-speaking parents to participate in their children's literacy development "when homework represents narrow definitions of literacy, such as spelling or decoding exercises" (p. 80). Therefore, the link that supports parents to guide and assist in their children's reading and writing development begins to deteriorate; family dynamics become disrupted; home–school relations begin to weaken; and, quite possibly, inaccurate and limiting notions of students as deficit learners may arise (Miramontes, 1991; Valdés, 1996).

Literacy Development as a Sociocultural Activity

Sociocultural theory is the proposal that individual learning and social interaction are connected (Vygotsky, 1934/1978). As it relates to education, learning is shaped by a mutual exchange of views and experiences by all parties involved; that is, children, parents, and teachers engage in the process of constructing their thoughts, ideas, and beliefs about school and learning through social activity within and outside the classroom context (Bakhurst, 1990; D'Andrade, 1995). Thus, literacy development is often defined within this sociocultural framework (Gee, 1992;

Snow, 1983). Sociocultural perspectives of literacy propose that reading, writing, and language are not isolated and decontextualized activities (McLaughlin, 1989). Perez (1998) added,

> nor are they generalized skills separate from specific contents, contexts, and social-communicative purposes; rather, there are multiple literacies and reading, writing, and language are embedded in and inextricable from discourses (the way the communicative systems are organized within social practices). (p. 23)

To understand the process of literacy development through social interaction, we suggest considering the sociocultural context of the community where families live and the goals parents wish to achieve in sharing literacy activities with their children (e.g., educational, recreational, political, or economic). For example, a parent might read the baseball scores of a favorite team, an article about the political turmoil in his or her homeland, a storybook to a child, and the current job advertisements—all to achieve separate but specific goals. And a child might be curious about the parent's reading and writing activity, as exemplified by this father's comment.

> He [child] is the driving force [to engage in joint early literacy activities]. Any kind of material, he always wants to know what it means or why people have to document so much. He's always looking at that. He's very curious. He wants me to explain all this to him. (A. Gomez [pseudonym], personal communication, March 4, 1993)

A parent might ask a child to write down a list of grocery items that the family needs or take down an important phone message. These activities, which are home- and community-based social interactions, can be incorporated into the teacher's literacy curricula. Thus the parent assists the child in developing reading and writing skills from familiar life events.

These literacy examples are effective learning methods that Moll and his associates have used to their fullest potential. For example, Moll (1999) explored ways of using information from home and community contexts in classroom homework assignments. He organized writing instruction to include assignments that not only produced literacy-related interactions in the home but also involved parents and community members. For example, an assignment on the topic of bilingualism required that students develop a brief survey and ask their parents for their opinions, feelings, and knowledge on the subject. Not only did the students gain a greater understanding of the topic of bilingualism, but also parents became involved in their children's writing development. Moll commented on the effectiveness of these types of school tasks, "Students who otherwise would do little, if any, classroom writing were able to produce essays in their second language that incorporated information collected from their community" (p. 82). Taylor (1997), in acknowledging the role of the community and culture on family literacy use, reminded us that

> It is essential that literacy programs recognize and honor not only the diversity of literacies that exist within families, but also the communities and cultures of which they are a part. The culture of the community and the experiences of the families who live in the community are an essential part of all literacy programs. (p. 4)

As such, family literacy should be viewed as an activity continually in flux—being changed and modified by a number of economic, social, political, and personal factors to fit the needs of the family as well as each family member. This process inextricably includes the culture of the family that by its very nature is woven into the fabric of everyday life. Hence, the need to reexamine the multitude of ways in which parents involve themselves in the literary lives of their children is warranted and should serve as the foundation for the development of comprehensive and culturally relevant family literacy initiatives.

Latino Families and Early Literacy: Reviewing Promising Practices

Current studies on early literacy practices of Latino families suggest that there is parental guidance, participation, and concern with children's reading and writing development. The findings from these studies suggest that Latino families engage in both traditional and nontraditional literacy practices to develop and maintain skills that are used in the school, home, and community. In a sample of immigrant Central and South American families, Reese, Goldenberg, Loucky, and Gallimore (1995) found that contributions and assistance to children's literacy progress were related to parents' scholastic achievement. Reese (1992) found a history of familial literacy practices in Mexican households. Parents', siblings', aunts', and uncles' educational levels were positively correlated with children's reading achievement.

Delgado-Gaitan (1994), in a study looking at the early reading and writing experiences of immigrant families from Mexico, found that all parents valued literacy skills for their children. The parents had definite opinions on who were the proficient and struggling readers, and most of them read with their early elementary age children regularly. Delgado-Gaitan (1990) also found that children's homework was the most common printed text and literacy practice among the working-class, Mexican immigrant families she investigated.

Goldenberg and Gallimore (1991) identified the school as a major contributor to the literacy interactions of Mexican and Central American kindergartners at home where almost half of observed literacy activities involved school materials. Moll and his colleagues (Moll, Amanti, Neff, & Gonzalez, 1992; Moll & Gonzalez, 2004; Moll, Velez-Ibanez, & Greenberg, 1990) examined and documented the origin, use, and distribution of literacy skills through "funds of knowledge" found in immigrant, Mexican households. They looked at the learning conditions in the classroom and the rich learning culture found in these homes. They suggested strategies that incorporated the knowledge found in the community and that children brought to the classroom, with the school's literacy curriculum.

Several studies of Mexican and Central American families (Goldenberg, Reese, & Gallimore, 1992; Mulhern, 1994) found that kin-

dergarten and first-grade children were the initiators of many of the home literacy activities, with the children reading and writing alone, with their mothers, and with siblings. Mulhern (1994) described how one child in her study invented her own homework to do with her mother and sisters using writing tasks to "establish or affirm relationships with them" (p. 275). Ortiz (1994) found similar results with the Mexican American parents he interviewed. In fulfilling their curiosity about the meaning of text and print in and around their neighborhood (e.g., street signs, billboards, and logos), young children generated numerous questions for their parents to answer. Ada (2003), Huerta-Macias (1995), and Valdés (1996) looked at Mexican and Mexican American families and how oral storytelling (e.g., folk tales, fables, family histories), language, and themes (e.g., herbal medicines) related to the home culture played a significant role in familial literacy practices.

Case studies conducted by Ordoñez-Jasis (2002) documented, for example, Mexican American mothers' quests to develop bonds of attachment with their children via literacy activities and events. One mother created Thursday "dates" with her son, which included cooking his favorite meal, reading the Harry Potter books, and incorporating *consejos* (moral teachings) into subsequent postreading conversations. Here, these planned reading events offered this Latina mother and her child insights on themselves and their worlds by allowing them to connect with the text and with each other in real and meaningful ways.

Although many parent participants in Ordoñez-Jasis's (2002) study took an active role in their children's schooling (particularly in relation to the child's progress in reading) due to time constraints, other children, and employment, not all mothers were able to devote an entire, uninterrupted evening to a specific literacy activity or event. For example, this single mother's narrative demonstrates a desire and ability to spontaneously engage, read, and discuss texts, in various contexts, despite overwhelming obstacles.

I had Gustavo when I was only a sophomore in high school and dropped out. Now I have a terrible job where I work nights from 3:30 p.m. to midnight. I try to do as much as I can on the weekends, my days off, and when I drop him off and pick him up from school. In the car we practice spelling words, or I have him read signs on the road. If we're waiting at the doctor's (office) we read books together, at the market we read labels. I do whatever I can. Sometimes I get really scared, but I have to work. I don't want him to fall behind. I want him to finish school. (A. Rodriquez [pseudonym], personal communication, October 5, 2002)

This example reveals how planned and spontaneous literacy practices—intricately tied to family dynamics, home culture, and parental aspirations—provide new understandings for educators of the nontraditional literacy forms and behaviors many parents engage in as they connect and interact with their children in the hope of creating more positive dispositions toward reading.

Studies show an array of literacy experiences occur among Latino families, including literacy for entertainment, daily living, general information, religion, and other experiences beyond practices involving books or schooling per se (Delgado-Gaitan, 1994; Gallimore & Goldenberg, 1993; Ortiz, 1992). More recent data have been collected on various aspects of Latino parents' early literacy usage, such as reading and writing activities, topics engaged in, time spent on these activities, and the reasons for participating in them (Ordoñez-Jasis, 2002, 2003; Ordoñez-Jasis & Jasis, 2004; Ortiz, 1992, 1996, 1998, 2000, 2001; Ortiz & McCarty, 1997).

Still other researchers attribute academic success in literacy development by English-language learners to the use and maintenance of the native language (Adams, Astone, Nunez-Wormack, & Smodlaka, 1994; Gandara, 1995). Williams (1991) suggested that native language use and maintenance often act as a cushion against academic failure by encouraging literacy in children's most developed language. Soto's (1997) research found that parents of high-achieving Latino children provided native language home environments more often than the parents of low-achieving students. Gandara (1995), in looking at the academic achievement

of Mexican American adults who grew up in poverty, found that 84% of them came from homes where Spanish was the primary language. Similarly, Zentella (1997), in a study of Puerto Rican American families, found that the most successful students were enrolled in bilingual programs. Snow (1997), a leader in the field of literacy and language acquisition, stated that "the greatest contribution that immigrant parents can make to their children's success is to ensure they maintain fluency and continue to develop the home language" (p. 29).

Finally, Kalman's (1997) case study demonstrates how a Mexican father with a fourth-grade education engaged in a multitude of literacy uses that involved work, recreation, church, home, and school. One of the father's daughters went on to become a physician, another an accountant, and another a translator. This, according to Kalman, breaks the rule of the intergenerational passing down of a weak, familial literacy legacy. Kalman suggested that reading and writing that are deeply embedded in the context of one's daily life point to evidence that literacy practices are constructed in response more to a "communicative need" (p. 55) than to unclear school reading assignments.

Clearly, the findings highlighted here suggest that Latino parents are involved in their children's literacy experiences and that there is diversity in their practices. Auerbach (1989), in a review of research, found that rather than being literacy impoverished, the home environments of poor, undereducated, and English-language learning children are rich with reading and writing practices and literacy tools and materials. Moreover, studies (Allen et al., 2002; Purcell-Gates, 1995) have documented that culturally and linguistically diverse parents not only value literacy but also see it as the single most powerful hope for their children.

Recommendations for Parent Early Literacy Involvement

Although the data presented here suggest that Latino parents are involved with their children's learning in a variety of ways, more work is need-ed to (a) help parents and educators recognize and broaden the role families have in their children's learning and (b) establish home–school relationships based on mutual respect and trust that support the attainment of literacy skills and goals. To more effectively promote comprehensive family literacy programs and initiatives, we offer the following recommendations.

1. *Reflect upon current notions of, and dispositions toward, parent involvement at the district, school, and classroom levels.* As mentioned previously, research suggests that despite high verbal support for parent involvement among educators, many schools and individual teachers tend to adopt an approach to family literacy based upon deficit assumptions, unequal power relations, and hierarchical structures that marginalize parental voices and efforts. Research conducted by Epstein and Dauber (1991) has demonstrated that few teachers receive systematic education on family involvement in schools. However, these researchers also found that when teachers were given the opportunity to engage in prolonged discussion and assessment of their school's family involvement programs and policies, positive relations and equal exchanges of knowledge between parents and educators occurred. Similarly, Ada et al. (2001) argued that teachers need to individually and collectively reflect upon the attitudes, practices, and assumptions they hold toward parent involvement. Next, they suggested that schools outline their focus, goals, orientation, and content related to family literacy agendas and objectively assess their strengths and weaknesses. Finally, Ada et al. (2001) emphasized the need for teachers to identify those variables that restrict schools from effectively reaching out to parents, such as time, resources, and school norms, and subsequently develop a joint action plan that addresses these barriers.

By engaging in collective reflection and schoolwide assessment, educators can develop meaningful dialogue whereby parents and teachers jointly explore ways to enhance literacy development within the classroom or via school-wide efforts. Literacy curricula, benchmarks, and assessment plans will be better suited for the child's learning style and particular needs when parents' ideas are included in the overall decision-making process.

2. *Obtain preliminary or background information from both parents.* Through parent surveys, individual interviews, focus groups, and home observations, a wealth of information can be obtained about specific family situations as well as parental perceptions and expectations on the uses and functions for literacy in their lives. As stated earlier, *Latinos* is a broad term used to describe a vast and diverse segment of the population, those who live under very different conditions, vary in socioeconomic status, and differ both in the needs they may have and the resources they can offer. The need to understand the uniqueness of community groups is paramount in developing a strength-based literacy program relevant to the lives of students and their families. Moll and Gonzalez (2004) strongly advocated that teachers discover the "funds of knowledge" that are accumulated over time in the homes of Latino families. Teachers can begin by entering their students' communities to observe how households function. For example, through social networks many families assist one another with finding jobs, taking care of children, and getting information for survival. Teachers can then take field notes, write personal journals, and hand out surveys to obtain a sense of the "funds of knowledge" in each household. After the in-home observations, teachers can come together in study groups to discuss their findings. With this information, teachers are able to create new teaching modules that use knowledge that children immediately recognize as significant in their lives.

The following questions may serve as a starting point in developing family literacy curricula based on parents' background information: From which Latin American country do families originate? In what language do they prefer to read? What interests does the family unit have? What type of materials do both parents enjoy reading? How comfortable are the parents in reading to their children? What are their goals for sharing literacy activities with their children?

In what ways do parents contribute to developing early reading skills? With this information, teachers, training personnel, and parents can construct a literacy agenda for children identifying fun, interesting, and meaningful reading activities to use at home and in school.

3. *Diversify reading materials. Latino parents in the studies cited chose reading materials they found interesting, helpful, and important to them.* The topics of their literacy interests varied widely, and it was through these "conduits" of reading interests that they explored text and print with their children (Ortiz, 1994). Consider including multicultural literature that reflects the rich and diverse realities and interests of Latino families. Family literacy programs have a greater chance of success and longevity when they attempt to tap into the wealth of background knowledge and experiences of the parent participants. Ada's (2003) historical analysis of books for children by Latino authors includes the following themes that have been found to be relevant for many families.

- Preserving tradition
- Celebrating the richness of culture
- Telling one's personal story
- Telling stories of people who share similar experiences
- Valuing family
- Addressing social issues and concerns

Ada (2003) further suggested that in facilitating dialogue with parents over literary selections, educators should consider a wide range of genres as possible reading materials for families: poetry, theater, biography, autobiography, history, and contemporary fiction and fantasy. Through a plan of reciprocity, parents can help schools identify texts that will enhance classrooms while educators, in turn, can seek out texts that can be shared with parents.

4. *Consider literacy as a means to parent empowerment.* Research findings suggest the attitudes that parents hold toward literacy will affect the type and amount of reading and writing they engage in with their children (Thornburg, 1993;

Yaden, Rowe, & MacGillivray, 2000). Although many parents expressed high expectations for the role of literacy in their children's lives, many felt they did not have enough information, training, or confidence to connect existing home literacy activities with academic achievement. Educators such as Freire and Macedo (1987) have written on the critical links between literacy, self-development, and empowerment. Literacy, according to these authors, holds the power to generate transformative thought and social action. Delgado-Gaitan's (1994) and Jasis's (2000) research with Latino families, for example, demonstrated how schools can play a role in establishing mutually empowering parent networks that can engage in educational decision making and improve schooling. Hence, educators can unveil and enhance the literate potential of Latino families by developing family literacy workshops where parents have an opportunity to reflect on and discuss among themselves the ways in which literacy affects their lives.

Beginning parent training with a safe place to share stories of triumphs, frustrations, and lessons learned will help build common ground among the participants and create an overall environment whereby parents develop agency and gain the confidence to construct new learning-based literacy activities with their children. It is important to note that educators need not abandon the goal of having all students attain traditional literacy skills; however, understanding, validating, and incorporating parents' diverse approaches to literacy acquisition builds a solid foundation for further learning to take place.

5. *Consider those parents who are not able to read or write.* Parents who cannot read or write fluently in their primary language or English still play a critical role in their child's literacy learning. The role of oral language development, in particular, should not be underestimated for it has been shown to be a strong precursor to early literacy (Burns, Griffin, & Snow, 1998). Children's oral, dramatic, and creative expressions also are enhanced when parents engage them in rhymes, songs, riddles, oral history, poetry, proverbs, and folklore (Ada, 2003; Snow, 1983). Literate and nonliterate parents alike should be encour-

aged to engage in enriching dialogue and language play with their children. Storytelling, for example, allows parents to create their own story with a beginning, middle, and end, referred to as sequencing. Storytelling prepares children to understand the complex components of literacy, such as motive for action, author/audience relationships, and the cultural definitions of a good story (Craig, Hull, Haggart, & Crowder, 2001). Invite family and community members to share stories with the class. Encourage them to share what they recall about being a child, coming to the United States, and learning how to read. Ask children to audiotape the guest storyteller, so that the stories can be listened to again and again (Craig et al.).

Educators also should model for parents how to share wordless picture books with their children to teach important early literacy skills: predicting, story sequencing, concepts of print, describing details within illustrations, and identifying key story elements or main characters. Using wordless picture books is also an excellent means for children and their parents to understand the aesthetic pleasures texts provide while they develop the critical tools of creativity and imagination.

6. *Take into consideration those parents with particular needs.* For a multitude of reasons, some parents may not involve themselves in their children's schooling (Lareau, 1994). For example, some parents must work two or more jobs, making it difficult to attend school functions. Recent Latino immigrant parents may be hesitant to attend school activities because they may be unfamiliar with the U.S. educational system; they may not understand or speak English well enough to communicate effectively with their child's classroom teacher. Second- or third-generation parents may not have had a positive educational experience themselves within U.S. schools and consequently may distrust school officials. For parent groups such as these, it is particularly important to create common ground and avoid making negative assumptions about their educational values and expectations (Nieto, 2002). A more comprehensive understanding and appreciation of others' insights, contributions, and perceptions are developed when parents and teachers reach a point of mutual understanding (Allen et al., 2002).

Educators should attempt a variety of approaches to effectively connect to parents. Send home translated materials such as surveys or invitations for special events. Parent workshops and conferences also should be conducted in the parents' primary language. When this is not possible, provide a translator, drawing upon the rich linguistic resources of potential parent liaisons within schools. In the research highlighted earlier, some parent participants expressed being "overwhelmed" with the amount of paperwork sent home from schools. Phone calls, scheduled home visits, or personal invitations to parents for school functions are positive additions to outreach efforts.

Teachers should be flexible in scheduling. The work schedule of the single mother in one case study (Ordoñez-Jasis, 2002) prevented her from attending parent–teacher conferences or family workshops held in the afternoon. An option is to vary the times of meetings and workshops offered throughout the year. Consider potluck activities such as a "Books and Breakfast" workshop one morning, a "Snack and Stories" on another afternoon, and possibly a "Dinner and Discoveries" later in the year. In addition, consider providing childcare services for those parents who would not otherwise be able to attend.

Finally, for many Latino households, *family* is a broad term that includes extended family members. Encourage older siblings, cousins, grandparents, aunts, uncles, and *padrinos* (godparents) to attend workshops or engage in home literacy activities, if the parents cannot.

7. *Build a strong community of learners.* It is essential for teachers to link literacy activities to the home and community environments. As mentioned earlier, teachers must integrate the families' "funds of knowledge" (Moll, 1992) into the classroom and make every attempt at understanding who parents are and where they are coming from. For example, investigate the interests that parents and children have, such as hobbies, sports, and celebrated cultural events. Build reading and writing assignments around

this information. Read literature that defines and describes the ethnicity of the family, but with the objective of moving beyond studying cultural artifacts to looking more closely at how families live culturally. For example, invite parents and students to bring photographs to class that they feel are important to them (Allen et al., 2002). Pictures can be of anyone or anything they feel has meaning not only from a cultural perspective but also from a personal one. Use these pictures to develop an understanding of and begin a relationship with families, thus having a "cultural" snapshot of the child sitting in the classroom.

Goldenberg and Gallimore (1991) concluded that Latino students attain higher achievement levels when their teachers actively attempt to make connections with their home and community values. Auerbach (1989) commented on the importance of these connections as follows:

> Literacy is meaningful to students to the extent that it relates to daily realities.... The teachers' role is to connect what happens inside the classroom to what happens outside so that literacy can become a meaningful tool for addressing the issues in students' lives. (p. 166)

As previously mentioned, reading and writing are often related to carrying out the numerous tasks demanded by the society and culture in which we live. And, as such, they should serve as the foundation for recommending strategies and techniques.

Shared Literacy Activities Foster Learning

Parents' involvement in their children's literacy experiences has been shown to have positive outcomes relative to academic achievement. Yet it also has been suggested that many Latino families have been unable to reap similar rewards when parents have engaged in shared literacy practices. The various reasons offered for this disparity include school personnel adhering to deficit-based theories and teachers failing to tap into the rich background experiences that these families bring with them.

We recommend that a sociocultural framework be applied when considering ways that teachers and parents can work together to build children's literacy skills. A sociocultural paradigm, in brief, is the premise that relationships are developed through an interactive process, one that is continually being defined and manipulated as families transact with the environment. Literacy within this framework is the construction of meaning from printed text in the world in which families live, and it is extended into the classroom (Perez, 1998). Learning, therefore, becomes a reciprocal "sharing" experience that benefits teachers, parents, and children.

Latino families form a heterogeneous group that differs in its experiences and literacy practices and varies in its understanding of learning processes. But families feel a tremendous sense of accomplishment when children succeed in school. By engaging in shared literacy practices, parents and their children undergo a metamorphosis, a transformation that is mutually rewarding. Parents take their children one step closer to realizing the importance of learning to read and write, and children are prepared to enter a literary world that is not only functional but also filled with amazing adventures and astonishing characters. In addition, parents and children experience a "bonding" relationship that fosters literacy interests and abilities. Parents then can monitor their children's literacy growth and share this valuable information—as well as their concerns—with school personnel. This type of shared event may have more of an impact on teaching children basic literacy skills than if they were formally instructed within the classroom.

Many parents engage in literacy activities every day without a second thought. But when mothers and fathers share print and text with a child, their role evolves from one of gaining knowledge at a personal level to becoming empowered resources for and "meaning makers" of their children's lives. Although parents may not fully realize the benefits associated with this type of shared activity, it is recognized that they are the most important influence and that to expect academic achievement they must be actively involved in their children's learning. Teachers play a crucial role in this process. The potential and promise of active parental involvement in children's early literacy development requires that educators connect with and expand the wealth of home-based knowledge to school-based practices in order to build a foundation for students' success.

References

Acuña, R. (1988). *Occupied America: A history of Chicanos.* New York: HarperCollins.

Ada, A.F. (2003). *A magical encounter: Latino children's literature in the classroom.* Boston: Allyn & Bacon.

Ada, A.F., Campoy, F.I., & Zubizarreta, R. (2001). Assessing our work with parents on behalf of children's literacy. In S. Hurley & J. Tinajero (Eds.), *Literacy assessment of second language learners* (pp. 160–182). Boston: Allyn & Bacon.

Adams, D., Astone, B., Nunez-Wormack, E., & Smodlaka, I. (1994). Predicting the academic achievement of Puerto Rican and Mexican American ninth-grade students. *The Urban Review, 26*(1), 1–14.

Allen, J., Fabregas, V., Hankins, K.H., Hull, G., Labbo, L., Lawson, H.S., et al. (2002). PhOLKS lore: Learning from photographs, families, and children. *Language Arts, 79,* 312–322.

Applebee, A.N. (1991). Literature: Whose heritage? In E.H. Hiebert (Ed.), *Literacy for a diverse society: Perspectives, practices, and policies* (pp. 228–252). New York: Teachers College Press.

Ardener, E. (1975). The "problem" revisited. In S. Ardener (Ed.), *Perceiving women* (pp. 19–27). London: Malaby Press.

Auerbach, E. (1989). Toward a socio-contextual approach to family literacy. *Harvard Educational Review, 59,* 165–181.

Auerbach, E. (1995). Deconstructing the discourse of strengths in family literacy. *Journal of Reading Behavior, 27,* 643–661.

Baca, L., & Almanza, E. (1991). *Language minority students with disabilities.* Reston, VA: Council for Exceptional Children. (ERIC Document Reproduction Service No. ED 339 171)

Bakhurst, D. (1990). *Consciousness and revolution in Soviet philosophy: From the Bolsheviks to Evald Ilyenkow.* Cambridge, England: Cambridge University Press.

Barrera, M. (1997). A theory of racial inequality. In A. Darder, R.D. Torres, & H. Gutierrez (Eds.), *Latinos and education: A critical reader* (pp. 3–44). New York: Routledge.

Burns, M.S., Griffin, P., & Snow, C.E. (1998). *Starting out right: A guide to promoting children's reading success.* New York: National Academy Press.

Cairney, T.H., & Munsie, L. (1995). *Beyond tokenism: Parents as partners in literacy.* Portsmouth, NH: Heinemann.

Craig, S., Hull, K., Haggart, A.G., & Crowder, E. (2001). Storytelling: Addressing the literacy needs of diverse learners. *Teaching Exceptional Children, 33*(5), 46–51.

CTB/McGraw-Hill. (1988). *SABE: Spanish Assessment of Basic Education* (Technical report). Monterey, CA: Author.

D'Andrade, R. (1995). *The development of cognitive anthropology.* New York: Cambridge University Press.

Darling, S. (1992). Family literacy: Parents and children learning together. *Principal, 72*(2), 10–12.

Daugherty, D. (2001). *IDEA '97 and disproportionate placement.* Retrieved June 17, 2003, from http://www.naspcenter.org/teachers/IDEA_disp.html de Castell, S., & Luke, A. (1988). Defining literacy in North American schools. In E.R. Kintgen, B.M. Kroll, & M. Rose (Eds.), *Perspectives on literacy* (pp. 159–174). Carbondale: Southern Illinois University Press.

Delgado-Gaitan, C. (1990). *Literacy for empowerment: The role of parents in children's education.* London: Falmer.

Delgado-Gaitan, C. (1994). Sociocultural change through literacy: Toward the empowerment of families. In B.M. Ferdman, R.M. Weber, & A.G. Ramirez (Eds.), *Literacy across languages and cultures* (pp. 143–169). Albany: State University of New York Press.

Devine, J. (1994). Literacy and social power. In B.M. Ferdman, R.M. Weber, & A.G. Ramirez (Eds.), *Literacy across languages and cultures* (pp. 221–237). Albany: State University of New York Press.

Donato, R. (1997). *The other struggle for equal schools: Mexican Americans during the civil rights era.* Albany: State University of New York Press.

Epstein, J.L., & Dauber, S.L. (1991). School programs and teacher practices of parent involvement in inner-city elementary and middle schools. *The Elementary School Journal, 91,* 289–305.

Freire, P., & Macedo, D. (1987). *Literacy: Reading the world and the word.* New York: Bergin & Garvey.

Gallimore, R., & Goldenberg, C.N. (1993). Activity settings of early literacy: Home and school factors in children's emergent literacy. In E. Forman, N. Minick, & C.A. Stone (Eds.), *Contexts for learning: Sociocultural dynamics in children's development* (pp. 315–335). New York: Oxford University Press.

Gandara, P. (1995). *Over the ivy walls: The educational mobility of low-income Chicanos.* Albany: State University of New York Press.

Garcia, E. (2001). *Hispanic education in the United States: Raices y alas.* Lanham, MD: Rowman & Littlefield.

Garcia, E. (2002). *Student cultural diversity: Understanding and meeting the challenge.* Boston: Houghton Mifflin.

Gee, J. (1992). Socio-cultural approaches to literacy (literacies). *Annual Review of Applied Linguistics, 12,* 31–48.

Genishi, C., Stires, S., & Yung-Chan, D. (2001). Writing in an integrated curriculum: Prekindergarten English language learners as symbol makers. *The Elementary School Journal, 101,* 399–414.

Goldenberg, C.N., & Gallimore, R. (1991). Local knowledge, research knowledge, and educational change: A case study of early Spanish reading improvement. *Educational Researcher, 20,* 2–14.

Goldenberg, C.N., Reese, L., & Gallimore, R. (1992). Effects of literacy materials from school on Latino children's home experiences and early reading achievement. *American Journal of Education, 100,* 497–536.

Green, J., & Dixon, C. (1996). Language of literacy dialogues: Facing the future or reproducing the past. *Journal of Literacy Research, 28,* 290–301.

Hero, R. (1992). *Latinos and the U.S. political system: Two-tiered pluralism.* Boston: Temple University Press.

Herrnstein, R.J., & Murray, C. (1994). *The bell curve: Intelligence and class structure in American life.* New York: Free Press Paperbacks.

Huerta-Macias, A. (1995). Literacy from within: The Project FIEL curriculum. In G. Weinstein-Shr & E. Quintero (Eds.), *Immigrant learners and their families: Literacy to connect generations* (pp. 91–99). McHenry, IL: Center for Applied Linguistics & Delta Systems.

Jasis, P. (2000). *Building la familia: Organization and empowerment with Latino parents in a public school.* Unpublished dissertation, University of California at Berkeley.

Jensen, A.R. (1973). *Educability and group differences.* Edinburgh, Scotland: Methuen.

Kaestle, C.F. (1988). The history of literacy and the history of readers. In E.R. Kintgen, B.M. Kroll, & M. Rose (Eds.), *Perspectives on literacy* (pp. 95–126). Carbondale: Southern Illinois University Press.

Kalman, J. (1997). Sr. Gonzalo and his daughters: A family tale from Mexico. In D. Taylor (Ed.), *Many families, many literacies* (pp. 51–55). Portsmouth, NH: Heinemann.

Lareau, A. (1994). Parent involvement in schooling: A dissenting view. In C. Fagnano & B. Werber (Eds.), *School, family and community interaction* (pp. 61–73). San Francisco: Westview Press.

Lewis, O. (1966). The culture of poverty. *Scientific American, 215*(4), 19–25.

McCarty, T.L., & Watahomigie, L.S. (1998). Language and literacy in American Indian and Alaska Native communities. In B. Perez (Ed.), *Sociocultural contexts of language and literacy* (pp. 69–98). Mahwah, NJ: Erlbaum.

McLaughlin, D. (1989). The sociolinguistics of Navajo literacy. *Anthropology and Education Quarterly, 20,* 275–290.

Miramontes, O.B. (1991). Organizing for effective paraprofessional services in special education: A multi-lingual/multi-ethnic instructional service (MMIS) team model. *Remedial and Special Education, 12,* 29–36.

Moll, L. (1992). Literacy research in community and classrooms: A sociocultural approach. In R. Beach, J.L. Green, M.L. Kamil, & T. Shanahan (Eds.), *Multidisciplinary perspectives on literacy research* (pp. 211–244). Urbana, IL: National Council of Teachers of English.

Moll, L. (1999). Writing as communication: Creating strategic learning environments for students. In E.R. Hollins & E.I. Oliver (Eds.), *Pathways to success in school: Culturally responsive teaching* (pp. 73–84). Mahwah, NJ: Erlbaum.

Moll, L., Amanti, C., Neff, D., & Gonzalez, N. (1992). Funds of knowledge for teaching: Using a qualitative approach to connect homes and classrooms. *Theory Into Practice, 31,* 132–141.

Moll, L., & Gonzalez, N. (2004). Beginning where children are. In O. Santa Ana (Ed.), *Tongue-tied: The lives of multilingual children in public education* (pp. 152–156). Lanham, MD: Rowman & Littlefield.

Moll, L., Velez-Ibanez, C., & Greenberg, J. (1990). *Community knowledge and classroom practice: Combining resources for literacy instruction.* Arlington, VA: Development Associates.

Morrow, L.M. (1997). *Literacy development in the early years: Helping children read and write* (3rd ed.). Boston: Allyn & Bacon.

Mulhern, M.M. (1994). *Webs of meaning: The literate lives of three Mexican-American kindergartners.* Unpublished doctoral dissertation, University of Illinois at Chicago.

National Center for Education Statistics. (2002). *Dropout rates in the United States: 2000.* Retrieved June 16, 2003, from http://nces.ed.gov/pubs2002/droppub_2001/

Nieto, S. (2002). *Language, culture, and teaching: Critical perspectives for a new century.* Mahwah, NJ: Erlbaum.

Ordoñez-Jasis, R. (2002). *Chicano families and schools: Tensions, transitions and transformations.* Unpublished doctoral dissertation, Graduate School of Education, University of California at Berkeley.

Ordoñez-Jasis, R. (2003, May). *Chicano families and special education: Reconstructing the "reluctant reader."* Paper presented at the annual meeting of the Linguistic Minority Research Association, San Diego, CA.

Ordoñez-Jasis, R., & Jasis, P. (2004). Rising with De Colores: Tapping into the resources of la comunidad to assist under-performing Chicano/Latino students. *Journal of Latinos and Education, 3*(1), 53–64.

Ortiz, R.W. (1992). *The unpackaging of generation and social class factors: A study on literacy activities and educational values of Mexican American fathers.* Unpublished doctoral dissertation, University of California at Los Angeles.

Ortiz, R.W. (1994). Fathers and children explore literacy. *The Kamehameha Journal of Education, 5,* 131–134.

Ortiz, R.W. (1996). Fathers' contribution to children's early literacy development: The relationship of marital role functions. *The Journal of Educational Issues of Language Minority Students, 16,* 131–148.

Ortiz, R.W. (1998). Chipping away at the monolith: Dispelling the myth of father noninvolvement in children's early literacy development. *Family Preservation Journal, 3*(2), 73–94.

Ortiz, R.W. (2000). The many faces of learning to read: The role of fathers in helping their children to develop early literacy skills. *Multicultural Perspectives, 2*(2), 10–17.

Ortiz, R.W. (2001). Pivotal parents: Emergent themes and implications on father involvement in children's early literacy experiences. *Reading Improvement, 38*(2), 132–144.

Ortiz, R.W., & McCarty, L.L. (1997). Daddy, read to me: Fathers helping their young children learn to read. *Reading Horizons, 38*(2), 108–115.

Perez, B. (1998). *Sociocultural contexts of language and literacy.* Mahwah, NJ: Erlbaum.

Purcell-Gates, V. (1995). *Other people's words: The cycle of low literacy.* Cambridge, MA: Harvard University Press.

Reese, L. (1992). *Ecocultural factors influencing the academic success of young Latino students.* Unpublished doctoral dissertation, University of California at Los Angeles.

Reese, L., Goldenberg, C., Loucky, J., & Gallimore, R. (1995). Ecocultural context, cultural activity, and emergent literacy: Sources of variation in home literacy experiences of Spanish-speaking children. In S.W. Rothstein (Ed.), *Class, culture, and race in American schools* (pp. 199–224). Westport, CT: Greenwood Press.

Slavin, R.E., Madden, N.A., Karweit, N.L., Dolan, L.J., & Wasik, B.A. (1994). Success for all: Getting reading right the first time. In E.H. Hiebert & B.M. Taylor (Eds.), *Getting reading right from the start* (pp. 125–147). Boston: Allyn & Bacon.

Snow, C.E. (1983). Literacy and language: Relationships during the preschool years. *Harvard Educational Review, 53,* 165–189.

Snow, C.E. (1997). The myths around bilingual education. *NABE News, 21*(2), 29.

Soto, L.D. (1997). *Language, culture, and power: Bilingual families and the struggle for quality education.* Albany: State University of New York Press.

Stewart, J. (1986). *Kindergarten children's awareness of how they are learning to read: Home and school context.* Unpublished doctoral dissertation, University of Illinois at Urbana-Champaign.

Taylor, D. (1997). *Many families, many literacies.* Portsmouth, NH: Heinemann.

Teale, W.H. (1986). Home background and young children's literacy development. In W.H. Teale & E. Sulzby (Eds.), *Emergent literacy: Writing and reading* (pp. 173–206). Norwood, NJ: Ablex.

Thornburg, D.G. (1993). Intergenerational literacy learning with bilingual families: A context for the analysis of social mediation of thought. *Journal of Reading Behavior, 25,* 323–352.

Valdés, G. (1996). *Con respeto: Bridging the distance between culturally diverse families and schools.* New York: Teachers College Press.

Vygotsky, L.S. (1978). *Mind and society: The development of higher psychological processes* (M. Cole, V. John-Steiner, S. Scribner, & E. Souberman, Eds. & Trans.). Cambridge, MA: Harvard University Press. (Original work published 1934)

Wells, G. (1985). *Learning, language, and education.* Philadelphia: NFER-Nelson.

Williams, S.W. (1991). Classroom use of African American language: Educational tool or social weapon? In C.E. Sleeter (Ed.), *Empowerment through multicultural education* (pp. 199–215). Albany: State University of New York Press.

Yaden, D., Rowe, D., & MacGillivray, L. (2000). Emergent literacy: A matter of (polyphony) of perspectives. In M. Kamil, P. Mosenthal, P.D. Pearson, & R. Barr (Eds.), *Handbook of reading research* (Vol. 3, pp. 425–454). Mahwah, NJ: Erlbaum.

Zentella, A.C. (1997). *Growing up bilingual: Puerto Rican children in New York.* Malden, MA: Blackwell.

Questions for Reflection

• The authors stress the importance of direct outreach to parents and of significant efforts in getting to know the family circumstances of young learners. Such activities obviously require considerable time and resources, but the authors suggest some ways that they can be effectively managed—by, for example, rethinking traditional evening parent–teacher conferences and scheduling instead morning coffee or afternoon snack time. Think about the resources available in your instructional setting. In what ways can you accomplish the goal of direct, personal, ongoing contact with parents and extended family while still managing the other demands of your job? What can other teachers, administrators, aides, or other families assist with? How can children themselves be enlisted in support of your efforts?

• This article focuses on Latino children and families in the United States. Do you have children from other cultural and linguistic backgrounds in your classroom? If so, how can learning from this article be extended to inform your work with those families?

Is Being Wild About Harry Enough?
Encouraging Independent
Reading at Home

Nancy Padak and Timothy Rasinski

We began drafting this column in the midst of the latest Harry Potter craze. The television news was full of countdowns to the availability of *Harry Potter and the Deathly Hallows* (Rowling, 2007). Videos showed long lines of children, many in costume, eagerly awaiting the chance to find out what happens to Harry and his Hogwarts friends. Early sales reports were amazing: 1.8 million copies were sold in the first 48 hours after release (home.businesswire.com, retrieved July 25, 2007).

But in the midst of all this "Potter mania," a few educators and reporters offered discouraging words. Although "many parents, teachers, librarians, and booksellers have credited [the Harry Potter series] with inspiring a generation of kids to read for pleasure" (Rich, 2007, para. 1), data about children's recreational reading outside of school in the United States paint a different picture. National Assessment of Educational Progress results, for example, show that the percentage of children who say they read for fun almost every day dropped from 43% at grade 4 to 19% at grade 8 (Rich, 2007).

Apparently, being wild about Harry isn't enough. Yet most educators agree that the goal of promoting children's outside-of-school literacy experiences is important. In this department for *The Reading Teacher* [the original source of publication of this article], we will address issues related to family literacy, particularly ways to encourage parents and other family members to engage children in reading and related activities outside of school. In this first column, we address the "whys" and "hows" of encouraging independent reading at home.

Why Is Reading at Home Important?

Family literacy professionals often point out that parents are their children's first and most important teachers. Indeed, research tells us that children whose families encourage at-home literacy activities have higher phonemic awareness and decoding skills (Burgess, 1999), higher reading achievement in the elementary grades (Cooter et al., 1999), and advanced oral language development (Sénéchal, LeFevre, & Thomas, 1998).

Two additional studies point to the "why" of reading at home. Durkin's (1966) classic study examined the reading achievement of more than 75 children who read before first grade. Durkin found that these early readers maintained higher achievement over time than children who were not early readers. In her search for family influences on early readers, Durkin found commonalities. For example, parents reported that their children remained engaged in self-initiated writing projects for long periods of time and that they frequently requested that parents read to them. In highlighting what she considered to be the most significant findings of her research, Durkin (1966) noted

> the presence of parents who spend time with their children; who read to them; who answer their questions and their requests for help; and who demonstrate in their own lives that reading is a rich source of relaxation, information, and contentment. (p. 136)

Reprinted from Padak, N., & Rasinski, T. (2007). Is being wild about Harry enough? Encouraging independent reading at home (Family Involvement department). *The Reading Teacher, 61*(4), 350–353.

Hart and Risley (1995) studied the early language interactions in families of varying socioeconomic status (SES). Their multiyear study involved 42 families who differed in socioeconomic status; gender composition and ethnic background (African American and Caucasian) were distributed among SES categories. For an hour each month (30 hours per family), Hart and Risley observed and tape-recorded family talk. They transcribed and analyzed the tapes to learn more about family conversations and children's opportunities to learn through language.

Hart and Risley (2003) found that "the 42 children [grew] more like their parents... in vocabulary resources, and in language and interaction styles...86–98% of the words in each child's vocabulary consisted of words also recorded in their parents' vocabularies" (p. 7). They also found a stunning difference in children's access to language, perhaps the major finding of this important study. In brief, children from the wealthiest families heard over 1,500 more words each hour, on average, than children from the poorest families (616 vs. 2,153). Over four years, this amounts to a 32-million-word difference! Moreover, a follow-up study of 29 of the original children showed that children's rate of vocabulary growth and vocabulary use at age 3 was strongly associated with their grade 3 standardized test scores in receptive vocabulary, listening, speaking, semantics, syntax, and reading comprehension (Hart & Risley, 2003).

Together, these studies build a strong rationale for parents' involvement in their children's reading. From this body of research we see that what happens in the home makes a difference, for better or for worse. Moreover, the research results should be comforting to parents; encouraging at-home reading need not be time consuming or complex. Instead, parents can talk, encourage, answer child-initiated questions, and model their own literate behaviors.

How to Encourage Independent Reading at Home

As we have seen, home involvement can provide rich opportunities for children to develop as readers. Instructing parents to simply, "Read to your child" or "Encourage your child to read at home"

may be a start, but it is not enough. Parents need specific suggestions and guidelines about what to do. We offer the following suggestions based on our own work with parents.

Keep It Simple

Many parents have limited time to devote to working with their children, so at-home activities must be easy to implement. In addition, you should help parents see that the recommended activities have been proven to make a positive difference in children's reading achievement.

Help Parents See Their Options

They may want to read to their children. Many parents believe this "reading to" should cease when their children begin to read independently. Not so! Help parents of older children see the value of continuing to read aloud, perhaps chapters at bedtime or an interesting article from the newspaper. Parents can also read with their children, perhaps alternating pages or paragraphs. They may want to listen to their children read. They may want to sit side by side with their children, each reading what he or she desires. They may even want to encourage their child to read to a family pet or even a stuffed animal. All these activities are legitimate forms of independent reading at home that will lead to success in children's literacy development.

Provide Texts or Booklists

Some at-home reading programs fail because parents lack appropriate texts or the time or resources to acquire them. Ideally, children should take books home from school. Some families may have time for trips to the public library, but these trips shouldn't be required for participation in the at-home reading program.

Teach Parents the Five-Finger Rule of Book Selection

(The child opens to a page in the middle of a book and begins to read, raising a finger each time he or she encounters an unknown word. If five fingers are raised before the page is complete, the book is probably too challenging for the child to read independently.) It may also be necessary to talk with parents about such issues as whether it's OK for a child to reread a favorite book or to read books that are "too easy." (In both cases, it's OK!) You may also need to think about whether Internet reading will "count" for purposes of your program.

Help Parents See and Use Print Wherever It May Be Found

Newspapers, magazines, mail, notes, shopping lists, bumper stickers, street and store signs, religious texts and hymnals are just a few types of print in addition to books that parents can use to make literacy a part of daily life for their families. Captioned television is particularly noteworthy. We know many families who claim that their children learned to read by being exposed to print while watching favorite television programs—the children simultaneously heard and saw the words in print on the television screen.

Provide Special Support for Children Who Are Learning English and for Their Families

Classroom volunteers can record texts in English for children to take home. Together, the parent and child can listen to the recording (several times, if necessary) and then read aloud along with the taped version.

Keep up With Children's Literature and Use Children's Interests to Make Book Recommendations

Read the Children's Choices lists (published in *The Reading Teacher* each October) and recurring columns about children's books in *Reading Today*, *The Reading Teacher*, and *Language Arts*. Look for book information on the Internet. Table 1 features valuable children's literature websites. All were active in July 2007 [and have been updated in October 2009 for this publication].

With these guidelines in mind, you are ready to plan the at-home reading program. The following are some things to think about.

Table 1
Great Websites for Learning About Children's Literature

Website	Description
www.ala.org/ala/mgrps/divs/rusa/awards /notablebooks/index.cfm	Notable children's books, shared by the American Library Association
www.monroe.lib.in.us/childrens/booklists.html	A list of web-based booklists for children
librarybooklists.org/	A variety of booklists for all ages and genres
www.reading.org/Resources/Booklists/ ChildrensChoices.aspx	Lists of good books selected by children themselves
www.nea.org/grants/13154.htm	Teachers' top 100 books, compiled by the National Education Association
www.carolhurst.com/titles/allreviewed.html	Carol Hurst's children's literature site
www.hbook.com/resources/books/default.asp	The Horn Book's list of recommended children's literature
www.cbcbooks.org/readinglists/	The Children's Book Council book lists
www.ucalgary.ca/~dkbrown/awards.html	Calls itself "the most comprehensive guide to English-language children's book awards on the Internet"
www.bookspot.com/readinglists/childrens.htm	A site that lists dozens of other sites

- What time range do you want to encourage? How long should children read each day? For how many days each week? Be realistic here, and keep families' busy schedules in mind.

- How will you explain the program to children? How will you help them see the value in outside-of-school reading?

- How will you explain the program to parents? How will you help them see the value in outside-of-school reading?

- How will you "launch" the program? What mechanisms can you put in place to answer parents' questions while the program is in process?

- What can you do to encourage long-term participation? Some teachers use log sheets that record at-home activity. Children then return these to school periodically.

Not Even Harry Potter Can Do It Alone

We are convinced that at-home independent reading programs can benefit children (Padak & Rasinski, 2003). We need to find ways to develop authentic partnerships with parents and other adults with whom children interact outside of school hours. Not even Harry the Wizard can do it alone.

References

Burgess, S.R. (1999). The influence of speech perception, oral language ability, the home literacy environment, and pre-reading knowledge on the growth of phonological sensitivity: A one-year longitudinal study. *Reading Research Quarterly, 34*, 400–402.

Cooter, R., Mills-House, E., Marrin, P., Mathews, B., Campbell, S., & Baker, T. (1999). Family and community involvement: The bedrock of reading success. *The Reading Teacher, 52*, 891–896.

Durkin, D. (1966). *Children who read early: Two longitudinal studies.* New York: Teachers College Press.

Hart, B., & Risley, T.R. (1995). *Meaningful differences in the everyday experiences of young American children.* Baltimore: Brookes.

Hart, B., & Risley, T.B. (2003). The early catastrophe: The 30 million word gap by age 3. *American Educator, 27*(1), 4–9.

Padak, N., & Rasinski, T. (2003). *Family literacy programs: Who benefits?* Kent, OH: Ohio Literacy Resource Center. Retrieved January 20, 2007, from literacy.kent.edu/Oasis/Pubs/WhoBenefits2003.pdf

Rich, M. (2007, July 11). Potter has limited effect on reading habits. *The New York Times.* Retrieved September 25, 2007, from www.nytimes.com/2007/07/11/books/11potter.html

Sénéchal, M., LeFevre, J., Thomas, E., & Daley, K.E. (1998). Differential effects of home literacy experiences on the development of oral and written language. *Reading Research Quarterly, 33*, 96–116.

Literature Cited

Rowling, J.K. (2007). *Harry Potter and the deathly hallows.* New York: Scholastic.

Questions for Reflection

- How much do you know about your students' out-of-school literacy experiences? Do you see differences in early literacy development among those who are exposed to lots of reading and writing at home and those who are not? Are there particular areas where those differences exist? If so, what can you do to encourage family involvement directed to growth in those areas?

- What mechanisms are in place in your school or district to facilitate communication with parents? Besides sending material home with the children in your classroom, are there other ways you can reach out to families?